Walk in the Light Series

Covenants

Understanding the Creator's Plan for the Redemption of Mankind

Todd D. Bennett

Shema Yisrael Publications

D1604029

Covenants
Understanding the Creator's Plan for the Redemption of
Mankind

First printing 2011
Second printing 2014

For information write: Shema Yisrael Publications, 123
Court Street, Herkimer, New York 13350.

ISBN: 0-9768659-7-1
Library of Congress Number: 2011900358

Printed in the United States of America.

Please visit our website for other titles:
www.shemayisrael.net

Covenants

Understanding the Creator's Plan for the Redemption of Mankind

"YHWH confides in those who fear Him.
He makes His Covenant known to them."
Psalms (Tehillim) 25:14

Table of Contents

Acknowledgments

I must first and foremost acknowledge my Creator, Redeemer and Savior who opened my eyes and showed me the Light. He never gave up on me even when, at times, it seemed that I gave up on Him. He is ever patient and truly awesome. His blessings, mercies and love endure forever and my gratitude and thanksgiving cannot be fully expressed in words.

Were it not for the patience, prayers, love and support of my beautiful wife Janet, and my extraordinary children Morgan and Shemuel, I would never have been able to accomplish this work. They gave me the freedom to pursue the vision and dreams that my Heavenly Father placed within me, and for that I am so very grateful. I love them all more than they will ever know.

Loving thanks to my father for his faithfulness along with his helpful comments and editing. He tirelessly watched and held things together at the office while I was away traveling, researching, speaking and writing.

Introduction

This book is part of a larger body of educational work called the "Walk in the Light" series. This book and the entire series were written as a result of my search for the truth. Having grown up in a major protestant denomination since I was a small child, I had been steeped in doctrine that often times seemed to contradict the very words contained within the Scriptures. I always considered myself to be a Christian although I never took the time to research the origins of Christianity or to understand exactly what the term Christian meant. I simply grew up believing that Christianity was right and every other religion was wrong or deficient.

Now my beliefs were founded on more than simply blind faith. I had experienced a "living God," my life had been transformed by a loving Redeemer and I had been filled with a powerful Spirit. I knew that I was on the right track, regrettably I always felt something was lacking. I was certain that there was something more to this religion called Christianity; not in terms of a different God, but what composed this belief system that I subscribed to, and this label that I wore like a badge.

Throughout my Christian walk I experienced many highs and some lows, but along the way I never felt like I fully understood what my faith was all about. Sure, I knew that "Jesus died on the cross for my sins" and that I needed to believe in my heart and confess with my mouth in order to "be saved." I "asked Jesus into my heart" when I was a child and sincerely believed in what I had done, but something always felt like it was missing. As I grew older, I found myself progressing through different denominations, each time learning and growing, always adding some pieces to the puzzle, but never seeing the entire picture.

College ministry brought me into contact with the baptism of the Holy Spirit and more charismatic assemblies yet, while these people seemed to practice a more complete faith than those in my previous denominations, many of my original questions remained unanswered and even more questions arose. It seemed that at each new step in my faith I added a new adjective to the already ambiguous label "Christian". I went from being a mere Christian to a Full Gospel, New Testament, Charismatic, Spirit Filled, Born Again Christian; although I could never get away from the lingering uneasiness that something was still missing.

For instance, when I read Matthew 7:21-23 I always felt uncomfortable. In that Scripture most English Bibles indicate that Jesus says: "*Not everyone who says to Me, Lord, Lord, will enter the kingdom of heaven, but he who does the will of My Father Who is in heaven. Many will say to Me on that day, Lord, Lord, have we not prophesied in Your name and driven out demons in Your name and done many mighty works in Your name? And then I will say to them openly (publicly), I never knew you; depart from Me, you who act wickedly [disregarding My commands].*" The Amplified Bible.

This passage of Scripture always bothered me because it sounded an awful lot like the modern day Christian Church, in particular, the charismatic churches which I had been attending where the gifts of the Spirit were operating. According to the Scripture passage it was

not the people who *believed* in the spiritual manifestations that were being rejected, it was those who were *actually doing* them. I would think that this would give every Christian pause for concern.

First of all "in that day" there are *many* people who will be calling Him "Lord." They will also be performing incredible spiritual acts in His Name. Ultimately though, the Messiah will openly and publicly tell them to depart from Him. He will tell them that He never knew them and specifically He defines them by their actions, which is the reason for their rejection; they acted wickedly or lawlessly. In short, they disobeyed His commandments. Also, it seems very possible that while they thought they were doing these things in His Name, they were not, because they may have never known His Name. In essence, they did not know Him and He did not know them.

I think that many Christians are haunted by this Scripture because they do not understand who it applies to or what it means and if they were truly honest they must admit that there is no other group on the face of the planet that it can refer to except for the "Christian Church." This series provides the answer to that question and should provide resolution for any who have suffered anxiety over this verse.

Ultimately, my search for answers brought me right back to the starting point of my faith. I was left with the question: "What is the origin and substance of this religion called Christianity?" I was forced to examine the very foundations of my faith and to examine many of the beliefs which I subscribed to and test them against the truth of the Scriptures.

What I found out was nothing short of earth shattering. I experienced a parapettio, which is a moment

in Greek tragedies where the hero realizes that everything he knew was wrong. I discovered that many of the foundations of my faith were not rocks of truth, but rather the sands of lies, deception, corruption and paganism. I saw the Scripture in Jeremiah come true right before my eyes. In many translations, this passage reads: *"O LORD, my strength and my fortress, My refuge in the day of affliction, The Gentiles shall come to You from the ends of the earth and say, "Surely our fathers have inherited lies, worthlessness and unprofitable things. Will a man make gods for himself, which are not gods?"* Jeremiah 16:19-20 NKJV

I discovered that I had inherited lies and false doctrines from the fathers of my faith. I discovered that the faith which I had been steeped in had made gods which were not gods and I saw very clearly how many could say "Lord, Lord" and not really know the Messiah. I discovered that these lies were not just minor discrepancies but critical errors which could possibly have the effect of keeping me out of the New Jerusalem if I continued to practice them. (Revelation 21:27; 22:15).

While part of the problem stemmed from false doctrines which have crept into the Christian religion, it also had to do with anti-Semitism imbedded throughout the centuries and even translation errors in the very Scriptures that I was basing may beliefs upon. A good example is the next verse from the Prophet Jeremiah (Yirmeyahu) where most translations provide: *"Therefore behold, I will this once cause them to know, I will cause them to know My hand and My might; and they shall know that My Name is the LORD."* Yirmeyahu 16:21 NKJV.

Could our Heavenly Father really be telling us that His Name is "The LORD"? This is a title, not a name and by the way, won't many people be crying out "Lord, Lord"

and be told that He never knew them? It is obvious that you should know someone's name in order to have a relationship with them. How could you possibly say that you know someone if you do not even know their name. So then we must ask: "What is the Name of our Heavenly Father?" The answer to this seeming mystery lies just beneath the surface of the translated text. In fact, if most people took the time to read the translators notes in the front of their "Bible" they would easily discover the problem.

You see the Name of our Creator is found in the Scriptures almost 7,000 times. Long ago a false doctrine was perpetrated regarding speaking the Name. It was determined that the Name either could not, or should not, be pronounced and therefore it was replaced. Thus, over the centuries the Name of the Creator which was given to us so that we could know Him and be, not only His children, but also His friends, was suppressed and altered. You will now find people using descriptions, titles and variations to replace the Name such as: God, Lord, Adonai, Jehovah and Ha Shem ("The Name") in place of the actual Name which was given in Scriptures. What a tragedy and what a mistake!

One of the Ten Commandments, also known as the Ten Words, specifically instructs us not to take the Name of the Creator "in vain" and *"He will not hold him guiltless who takes His Name in vain."* (Exodus 20:7). Most Christians have been taught that this simply warns of using the Name lightly or in the context of swearing or in some other disrespectful manner. This certainly is one aspect of the commandment, but if we look further into the Hebrew word for vain - שוא (pronounced shav) we find that it has a deeper meaning in the sense of "desolating, uselessness or

naught."

Therefore, we have been warned not only to avoid using the Name lightly or disrespectfully, but also not to bring it to naught, which is exactly what has been done over the centuries. The Name of our Creator that we have the privilege of calling on and praising has been suppressed to the point where most Believers do not even know the Name, let alone use it.

This sounds like a conspiracy of cosmic proportions and it is. Anyone who believes in the Scriptures must understand that there is a battle between good and evil. There is an enemy, ha'shatan, who understands very well the battle that has been raging since the creation of time. He will do anything to distract or destroy those searching for the truth and he is very good at what he does. As you read this book I hope that you will see how people have been deceived regarding the Scriptural Covenants.

My hope is that every reader has an eye opening experience and is forever changed. I sincerely believe that the truths which are contained in this book and the "Walk in the Light Series" are essential to avoid the great deception which is being perpetrated upon those who profess to believe in, and follow the Holy One of Yisrael.

This book, and the entire series, is intended to be read by anyone who is searching for the truth. Depending upon your particular religion, customs and traditions, you may find some of the information offensive, difficult to believe or contrary to the doctrines and teachings that you have read or heard throughout your life. This is to be expected and is perfectly understandable, but please realize that none of the information is meant to criticize anyone or any faith, but merely to reveal truth.

The information contained in this book had better

stir up some things or else there would be no reason to write it in the first place. The ultimate question is whether the contents align with the Scriptures and the will of the Creator. My goal is to strip away the layers of tradition that many of us have inherited and get to the core of the faith which is described in the Scriptures.

This book should challenge your thinking and your beliefs and hopefully aid you on your search for truth. May you be blessed in your journey of faith as you endeavor to Walk in the Light.

I

In the Beginning

The thought of reading a book entirely focused on covenants may sound rather dry and boring to most people - possibly something suitable for a lawyer, but certainly not a pleasure read. This is the result of a common perception that a covenant is simply a contract. As a result, some might initially view this book in the same light as a legal treatise on contracts.

Nothing could be further from the truth. Rather than being tedious or boring, the subject of Scriptural Covenants is exciting and vital for every person who believes in a Creator and desires to enter into relationship with God, more accurately referred to as Elohim.[1]

The Scriptural Covenants tell a story and actually provide the framework for the redemption of all mankind. As with any story, this one has a beginning. We read about it in the text commonly referred to as Genesis, better known as Beresheet in Hebrew. The word Beresheet literally means: "in Beginning" and it is the first word found in the Scriptures.

There is something very interesting about this word, but you will only see it in a Hebrew manuscript. The word will look something like this in modern Hebrew script:

בְּרֵאשִׁית

It is important to know that Hebrew reads from right to left. Something that becomes immediately noticeable about this word is the fact that it begins with what is known as the Enlarged Bet. The bet (בּ) is larger than the rest of the Hebrew characters, but it should not to be confused with illuminated letters that often decorated older manuscripts. It is enlarged to draw the reader's attention, and it actually has great significance.

In ancient Hebrew the character "bet" (⅁) represents a tent or a floor plan of a house. The letter "bet" (בּ) actually means "house." So the presence of the enlarged bet (בּ) appears to be emphasizing, at the beginning, the fact that the story is about a house.

The word beresheet ends with the letter "taw" (ת), which in ancient pictograph form represents an "x" or a mark (X). To this day the "x" is a legally acceptable form for a persons autograph or signature. In ancient Hebrew the character actually means: "completion" or "covenant," which is the subject of this book.[2]

So the word "beresheet" (בְּרֵאשִׁית) begins with a house and ends with a covenant. Amazingly, the Hebrew word for covenant – "brit" (בְּרִית), constitutes the second layer surrounding the word beresheet (בְּרֵאשִׁית). So we know that a covenant is going to be a very significant part of the text.

Interestingly, there is a word found between "brit" (בְּרִית). That word is "esh" (אֵשׁ) in Hebrew, and it means: "fire." So at the center of this covenant is fire. The letters for the word "man" are also plainly located in

the word. The Hebrew word for man is "aish" (אִישׁ).

A considerable amount of time could be spent looking at this one word, but the point should be clear - this one word contains quite a story. It actually sets the stage for the rest of the text. So "In the beginning" – even before there was any mention of mankind, the text is telling us that a covenant involving fire and man is one of the prominent themes, and it all revolves around a house.

A bit further in the text of Beresheet we end up reading about the creation of man and woman. We also read about the special garden where they were placed which was, in essence, their house. Most readers are probably familiar with the story of the Garden and the fall of man.

It is essentially a simple story that details how Elohim created man from the dust of the earth and breathed life into him. The Creator called the man Adam,[3] and placed him in the garden known as Eden. The Hebrew word for garden is "gan" (גן) and it refers to an enclosed or protected space.

Therefore we see this particular Garden as separate from the rest of the planet. Eden (עֵדֶן) literally means: "paradise" or "pleasure" and must have been quite a place to live in. It was a place where Adam and his mate, Hawah[4] lived in perfect harmony with creation and their Creator.

Hawah was not created from the ground, nor was the breath of life breathed directly into her, as was the case with Adam. She was taken from Adam. This first woman was literally birthed from the man.

We are told that during this "birthing process" Adam was placed in a "deep sleep." The Hebrew word used to describe his condition is tardemah (הרדמה) - which means more than just deep sleep. In fact, it means: "trance or stunned - like death." So what we see is a picture of Adam dying so that his bride could live. Adam was then "brought back to life," or "resurrected" so that he and his bride could dwell together in paradise. This was a pattern established at the very beginning that would have profound implications in the future.

As stated, the word for man is "aish" (איש) in Hebrew. The word for woman is "aishah" (אשׁה). Aishah means: "taken out of man." Notice that there is a Hebrew letter hey (ה) added to the word for woman. The hey (ה) has changed over the centuries and in an ancient paleo script it symbolizes a man standing with arms raised (𐤄) and means: "behold." It is intended to announce something and can also mean: "to reveal." The hey (ה) also represents breath, which is life - the Spirit of Elohim.

Interestingly, the passage of Scripture detailing the birthing of of the woman includes something that can only be seen in the Hebrew text. Located within the passage is an un-translated word spelled Aleph Taw (את). Now this is by no means the only place in the Scriptures where it is found. In fact, it is found all throughout the Hebrew Scriptures and it is a great mystery, because it is rarely ever translated.

It is usually there to draw our attention to a deeper meaning hidden within the text. Some believe that it points to the Messiah.[5] The Aleph Taw (את) will be discussed throughout this book, and it demonstrates the importance of studying the Scriptures in the original Hebrew. There are great mysteries and treasures hidden

within the text that can only be seen in the Hebrew.

As it turns out, the entire birthing process is an important event that we are meant to learn from. Elohim could have merely created a woman from scratch. Instead He chose to create a new being, similar, but very different from Adam. Both the man and the woman were unique in their beings, and the fashion in which they were created.

Before the woman was taken from Adam he was "echad" (אחד) – united as a single being. When Elohim took Hawah from him, Adam was thereafter divided. He was later closed up, which means his flesh had to be opened up to take the part of him - which became Hawah. As a result, blood was likely shed. This, as we shall see, is the mark of a blood covenant – the shedding of blood.

From this event we actually see the foundation of a very important covenant – the marriage relationship. If this were a book on contracts we could discuss the legal requisites of a marriage contract, since most governments treat marriage as a mere contract. Because of that designation, a divorce is typically treated as a list of legal decisions that must be made when the marriage "contract" is breached.

As a lawyer and a husband I can attest to the fact that marriage is much more than a mere contract. In a Scriptural sense, marriage is a covenant. It is a special relationship, the formation of which involves more than ink on paper. It is when two lives are spiritually and physically joined together as one.

The Hebrew word that epitomizes this concept is echad (אחד), and it means, not just the numeral one, but more specifically - "unity." When this Covenant is broken, the two lives that have been knit together and unified are ripped apart. There is no perforated line to make this tear, and there is no simple or clean way to separate those two lives that have literally been woven together as one. Divorce is messy and destructive.

This is where we start to see the difference between a contract and a covenant. This new relationship created between the man and the woman is an important pattern established by the Creator. It essentially would teach mankind the type of intimate relationship that He would seek to have with them.

Thus, this first bloodshedding event in the Scriptures points to one of the most important covenant concepts found within the Scriptures – the Marriage Covenant.

It is important that this marriage occurred in a very specific and important place – the garden. The garden was a place where mankind was permitted to partake from the Tree of Life, which provided him with an eternal existence. It was therefore a place of life, where man could dwell and commune with the Creator forever.

It was not all fun and games though. Man was given a mandate to be fruitful and multiply. He was to fill the Earth, subdue it and rule over the creatures of the earth. (Beresheet 1:28). The garden would be his castle – the capital of his new kingdom. He was essentially the king of a new kingdom given to him by his Creator. He was given a place of reprieve and a commission of authority.

Along with these great gifts he was also given great responsibility to care for this new home – the garden. Elohim commanded him to "*to tend it and keep it.*"

Beresheet 2:15. In the Hebrew text we read two very important words - "abad" (עבד) which means: "to work, to serve, to tend," and "shamar" (שמר) which means: "to hedge about (as with thorns), to keep, to guard, to protect." The underlying Hebrew text implies that Adam was to act as a servant and a watchman.

This is important to understand because, as we already saw, the word for garden in Hebrew is "gan" (גן) which means: "an enclosed space." The word provides a picture of a place surrounded by a hedge. Adam was charged with the cultivation and the protection of this place.

Adam was given very specific and simple instructions on how to live, so that he could continue in relationship with Elohim. The Scriptures provide details concerning what man could eat and what he could not eat. It is significant to note that the first recorded commandment given to man by Elohim concerned his diet.[6]

It is also important to note that Adam was given these instructions prior to the creation of Hawah. The Scriptures record: *"[16] And YHWH Elohim commanded the man, saying, 'Of every tree of the garden you may freely eat; [17] but of the tree of the knowledge of good and evil you shall not eat, for in the day that you eat of it you shall surely die.'"* Beresheet 2:16-17. Notice the Name of the Creator – YHWH.[7] Many English translations replace this Name with the title The LORD, but that is an erroneous tradition.[8] Throughout this book we will use an English transliteration of the Hebrew Name designated יהוה in modern Hebrew.

Now this was by no means the only command given to man, but it happened to be the first one that was transgressed - that is why we are provided the specific details of this particular command. Adam was surely given instructions concerning his duties and what was expected of him as he and his Creator walked and fellowshipped together in the Garden.

Since this command was given to Adam prior to the creation of Hawah, it would have been his duty to teach his wife the instructions so that she too could obey them. This is where we start to see a problem, either Adam did not properly instruct the woman or she did not understand the instructions.

The Scriptures record an incident when the woman was deceived by a serpent that had entered the Garden. This serpent first approached the woman and convinced her to eat "fruit" from the forbidden tree. The woman then convinced the man to do the same. Adam and the woman both transgressed a command – they partook of the fruit of the tree of knowledge of good and evil - better known as the tree of all knowledge.

It has been suggested that: "the phrase [tov v'ra] טוב ורע translated *good and evil*, is a merism. This is a figure of speech whereby a pair of opposites are used together to create the meaning *all* or *everything*, as in the English phrase, 'they came, great and small', meaning just that they all came. So the *Tree of Knowledge of Good and Evil* they take to mean the *Tree of All Knowledge*. This meaning can be brought out by the alternative translations *Tree of Knowledge of Good and of Evil* (the word *of* not being expressed in the Hebrew) or *Tree of Knowledge, both Good and Evil*."[9]

The word "knowledge" comes from "yada" (ידע) "to know" which is the same word used to describe a man having intercourse with his wife. This is a very

intimate word and describes something physical and experiential – not just head knowledge, such as "knowing" a persons name.

Therefore, whether or not this tree contained actual fruit that was eaten, it definitely involved an experience of "knowing" evil. In other words, it involved man actively disobeying the Commandment which is, in fact, evil. So it was not as if their eyes were simply opened and they then cognitively recognized both good and evil, they had experienced it.

Most people who read this account will ask: "What could have possibly happened to cause such a sudden change in their perception and how could eating a piece of fruit do such a thing?" While the fruit of that particular tree may have had special "powers" there is likely more to the story than meets the eye. This episode was a sensual event and we read in the text the emphasis placed upon the senses of touching, tasting and seeing.

The act of eating, drinking and tasting is at times used in the Scriptures in a metaphorical fashion to describe intimacy. For example, in Song of Solomon we read *"Like an apple tree among the trees of the woods, so is my beloved among the sons. I sat down in his shade with great delight, and his fruit was sweet to my taste."* Song of Solomon 2:3 NKJV. The Proverbs speak about a man drinking water from his own cisterns and not being enraptured by an immoral woman. Proverbs 5:15. We are encouraged to: *"Taste and see that YHWH is good."* Psalms 34:8

Prior to the incident involving the Tree of All Knowledge, the Scriptures provide that *"they were both naked, the man and his wife, and they were not ashamed."* Beresheet 2:25. When Adam and the woman partook of this forbidden fruit, their eyes were suddenly opened to their "nakedness" which is arom (עֲרוֹם) in Hebrew. They were suddenly afraid and made for themselves coverings of leaves, likely leaves from the very tree from which they partook the fruit.[10]

The key is that they now "knew" that they were naked. The fact that they were naked had not changed, rather the fact that they "knew," which again is "yada" (יָדַע) in Hebrew. It was now their nakedness that caused them to be ashamed.

Interestingly, the man and the woman were not the only ones who were naked during this event. The Scriptures record that the serpent was also "arom" (עָרוּם), which was the same word to describe the man and woman as naked. Relative to the serpent, the word "arom" (עָרוּם) is usually translated as "cunning."

The word translated "the serpent" is "ha'nachash" (הַנָּחָשׁ) in Hebrew. The noun "nachash" (נָחָשׁ) can mean a "snake, serpent or one who practices divination." The adjective "nachash" (נָחָשׁ) means: "bright or brazen."

Therefore, this intruder is often referred to as a serpent, but should actually be referred to as the "nachash" (נָחָשׁ). There is much mystery surrounding this word, which is strongly associated with "sorcery" and "divination." It is possible that this was the first instance of misappropriating the power of the divine.

It appears that Hawah was essentially placed under a "spell." It could be that she was not protected by Adam – her covering. The instructions of the Creator were being misappropriated and twisted. While the Creator had told the man that "in the day that he ate from the tree of all knowledge he would certainly die"

we later see the nachash instructing the woman concerning these same commands.

It is interesting to note that the woman does not provide an accurate understanding of the command concerning this particular tree. When asked by the nachash, "Is it true that Elohim has said 'Do not eat of every tree of the garden,'" her reply was not accurate. She told the nachash, "*We are to eat of the fruit of the trees of the garden but the fruit of the tree which is in the midst of the garden, Elohim has said 'Do not eat of it, <u>nor touch it</u>, lest you die.'*" Beresheet 3:1-3.

She added to the command given to the man by Elohim. Adam was only told not to eat of the fruit. Hawah added to the command by stating they could not "touch" the fruit. As a result of her adding to the command she opened herself to deception. She was no longer on "doctrinal" solid ground.

The nachash then seized upon this opportunity and proclaimed: "You shall certainly not die." The nachash directly contradicted Elohim. He lied to the woman and indicated that, in fact, Elohim was the liar, merely hiding valuable information from them.

Now the woman looked at this tree and saw that the tree was "good" and "pleasant" and "desirable" so she indulged. She believed the words of the nachash and was influenced to disobey the commandment of Elohim. She took of the tree and thereafter encouraged Adam to transgress the commandment of Elohim by eating from the tree.

An entire book could be written on the dynamics of this interchange, but that is not the specific purpose of this text. The point is that the "act" of partaking of the "forbidden fruit," whatever that might have entailed, was obviously an "eye opening" experience, because it resulted in their desire to cover themselves. The nachash had promised that their "eyes would be opened" and that did indeed happen. The question is: What did it mean?

Their thinking and perception had been changed. They hid their bodies, particularly their sexual organs, because they knew that they had done wrong. Something drastically wrong happened between mankind and the Creator. Their relationship was now different. The seemingly simple act of curiosity and defiance altered the course of creation and sets the tone for the rest of this book.

The transgression of the commandment resulted in punishment. All three of the participants were meted out judgment as follows:

"[14] . . . to the nachash, 'Because you have done this, Cursed are you above all the livestock and all the wild animals! You will crawl on your belly and you will eat dust all the days of your life. [15] And I will put enmity between you and the woman, and between your offspring and hers; he will crush your head, and you will strike his heel.' [16] To the woman He said, 'I will greatly increase your pains in childbearing; with pain you will give birth to children. Your desire will be for your husband, and he will rule over you.' [17] To Adam He said, 'Because you listened to your wife and ate from the tree about which I commanded you, you must not eat of it, cursed is the ground because of you; through painful toil you will eat of it all the days of your life. [18] It will produce thorns and thistles for you, and you will eat the plants of the field. [19] By the sweat of your brow you will eat your food until you return to the ground, since from it you were taken; for dust you are and to dust you will return.'" Beresheet 3:14-19.

Adam and Hawah were thereafter provided

animal pelts as garments, which means that blood was shed to cover their shame. That shed blood did not solve the problem. It did not cleanse them from their transgression, it merely provided a temporary atonement. They still received punishment, so what was the reason for the shedding of the blood? That will be a major part of the discussion in this book.

This is where the need for a "new" or "renewed" Covenant arises. Had this incident never occurred there would never have been a need for this book, because the relationship between man and the Creator would have remained unchanged. There would be no need to explain or define the relationship between mankind and the Creator, because the ground rules had already been established in the beginning – obey and live, disobey and die. Life is represented as dwelling with the Creator, and death is represented by separation from the Creator.

One could argue that this, in and of itself, was the original and ultimate Covenant. There were terms and conditions that defined a relationship between different parties, and there was a punishment for violating those terms - death. We see the union between man, woman and their Creator ruling a kingdom from paradise as the essential picture provided from the beginning. It was the Marriage Covenant that was at the core of everything at the beginning and man proved to be unfaithful and adulterous. Man was therefore essentially given a divorce and expelled from the marital residence.

Most studies on the covenants found within the Scriptures will begin with an analysis of the Edenic and Adamic covenants. They claim that Elohim established a covenant with Adam both before and after the Tree incident. While the Scriptures do not specifically define

different covenants there is validity in making these distinctions, because they essentially reveal differing conditions of the relationship between the Creator and man. Covenants, after all, are about defining relationships.

The problem that I have with naming the differing relationships is that it gives the impression that these were different covenants. That can lead a person down a dangerous doctrinal road, if they interpret the Creator as changing His mind every thousand years by implementing new covenants.[11]

I do not believe that the Scriptures support such an interpretation. Rather, they reveal a relationship that was broken and needs to be restored. This is the underlying theme of all of the Scriptural texts – the restoration of the relationship between the Creator and mankind, which is defined through covenants.

2

Covenants

Many people think of a covenant as a contract or an agreement, but as we have already seen, it has a much deeper meaning. In Hebrew the word for covenant is brit (ברית) and it literally means "cutting." This is why we often see the shedding of blood associated with the formation of a covenant. As mentioned, we can infer blood being shed when Hawah was taken from Adam's side, thus establishing the Marriage Covenant.[12]

Interestingly, when we look at the name Adam we see a vivid picture of Adam's role. In modern Hebrew Adam is spelled אדם. In ancient Hebrew we see 𐤌𐤃𐤀. The name begins with an aleph (𐤀) and ends with a mem (𐤌). The word "am" (𐤌𐤀) actually means: "nation, peoples, large city or womb." So from this man we see that he would be the "womb" which would come nations and peoples. The letter in the middle is dalet (𐤃) which means: "door." So Adam is the door to the nations – the peoples. We will also see very important covenant events involving "the door" as this discussion continues.

After the transgression in the Garden, blood was shed allowing mankind to live, albeit outside the garden. It was not the blood of the perpetrators, but rather blood from animals. The skin of these slaughtered animals was thereafter used to cover the wrongdoers.

This event provided a picture of atonement and seemed to provide a picture of how the Creator would deal with the problem of transgression. Blood would now be shed to atone or "cover" the transgression. Sinful man was still underneath that covering, so the shedding of blood from animals would not be a permanent solution. Nevertheless, it provided the pattern and the means to a more perfect solution.

So this bloody event showed the way for man to continue to live, despite their transgression, but it would be a different existence, separated from their Creator. It was likely the source of the ancient blood covenant, which grew to become an integral aspect of relationships between the Creator and mankind, as well as between individuals.

Typically, when making an ancient blood covenant, the parties to the covenant would cut the sacrifice in two and then pass between the pieces – literally walking in the blood of the covenant.

This was intended to symbolize the consequences to anyone who broke the covenant. They would be treated as the slaughtered animal that was split in half, so they could walk between the pieces. (see Jeremiah 34:18) If you break a contract in most societies it is deemed a civil matter, and there are usually monetary damages assessed for the breach. When you break a blood covenant, someone is supposed to die - just as the sacrifice died when the covenant was established. Due to the severity of the breach, it elevates covenants beyond a mere contract.

Covenants would often involve life or death issues, and they were not entered into lightly. A relationship was forged with consequences for violating

the terms of the trust that was created. These were serious events with very ancient, and sometimes elaborate rituals associated with them.

If we look at the Ancient Hebrew Script we can see that this word "brit" also provides us with a story. The bet (ב) in Ancient Hebrew represents a house or a tent - (𝋉). The resh (ר) is a head - (𝋨). The yod (י) is an arm - (𝋉) and the taw (ת) is a cross, or a mark - (X), which actually means: "completion" or "covenant." Therefore, in the ancient script the word "brit" would appear as X𝋉𝋨𝋉.

The fact that the word for "covenant" ends with a symbol (X), which represents "completion" or "covenant," exemplifies the very fact of the perpetual nature of a covenant. Through this representation it is distinguished as a very Hebrew or "eastern" concept, and as we shall see, it is very different from the "western" idea of a contract. When studying the Scriptures it is particularly important to recognize this east-west dichotomy.

The events described in the Scriptures took place in an eastern culture involving eastern individuals who spoke and thought from an eastern perspective. Much of the "modern" world looks at life from a western perspective and this is often at the root of many of the culture clashes that we see in "developing" eastern societies that are being influenced by the west.

Eastern thought tends to be very concrete and cyclical, while western thought tends to be abstract and linear. The distinction between the eastern concept of a covenant and the western concept of a contract clearly demonstrates this divergence of cultures.

This is an important distinction to understand

when examining the subject of Scriptural Covenants. Instead of a string of different Covenants lined up one after another, as a western mind might perceive them, Scriptural Covenants operate cyclically and overlap - thus leading to the same end and creating one unified Covenant. It should become clear throughout this text that while there are different covenants described in the Scriptures made with various individuals, they all essentially become one - echad.

Understanding eastern thought and language is vital for a proper understanding of the Scriptural Covenants. Since Hebrew originated as a pictographic language, it is often helpful to examine the pictographs that make up a word in order to discern the breadth and depth of a word. When we examine the ancient script we begin to get the picture - literally. As we see with the word "brit," it has a much deeper meaning than simply interpreting it as "cutting" or "covenant."

Examining the original language is a very important part of Scriptural studies, and it is critical to understand that the so-called "modern" Hebrew script actually originated in Babylon after Yisrael had been divided into two separate Kingdoms: 1) the Southern Kingdom known as the House of Judah, and 2) the Northern Kingdom known as the House of Yisrael. Both of these Kingdoms were conquered and exiled for reasons that will be discussed further on in this book. The House of Yisrael was exiled by the Assyrians, and the House of Judah was exiled by the Babylonians.

During the time the House of Judah was in exile, between 618 - 526 BCE, they ended up with a brand new character set for their language.[13] Just how the new language developed is a bit of a mystery, but one thing is

certain – it is not the original Hebrew language.

It is a hybrid language whose creation and implementation has significantly neutered the original Hebrew language by diminishing, to a great extent, the original pictographic symbols. While certain symbols are still recognizable, the Babylonian derived script does not always carry the weight, or tell the story that was originally intended.

Instead of symbols with complex meanings and combinations of meanings that paint a visible and living picture, the modern characters are generally viewed as mere letters that combine to spell various words. Only when combined in recognized patterns do the words then take on meaning. Many attempt to discern the deeper meanings, but again, the symbols are not always recognizable, nor are they directly related to the ancient language.

In the original Hebrew language, each symbol is alive with meaning and has a relationship with all of the others. It is visual and vibrant and instead of memorizing combinations of letter patterns to discern words, the reader of ancient pictographic Hebrew combines the meanings of the symbols, and works them together to discern very detailed concepts. One word in ancient Hebrew can actually be translated into a sentence or a paragraph in English.

We already saw that the first letter in the word "brit" (𐤕𐤉𐤓𐤁) is bet (𐤁), which originally represented a house or a tent. The second letter resh (𐤓) symbolized the head of a man. The third letter yud (𐤉) originally represented an arm. The final letter taw (𐤕) was represented by a cross or a mark, and literally meant "completion" or "covenant."

So looking at the original Hebrew pictographs, which essentially tell a story, it appears that a covenant involves relationship and living with Elohim. He first provides a house. We then see two different aspects of the body: 1) the head, and 2) the arm. Somehow the head and the arm will lead to the covenant.

We come to that conclusion by looking at these symbols in a linear or western fashion. The interesting thing about the ancient language is that the symbols take on other meanings when combined with each other. For instance, when you combine the bet ($\mathcal{Y}$) and the resh ($\mathcal{A}$) you have the word "bar" ($\mathcal{A}\mathcal{Y}$), which is a common word for "son."[14]

When you combine the bet ($\mathcal{Y}$) and the taw (X) you have the word "bet" ($\mathsf{X}\mathcal{Y}$), which is a common word for "daughter." When you combine the bet ($\mathcal{Y}$), the yud (Z) and the taw (X) you have the word "beit" ($\mathsf{X}\mathsf{Z}\mathcal{Y}$), which is a common word for "house" or to "domesticate."

When we look at the various combinations, and the words within the word, we see a more full and comprehensive definition of the source word.[15] So through the word "brit," and the various words contained therein, we lear an important truth. We can see that there is a process where we become "domesticated," or learn behavior that allows us to join the family of YHWH as sons and daughters. We are then in a position to gain entry into the House.

Thus a covenant is ultimately a means to an end. It is a way of life that teaches us how to be sons and daughters and leads us into our home, our inheritance.

Hopefully this method of analysis gives the reader a better understanding of this most important

word. A word which is unique due to the fact that it ends with the symbol taw (X), which is the very meaning of the word, thus creating a sense of perpetuity and elevating it to the eternal.

The notion of a covenant forming an eternal family is a common, repeating theme that we will see interlaced throughout all of the Scriptures. We shall see how the covenant process was and is used by the Creator to establish and build relationships with His creation.

As stated previously, many people view covenants as strictly contracts, which are bargained agreements involving the exchange of consideration. While there are definitely some similarities between contracts and covenants, the covenant goes far deeper and extends beyond the bounds of a contract.

Let us look at a common definition of a Covenant from a traditional source.

> "Covenant involves a stipulation of something to be done by the person offering the covenant, there is a restipulation by the other party of something to be done or given in consideration which constitutes acceptance and which forms the essence of the agreement. Finally, there must be some penalty to the party that violates the agreement. The notion of a covenant in the strict sense, as requiring two independent contracting parties, cannot apply to a covenant between [Elohim] and man. His covenant must be essentially one of gratuitous promise, an act of pure grace on His part . . . So in Psalms 89:28

'covenant' is explained by the parallel word 'mercy.'"[16]

Notice that this definition makes a distinction between covenants involving men, and a Covenant made with Elohim. Many discussions on Scriptural Covenants make the comparison with a suzerainty treaty because in Hebrew, the same word "brit" is used to describe a Covenant with Elohim and treaties between kings.

The point is that a covenant with the Creator is clearly a lopsided arrangement – the parties are by no means equal in strength or status. The "treaty" is not negotiated. The suzerain, Elohim, simply offers His terms. The other party needs to decide whether or not to accept the terms and enter into the relationship.[17]

So a covenant is an agreement that establishes a relationship and forms a bond between different parties – sometimes between individual men, and sometimes between men and Elohim. Despite the fact that Elohim and man are not on equal footing, Elohim, as a demonstration of His mercy and desire to commune with man, still makes covenants with him. This simple fact demonstrates the love and mercy of YHWH - it reveals His nature. He continually reaches down to mankind and deals with man on his level.

There are various covenants described in the Scriptures. Not all of them will be discussed in this text at length. For the purpose of this discussion we are concerned primarily with the Covenants that YHWH makes with men, and mankind as a whole.

It is important to understand that some covenants come with conditions while others are unconditional. This is an important fact that distinguishes a covenant from a contract. Contracts, by their very definition,

come with conditions. Covenants do not need conditions – they can be made simply because the parties desire to do so. There can be unilateral benefits and/or obligations that define the relationship.

An examination of the Scriptures reveals that some covenants are made with mankind and others are made with a select group. When we look at these covenants we must keep in mind the concept that YHWH is building a House, and entrance into this House and relationship with Him is the essential part of the Covenant. This is the context within which we will view the Scriptural Covenants.

If we consider what is traditionally called the Adamic Covenant, we can see what is commonly referred to as the threshold covenant. This was an ancient tradition that possibly began at the Garden of Eden.

When the blood was shed to provide the skins for Adam and Hawah. It was likely done at the gate, or rather, the door, where the man and the woman were expelled. The blood was there as a reminder of the transgression and Cherubims were thereafter posted at the door, or entrance to the East with a "flaming" or "enchanting" knife or sword.

Here is the passage that describes the event. "²³ therefore YHWH Elohim sent him out of the garden of Eden to till ✗ℓ the ground from which he was taken. ²⁴ So He drove out ✗ℓ the man; and He placed at the east of the garden of Eden ✗ℓ Cherubims and a flaming sword which turned every way, to guard ✗ℓ the way to the tree of life." Beresheet 3:23-24.

Interestingly, the two things that Adam was to do in the Garden are present in this passage. Remember he was to "tend or till" (עבד) the ground in the Garden, and he was to "watch or guard" (שׁמר) the garden – the house. Adam, still had to work, but he had to till the ground outside the garden. His responsibility to watch and guard was taken away from him. The privilege of guarding and protecting was given to Cherubims, and now Adam was the one being kept out. His role had been completely reversed.

In the passage describing this event there are four instances of the un-translated Aleph Taw (𐤗𐤊). We already briefly touched upon this mysterious Aleph Taw (𐤗𐤊) that is located throughout the Hebrew text. Since it is not translated, it is never seen by those who rely solely upon a translated text.

The aleph (𐤊) is the first symbol in the Hebrew alephbet (alphabet). It represents the head of an ox and symbolizes "strength." The taw (𐤗), once again, is the last letter in the Hebrew alephbet. It represents a "mark" and means "completion" or "covenant."

To a western mind, the Aleph Taw (𐤗𐤊) would appear to symbolize "the beginning and the end" as two distinct points on a line. In eastern thought the Aleph Taw (𐤗𐤊) has much more meaning. The Aleph Taw (𐤗𐤊) must be viewed in a cyclical sense. It is the beginning and end of a cycle, which could be the same point – one. It could also contain everything within that cycle. Since the cycle ends with the taw (𐤗), the covenant, the implications are profound. A simple definition of this concept could be "strength of the covenant" or "the power that completes."

The Aleph Taw (𐤗𐤊) represents all of the letters (symbols) in the Hebrew alephbet so it could represent "The Word" – the creative force of YHWH that is

responsible for all that exists. The Aleph Taw (X✗) is often associated with the Messiah, as is the number four (4). Since the Aleph Taw (X✗) is intimately tied with the Covenant then we should expect to see the Messiah associated with the Covenant as "the strength of the Covenant throughout the entire cycle."

The existence of the Aleph Taw (X✗) on four (4) occasions, at the entrance of the garden during this Threshold Covenant event points to the Messiah having a role in mankind gaining entrance back through the "door" into the House of Elohim. This concept will be developed further throughout the discussion as we continue to examine the different Covenants described in the Scriptures.

We will see that this ancient practice developed wherein blood was spread on the threshold of a door to cover the inhabitants of the house. Obviously, for blood to be placed on a doorpost a sacrifice needed to be performed. This bloodshedding event is closely linked with the most prevalent covenant in the Scriptures referred to as the Blood Covenant.

For the purposes of this discussion we will be focused primarily on blood covenants found in the Scriptures, although an attempt will be made to touch upon all of the covenants described in the Scriptures, such as the Salt Covenant.[18]

The irony of a blood covenant is that it is established through death, but it involves a relationship between the living participants. The Scriptures record that "the life is in the blood," so a life is taken by the shedding of blood. (Vayiqra 17:11-14). The shed blood of the covenant is also representative of the punishment resulting from one of the parties breaking the covenant.

Along with the punishment for breaking the covenant there is generally a "sakar" (ᕼᒋ) or rather, a payment, reward or benefit, associated with the Covenant. That benefit may be to one or both of the parties, but there would be no covenant unless there was some sort of resulting benefit.

It is vital to understand that through the blood covenant, Elohim establishes His relationship with Creation. It is through His Covenants that He directs Creation back to Him – back to the Garden. We mentioned the Threshold Covenant at the Garden entrance, but there is much speculation whether there was actually a covenant established with Adam.

The word "brit" is not included in the text, but that, in and of itself, is not conclusive. We know there were terms – obey and live, disobey and die. While man obeyed he was permitted to live in paradise. We know that those terms were eventually breached and there was punishment – the punishment of death. The Creator threw in an interesting twist by introducing the concept of atonement. As a result, the immediate punishment of death was executed on innocent animals – not the actual violators.

There was also punishment meted out to the guilty parties, just not the promised death sentence. Adam and Hawah were permitted to continue their physical existence. They were told their new fates, but they were also given some hope. While they were allowed to live, they would eventually experience physical death. They also experienced spiritual death, which is separation from the source of life – the Creator. Their relationship with Elohim had been severely altered, and because of their conduct they were ejected

from the house – the garden.

     We see hints of a covenant made with Adam and Hawah prior to and during their existence in the Garden, although it is never specifically stated as such. In fact, it is not until after the death of Adam, during the life of Noah that we specifically read about a Covenant.

3

Noah

It is not until the account of a man named Noah that the Scriptures specifically refer to a covenant. We know that after the transgression in the Garden the earth was under a curse. The transgression of Adam and Hawah continued, like a virus, through the man named Qayin. Qayin,[19] the first son of Hawah, killed his brother Hebel.[20]

Hebel had offered up a blood sacrifice with fat from his firstfruits, while Qayin offered only grain offerings that were not designated as firstfruits. YHWH had respect for Hebel's offering, but He did not have respect for the offering of Qayin.

Hebel did what was right in the eyes of YHWH. He presented the proper sacrifice at the Appointed Time while Qayin did not. [21] As a result, Qayin became very angry and killed Hebel.

We are not given much detail in the Scriptures about the life of Adam beyond the fact that he had sons and daughters who then populated the planet. Despite the fact that Adam lived for a period of nine hundred and thirty years, and could personally testify to the effect of sin, the condition of mankind continued to worsen.

The Scriptures record ten generations from Adam to Noah, when the planet was in a terrible state. The

original transgression of Adam and Hawah had spread like a virus with the expansion of men. "¹¹ *The earth also was corrupt before Elohim, and the earth was filled with violence.* ¹² *So Elohim looked upon the earth, and indeed it was corrupt; for all flesh had corrupted their way on the earth.*" Beresheet 6:11-12.

Despite the condition of the planet, we know that Noah was different. "⁵ *YHWH saw that the wickedness of man was great in the earth, and that every intent of the thoughts of his heart was only evil continually.* ⁶ *And YHWH was sorry that He had made man on the earth, and He was grieved in His heart.* ⁷ *So YHWH said, I will destroy man whom I have created from the face of the earth, both man and beast, creeping thing and birds of the air, for I am sorry that I have made them.* ⁸ *But Noah found favour in the eyes of YHWH.*" Beresheet 6:5-8.

The account of Noah continues by stating: "*Noah was a just man, perfect in his generations. Noah walked with Elohim.*" Beresheet 6:9. The Hebrew word translated as "just" is "tzedek" (𐤐𐤆𐤃𐤂𐤍) which means: "*straight or righteous.*" The Hebrew word translated as "perfect" is "tamiyim" (𐤅𐤆𐤅𐤗) which means: "*clean or unblemished.*"

The Hebrew word translated as "walked" is "halak" (𐤇𐤋𐤀), which is where we get "halakah" - a word used to describe our walk with Elohim. Our halakah is the way we live in a manner that is pleasing to Him according to His instructions found within the Scriptures.

Noah obviously knew the way that YHWH had established for men to live. The commands that were given in the Garden were surely transmitted by Adam through his descendants. As a result, Noah walked with

YHWH and was righteous. That meant he followed the instructions of YHWH and was obedient. This provides us with some interesting insight into who YHWH decides to establish His Covenant with.

We have already discussed the "cutting" aspect of the word "brit," and we shall continue to see that throughout the text. The word "brit" also derives from the word "bara" (𐤊𐤀𐤁) which means to "select" or "create." Thus the party to a covenant with YHWH must be selected or "chosen." So in the Scriptural sense, when we talk about a "chosen people" or a "chosen generation" we are talking about those who are in a Covenant relationship with YHWH, and as such, those who walk according to His ways.

Noah was chosen by YHWH to enter into a Covenant relationship. He was told about a covenant that YHWH would establish with him. "*[17] I am going to bring floodwaters on the earth to destroy all life under the heavens, every creature that has the breath of life in it. Everything on earth will perish. [18] But I will establish* ✗✗ *My Covenant with you, and you will enter the Ark - you and your sons and your wife and your sons' wives with you. [19] You are to bring into the ark two of all living creatures, male and female, to keep them alive with you. [20] Two of every kind of bird, of every kind of animal and of every kind of creature that moves along the ground will come to you to be kept alive. [21] You are to take every kind of food that is to be eaten and store it away as food for you and for them. [22] Noah did everything just as Elohim commanded him.*" Beresheet 6:17-22.

YHWH informed Noah that He was going to wipe out life on the planet. YHWH would establish His Covenant with Noah. The word "establish" derives from the Hebrew word "quwm" (𐤒𐤅), which means "to

stand" or "raise up." The Aleph Taw (𐤗𐤀) is an integral element of "establishing" the Covenant that specifically belonged to YHWH. He chose Noah to enter into His Covenant relationship.

As a result, Noah would be saved along with his family and some select creatures. While this was certainly good news for Noah, it was only the beginning of the Covenant process. It was simply a promise that came with conditions. Noah was required to perform his part - he had to build the vessel of his deliverance, which would protect him from the judgment of YHWH. It was also incumbent upon him to store all of the food required for the Ark's passengers. This was a lot of hard work.

If Noah did not build the Ark, he would have been killed along with the rest of mankind. Instead, Noah believed the promise, and his actions were consistent with his belief. Thus, through the obedience of Noah we see the continuation of man and animals. Noah was, in essence, like Adam. He was the father of all of mankind, and because of his obedience, man would continue to physically exist.

When Adam disobeyed, mankind experienced a separation from YHWH and separation from the Tree of Life, the life-giving source of YHWH on planet Earth. The expulsion from the Garden exposed mankind to both physical death and spiritual death. Due to the deterioration of the inhabitants of the planet, YHWH was prepared to wipe them out. Because of the obedience of Noah, mankind would be spared annihilation and all subsequent generations owe their existence to the mercy of YHWH, and the obedience of Noah.

Because of his walk, he found favour in the eyes of YHWH, and he and his family would be spared from the flood. Noah was not an arbitrary choice, he was chosen because of his walk, to build an Ark - a vessel that would save a portion of creation.

The word "ark" in the Hebrew text is "tebah" (ᴬᵍX). It is a very curious and unique word, and if you look at most Hebrew dictionaries you will find that the origin of the word is at question. Some actually believe that it is borrowed from Egyptian or Arabic where similar sounding words refer to a "chest" or a "coffin." Essentially the word has been given its meaning from the context of the passage, not necessarily because of the root meaning.

In cases like this it is especially helpful to look at the ancient language, and in the case of "tebah" (ᴬᵍX) we see the taw (X), the bet (ᵍ) and the hey (ᴬ). Once again, the taw (X) represents a mark and it means: "covenant." The bet (ᵍ) means: "house" and the hey (ᴬ) represents a "window." The pictograph appears as a man with his arms upstretched and it means: "behold." It shows that something important is being revealed.

This word "tebah" (ᴬᵍX) seems to be describing much more than a boat, it is pointing us to something important. A literal definition from the ancient script could mean: "behold the covenant house." It is demonstrating that if we follow the instructions of YHWH, and remain in Covenant with Him, we can enter into His House, where there is protection from the waters of judgment.

There was a window, so this was not a coffin, as many liken the word. In this protected place, man could see and be seen - it was a place of safety meant for the living. It was not a place for the dead, it was a place separated and apart from judgment and death. Death was

on the outside, and life was on the inside.

After YHWH gave the promise, there came a time when He commanded Noah to actually build the Ark. According to the Dead Sea Scrolls, Noah was told by an angel that a flood would occur after a certain number of Shemitah cycles. Most people are unfamiliar with the concept of Shemitah cycles, but it is a most important pattern established on the first week of creation – the pattern of sevens. In the case of the Shemitah cycle, it is a pattern of seven years.

Every seventh year in the count is a Shemitah year which, essentially is a Sabbath year – a year of rest. These Shemitah years are then counted seven times and after the seventh Shemitah year is a Jubilee year. This is how the Creator gauges time, and it is this calculation of time that is imbedded within the Covenant relationship with YHWH.

Therefore, every Jubilee cycle contains seven Shemitah Cycles each consisting of seven years. The seven Shemitah cycles, totaling 49 years, are followed by one Jubilee Year. These 50 years form a Jubilee cycle. You might be wondering why this is important when talking about the story of the flood. The reason why it is mentioned here is because, according to the Dead Sea Scrolls 1 QapGen Col. 6, the flood was to occur in the year that followed a Shemitah cycle.[22]

This would have either been Year 1 of a new Shemitah cycle or a Jubilee Year. The point is that YHWH had Noah counting Shemitah cycles. The importance of the Shemitah count is extremely significant when examining time and creation.[23]

In fact, through this system of reckoning time it was actually revealed how much time man would be given on Earth. The Scriptures record that when YHWH saw the condition of things He declared: *"My Spirit shall not strive with man forever, for he is indeed flesh; yet his days shall be one hundred and twenty (120) years."* Beresheet 6:3.

Many believe that YHWH was giving a limit to the number of years that individual men would be allowed to live, but that is clearly not the context nor is it true since men were recorded as living far longer than 120 years after that declaration. YHWH was speaking of mankind and indicated that he was not going to allow their existence to continue forever.

Clearly men were rebellious and He was not going to contend with them forever. He was establishing a limit and it would be within that period of time He would gather His chosen into His Kingdom through His Covenant. The 120 "years" that YHWH was referring to are actually 120 "cycles" – more specifically – Jubilee Cycles. Since a Jubilee Cycle is 50 years we can discern that YHWH was giving mankind 6,000 years.

This pattern was, of course, established during the first week of creation. As a result, many understand that YHWH would allow men 6,000 years until He would establish His Sabbath reign – the millenial Kingdom. For the time being, He was going to allow them to continue, but He would start over with a righteous man and his seed.

The Scriptures record that: *"Noah did everything just as Elohim commanded him."* Beresheet 6:22. As a result, the Ark was ready to deliver him and his family when the flood waters came. *"¹ YHWH then said to Noah, 'Go into the Ark, you and your whole family, because I have found you righteous in this generation. ² Take with you seven (7) of*

every kind of clean animal, a male and its
mate, and two (2) of every kind of unclean
animal, a male and its mate, ³ *and also seven*
(7) of every kind of bird, male and female, to
keep their various kinds alive throughout the
earth. ⁴ *Seven (7) days from now I will send*
rain on the earth for forty (40) days and
forty (40) nights, and I will wipe from the
face of the earth every living creature I have
made." Beresheet 7:1-4.

    The text then specifically reports the fact that: "*Noah did all that YHWH commanded him.*" Beresheet 7:5. The point is quite clear, Noah obeyed the instructions of YHWH. Notice that Noah was commanded to take seven (7) pairs of clean animals. Previously we read about two (2) of each animal and now we read about seven (7) clean animals. It is important to understand that there is, and always was, a distinction between clean and unclean, righteousness and sin. We currently find those instructions written in the Torah, but they were ever present before mankind.[24]

    Noah knew those distinctions and we already discussed that he was literally described as "righteous" and "clean." The instructions of YHWH were no doubt handed down by Adam, although by this time, very few were actually following them.

    Besides these distinctions, it is also interesting to look at the significance of numbers in the text. Numbers are very prominent and significant in the account of the flood. The Scriptures specifically provide that Noah was six hundred (600) years old when the floodwaters came. The number six (6) is closely tied with man, and we saw that six thousand (6,000) is the number of years given to man.

It is striking to note that Noah lived the equivalent of twelve (12) Jubilee cycles before the flood. As we shall see, the Jubilee is intimately connected with restoration, as is the number twelve (12). This will become even more significant when we examine the role of Israel in the restoration of Creation. We will also see how Noah is a type of savior for mankind and creation.[25]

There is another number that stands out in the story of Noah. The Scriptures record that Noah obeyed YHWH. As a result, he and his wife along with their three sons and their wives were saved from a flood that wiped out the inhabitants of the Earth. The number of people on board the ark was (8) eight.

This number is significant because eight means: "new beginnings." This was to be a new beginning for mankind. We see this in the patterns of seven (7) provided through the Scriptures, so the number eight (8) is essentially the "beginning" of a new cycle, after seven (7). The eighth letter in the Hebrew alephet is het (ח), which means: "fence." This can be seen in the Ancient Hebrew pictograph (𐤇), that actually looks like a fence. The number eight is also closely linked with covenants.

When all preparations were completed YHWH closed the door of the Ark, sealing the eight (8) beings along with the animals inside the "House of the Covenant."

The rains began to fall: "[17] *For forty (40) days the flood kept coming on the earth, and as the waters increased they lifted the Ark high above the earth.* [18] *The waters rose and increased greatly on the earth, and the Ark floated on the surface of the water.* [19] *They rose greatly on the earth, and all the high mountains under the entire heavens were covered.* [20]

The waters rose and covered the mountains to a depth of more than twenty feet. ^{21} *Every living thing that moved on the earth perished - birds, livestock, wild animals, all the creatures that swarm over the earth, and all mankind.* ^{22} *Everything on dry land that had the breath of life in its nostrils died.* ^{23} *Every living thing on the face of the earth was wiped out; men and animals and the creatures that move along the ground and the birds of the air were wiped from the earth. Only Noah was left, and those with him in the Ark.* ^{24} *The waters flooded the earth for a hundred and fifty (150) days.* $^{8:1}$ *But Elohim remembered Noah and all the wild animals and the livestock that were with him in the Ark, and He sent a wind over the earth, and the waters receded.* ^{2} *Now the springs of the deep and the floodgates of the heavens had been closed, and the rain had stopped falling from the sky.* ^{3} *The water receded steadily from the earth. At the end of the hundred and fifty (150) days the water had gone down,* ^{4} *and on the seventeenth day of the seventh month the ark came to rest on the mountains of Ararat.* ^{5} *The waters continued to recede until the tenth month, and on the first day of the tenth month the tops of the mountains became visible.* ^{6} *After forty (40) days Noah opened the window he had made in the ark* ^{7} *and sent out a raven . . ."*
Beresheet 7:17-8:7.

The floodwaters receded and Noah, along with the occupants, exited the Ark safely. It is then that we are told of a Covenant established by Elohim. *"^{8} Then Elohim spoke to Noah and to his sons with him, saying: ^{9} 'And as for Me, behold, I establish My Covenant with you and with your descendants after you, ^{10} and with every living creature that is with you: the birds, the cattle, and every beast of the earth with you, of all that go out of the ark, every beast of the earth. ^{11} Thus I establish My Covenant with you: Never again shall all flesh be cut off by the waters of the flood; never again* *shall there be a flood to destroy the earth.'* [12] *And Elohim said: 'This is the sign of the Covenant which I make between Me and you, and every living creature that is with you, for perpetual generations:* [13] *I set My rainbow in the cloud, and it shall be for the sign of the Covenant between Me and the earth.* [14] *It shall be, when I bring a cloud over the earth, that the rainbow shall be seen in the cloud;* [15] *and <u>I will remember My Covenant which is between Me and you and every living creature of all flesh</u>; the waters shall never again become a flood to destroy all flesh.* [16] *The rainbow shall be in the cloud, and I will look on it to remember the everlasting Covenant between Elohim and every living creature of all flesh that is on the earth.'* [17] *And Elohim said to Noah, 'This is the sign of the Covenant which I have established between Me and all flesh that is on the earth.'"* Beresheet 9:8-17.

It is important, once again, to note that YHWH repeatedly refers to the Covenant as "My Covenant." In other words, it belongs to Him and no one else. This Covenant is an everlasting Covenant. It went beyond the life of Noah, or his immediate descendents for that matter. YHWH promised that He would never again cut off all flesh by a flood, and never again would He use a flood to destroy the whole earth.

There was no corresponding duty or obligation required from man or the animals. It was a promise

accompanied by a sign – the bow. So the ultimate blessing associated with this Covenant was unconditional. There was no further obligation from mankind. Noah had done the work to get them to the point of the Covenant. He had paid the price, and now the rest of mankind and creation would reap the reward –

the sakar.

The fact that there was a sign attached to the Covenant is significant. The Hebrew word for sign is owt, spelled אות in the Babylonian derived modern Hebrew Script and XY𐤊 in ancient Hebrew. It can mean a "mark" or a "token" and is intended to be a visible sign or reminder of the Covenant. We shall see that YHWH often attaches these marks or signs to His Covenants. In the case of the Covenant with Noah and creation, we see the bow as the sign of that particular Covenant. It was a sign placed in the sky visible to all creation.

The word for bow in Hebrew is "qesheth" (XW𐤒). It is interesting that the bow consists of seven colors which correlate to the seven Spirits described by the Prophet Isaiah (Yeshayahu)[26] in Chapter 11 and verse 2 of the text attributed to him. The sign of the Covenant is also the same bow described as being in the Throne Room of Heaven.[27] There is meaning to every color in the rainbow and I encourage the reader to examine this subject deeper.

In addition, from Elohim's perspective in the heavens, the bow was held backward, an ancient sign by which warriors often indicated that a battle was over.[28] We can still see the bow to this day. It is a reminder of His Covenant, which is essentially a demonstration of His mercy and restraint.

While we continue to see floods on the Earth, we have never seen the entire planet judged by water since the time of Noah – a promise kept. The Earth is full of sin, which cries out for judgment. This cry is heard in the Throne Room of YHWH, which is colored by the sign of the promise as a continual reminder. As a result,

YHWH remembers His Covenant and keeps His promise by not judging the Earth by a flood.

There is a pattern established here. As YHWH makes Covenant with His creation, He uses a man as the mediator. In this instance, Noah represented mankind and creation. Part of this Covenant process also involved the shedding of blood.

The Scriptures record that: "*²⁰ Noah built an altar to YHWH, and took of every clean animal and of every clean bird, and offered burnt offerings on the altar. ²¹ And smelled YHWH ✗✦ a soothing aroma. Then YHWH said in His heart, 'I will never again curse ✗✦ the ground for man's sake, although the imagination of man's heart is evil from his youth; nor will I again destroy ✗✦ every living thing as I have done.'"* Beresheet 8:20-21.

Noah had already been saved, but the future promise was sealed by the shedding of the blood. So the Covenant with Noah was essentially two fold. First, Noah had to obey and act in faith in order to be in a place where he and his family, along with the animals, could be saved. Second, YHWH promised that He would never again destroy the planet by a flood.

This was an everlasting Covenant made for all of mankind as Elohim had done with Adam, except that this Covenant was unconditional. It is a unilateral Covenant made between YHWH and mankind. Only YHWH has to keep the Covenant, and He gave a continuing sign of this Covenant for all future generations to see.

Man could not save himself from judgment, and the only way to life was through obedience. Ultimately, it was YHWH Who provided the salvation. To emphasize this point, there are three instances of the un-

translated Aleph Taw (𐤗𐤘) in Beresheet 8:21 when the burnt offerings were being made to YHWH. There are also three instances of the Aleph Taw (𐤗𐤘) when YHWH declares that He will make a covenant. (Beresheet 9:9-10).[29]

YHWH did not have to enter into this Covenant with man. He could have easily stated, "If you continue to sin I will flood the planet again until you learn your lesson." On the contrary, He unilaterally stated that He would never do such a thing again. This is very telling.

It must have grieved the Creator to destroy His creation through the flood. As bad as things had deteriorated, it was still His creation. It was a very difficult decision, and He waited a long time before He finally rendered judgment, which demonstrates His patience. The fact that He made this Covenant with man immediately after the judgment by water is a demonstration that YHWH is a merciful Elohim. He made this Covenant as part of His plan to restore His creation, which reveals His mercy and love.

When Adam and Hawah transgressed His commandments, YHWH could have just killed them and scrapped all of creation. Likewise when the planet was corrupted during the age of Noah, He could have just destroyed everything. Instead He continued to work with certain men to bring about a restoration.

This is the repeating theme that we shall see throughout the Scriptures - the Covenants are specifically designed to bring about the restoration of all things, and YHWH always preserves a righteous line through which He operates His Covenant promises. Thanks to the mercy of the Almighty and the obedience of Noah we are alive today to participate in this process.

There are some who teach that through this Covenant, YHWH established what are commonly referred to as The 7 Noahic Laws. This is an erroneous doctrine which teaches that Gentiles are only required to obey 7 laws to be deemed righteous, while only Jews are required to obey the Commandments of YHWH outlined in the Torah.

Those who teach and believe this doctrine believe that the world is essentially divided into two categories: 1) Jews, and 2) non-Jews - called Gentiles. This is simply preposterous and is not supported by the Scriptures.[30]

The label "gentile" is actually equivalent in meaning to the word "heathen." It means "the nations" and refers to those who are not in Covenant with YHWH. A fundamental teaching in the Scriptures is that righteousness is determined by the heart, and is demonstrated through a persons conduct - whether they obey the instructions of YHWH.

As we shall see, there is no special provision made for Gentiles. There was no such thing as a Jew or even a Hebrew, when Noah participated in this Covenant. In fact, the first Hebrew would not arrive on the scene for another ten (10) generations through Noah's son Shem. That man was named Abram and his name was later changed to Abraham after he too was chosen by YHWH and entered into Covenant with YHWH.

4

Abraham

The Scriptures describe a man named Abram who dwelled in the city called Ur of the Chaldees. This man, while living in the midst of a pagan society, was called out by YHWH Who told him to leave his father's household and travel to the Land of Canaan.

As with Noah, a promise was first given which required action on the part of this man. YHWH gave the following promise and instruction to Abram:

"¹ Go yourself out of your land, from your relatives and from your father's house, to a land which I will show you. ² I will make you into a great nation and I will bless you; I will make your name great, and you will be a blessing. ³ I will bless those who bless you, and whoever curses you I will curse; and all peoples on earth will be blessed through you."
Beresheet 12:1-3.

This was literally a "great" promise. It involved land, and not only would his name be great, but his descendants would become a great nation. In Modern Hebrew, "great nation" is "goy gadol" (ל Y ◁ 7 ז Y 7). The word "gadol" (ל Y ◁ 7) means: "great." The word "goy" (ז Y 7) means: "nations."

Interestingly, the term "goy" is often used to refer

to "gentiles or heathens" – the peoples or nations walking outside of the covenant. This will become more significant as our discussion continues. For the time being, it is important to recognize that Abram is not just a simple man who was randomly chosen to be blessed with wealth and favor. Rather, he was being chosen to establish a kingdom. He was even married to a woman named Sarai (ㄥ⅁W) whose name actually means: "princess."

This promise involved blessings and favor from the Creator. It was an unconditional promise in that Abram did nothing that we know of to earn the blessings, although it was conditioned upon him acting. In fact, the very first word in the promise was "go."

Abram had to leave his home, which surely was no small thing, and go to this land of promise that he presumably had never seen. It meant leaving the life that he knew and had labored to build. It meant leaving the security of the position that he held in his society. It meant travelling through unknown lands, and dwelling in those lands as a stranger.

There were pros and there were cons that Abram may have considered. First and foremost, there was a promise of offspring. This was surely significant, since he had no children at that time. The promise involved a land grant. That was also very significant to a man who raised herds, likely on other people's land.

We do not know if Abram struggled with this decision, all we know is that he obeyed by going. Prior to travelling to the land of Canaan, his father Terah moved the family to Haran, where he lived until his death.

The Scriptures record the following: "*⁴ So Abram departed as YHWH had spoken to him, and Lot went with*

him. And Abram was seventy-five years old when he departed from Haran. ⁵ Then Abram took ✗𝕶 Sarai his wife and ✗𝕶 Lot his brother's son, and ✗𝕶 all their possessions that they had gathered, and ✗𝕶 the people whom they had acquired in Haran, and they departed to go to the land of Canaan. So they came to the land of Canaan. ⁶ Abram passed through the land to the place of Shechem, as far as the terebinth tree of Moreh. And the Canaanites were then in the land. ⁷ Then YHWH appeared to Abram and said, 'To your seed I will give ✗𝕶 this Land.' And there he built an altar to YHWH, Who had appeared to him." Beresheet 12:4-7.

The above Scripture passage that details Abram's departure includes the Aleph Taw (✗𝕶).³¹ Notice that the text describes how he left with "the people they had acquired." The household of Abram included more than just his wife and his nephew. There were many others who travelled with him.

The first location where Abram actually built an altar was in Shechem. This is also the location where YHWH appeared to Abram. YHWH specifically told him that this land would be given to his seed. It was obviously a special place of great significance.³²

Notice that even though Abram was there in the land, it was not immediately given to him. It was for his seed that he did not yet have. Thus, the promise was made to a specific people at a future time. This required faith on the part of Abram. Faith to believe that he would actually have seed, and then faith to believe that the land would be given to that seed.

After his experience with YHWH at Shechem, Abram then moved near Beth El, built another altar and called on the Name of YHWH. He then proceeded further south. (Beresheet 12:5-9).

Abram was on the move much of his life after leaving Haran, and his travels and experiences provide a pattern for future events. One very important pattern was established when he went to Egypt during a terrible famine. There is something important in the Scriptures that is often overlooked. We read the following in English: "*And there was a famine in the land: and Abram went down into Egypt to sojourn there; for the famine was grievous in the land.*" Beresheet 12:10 KJV. The word for "sojourn" is "gowr" (ٹݐٹ) in Ancient Hebrew, which shares the same root as "ger" (ٹٹ). So we see Abram, as a ger, dwelling in Egypt.

While in Egypt, Pharaoh took Sarai captive. The bride of Abram was literally a slave of Pharaoh. Pharaoh held her captive until he experienced great plagues from YHWH. After being plagued, Pharaoh released the bride of Abram and she departed Egypt with Abram, along with great wealth given to them by the Egyptians.

Abram returned to the land of Canaan when instructed. He went to the altar near Beth El and again called on the Name of YHWH. (Beresheet 13:3-4).

There came a time when he and Lot separated. After that time YHWH said to Abram: "*[14] Now lift up your eyes and look from the place where you are, northward and southward and eastward and westward, [15] for all the land which you see I shall give to you and your seed forever. [16] And I shall make your seed as the dust of the earth, so that, if a man could count the dust of the earth, then your seed could also be counted. [17] Arise, walk in the land through its length and its width, for I give it to you. [18] So Abram moved his tent, and went and dwelt by the terebinth trees of Mamre, which are in Hebron, and built an altar there to YHWH.*" Beresheet 13:14-18.

Once again we see a promise of land and of seed. This time it involved a great multitude of seed, as much as the dust of the earth. Abram's entourage grew in size and stature in the land of Canaan. So much so, that he was on the same level as the Canaanite Kings. He had an army and was able to defeat coalitions of sovereigns. (see Beresheet 14). He made a point not to owe homage to any of them, he only paid tithes to the mysterious Melchizedek – The King of Shalom.

Here is the brief account of their interchange. *"18 Then Melchizedek king of Salem brought out bread and wine; he was the priest of El Most High. 19 And he blessed him and said: Blessed be Abram of El Most High, Possessor of heaven and earth; 20 And blessed be El Most High, Who has delivered your enemies into your hand. And he gave him a tithe of all."* Beresheet 14:18-20.

This King was the priest of El Most High (El Eliyon) – the same El that Abram was following and receiving promises from. They broke bread together and drank wine. This King and Priest blessed Abram and he blessed El Eliyon.[33] It is only after this important encounter that we read about Abram entering into Covenant with YHWH in the Scriptures.

"1 After these things the Word of YHWH came unto Abram in a vision, saying, Fear not, Abram: I am your shield, and your exceeding great reward. 2 And Abram said, Master YHWH, what wilt thou give me, seeing I go childless, and the steward of my house is this Eliezer of Damascus? 3 And Abram said, Behold, to me you have given no seed: and, lo, one born in my house is my heir. 4 And, behold, the Word of YHWH came unto him, saying, This shall not be your heir; but he that shall come forth out of your own bowels shall be your heir. 5 And He brought him forth abroad, and said, Look now toward heaven,

and tell the stars, if thou be able to number them: and He said unto him, So shall thy seed be. [6] And he believed in YHWH; and He counted it to him for righteousness. [7] And He said unto him, I am YHWH that brought you out of Ur of the Chaldees, to give you this land to inherit it. [8] And he said, Master YHWH, whereby shall I know that I shall inherit it? [9] And He said unto him, Take me an heifer of three years old, and a she goat of three years old, and a ram of three years old, and a turtledove, and a young pigeon. [10] And he took unto Him all these, and divided them in the midst, and laid each piece one against another: but the birds divided he not. [11] And when the fowls came down upon the carcasses, Abram drove them away. [12] And when the sun was going down, a deep sleep fell upon Abram; and, lo, a terrible great darkness fell upon him. [13] And He said unto Abram, Know of a surety that your seed shall be a stranger (ger) in a land that is not theirs, and shall serve them; and they shall afflict them four (400) hundred years; [14] And also that nation, whom they shall serve, will I judge: and afterward shall they come out with great substance. [15] And you shall go to your fathers in peace; you shall be buried in a good old age. [16] But in the fourth generation they shall come hither again: for the iniquity of the Amorites is not yet full. [17] And it came to pass, that, when the sun went down, and it was dark, behold a smoking furnace, and a burning lamp that passed between those pieces. [18] In the same day YHWH made a Covenant with Abram, saying, Unto your seed have I given this land, from the river of Egypt unto the great river, the river Euphrates: [19] The Kenites, and the Kenizzites, and the Kadmonites, [20] and the Hittites, and the Perizzites, and the Rephaims, [21] And the Amorites, and the Canaanites, and the Girgashites, and the Jebusites." Beresheet 15:1-21.

This is the first time that we read of a Covenant actually being made with this man named Abram. Here

are the essential elements of the Covenant: His offspring would come from his body and they would be very numerous. There was the repeated promise that they would inherit land.

Within the Covenant process Abram was told

that his seed would be strangers in a land not their own, they would be afflicted, but the nation that afflicted them would be judged and his seed would come out with great wealth. In the fourth generation they would come out.[34] He was then provided a description of the borders, which spanned a very large area, well beyond the land of Canaan. He was also promised a long life and a peaceful death.

This is a very important passage that deserves much attention. First, it is important to recognize that "The Word of YHWH" came to Abram in a vision and spoke to him. So the Word of YHWH was visible and audible. Many read right past the powerful realization in this verse. Typically, a word is something spoken which is heard – not seen. Here "the Word of YHWH" came in a vision. It was something or someone that Abram saw.

It was this Word that then introduced Himself by stating: *"I am your shield and your exceedingly great reward."* The word for reward is "sakar," which is the Covenant language we saw earlier. The Word of YHWH is the sakar of the Covenant established with Abram.

There are many who believe that "The Word" was the Messiah. If so, then we have the Messiah stating that He was the payment for the agreement. This appears to be reinforced by the fact that when we are told about the actual terms of the Covenant, the Aleph Taw (✗𝑘) stands between YHWH and Abram. The Hebrew text literally reads: *"In day the same made YHWH ✗𝑘 Abram a Covenant."* (Bersheet 15:18).

Amazingly, in the portion that describes the Covenant that YHWH made with Abram, there are twelve (12) instances of the untranslated Aleph Taw (✗𝑘). Because of this we see a picture of the Messiah passing through the pieces. Therefore, the message is clear that the Messiah would carry the punishment for either party breaking the Covenant. These twelve (12) instances of the Aleph Taw (✗𝑘) appear to reveal that the punishment inflicted upon the Messiah will save the seed. The number twelve (12), as we shall see, is directly related to that seed.

The Word is very active and present during this encounter. The Word is unique and special and the Aramaic Targums refer to "the Memra."[35] Notice that the Word tells Abram that his heir shall come from his own body, not his servant Eliezer. The Word then takes Abram outside and shows him the night sky. Once again there is a promise of a large number of offspring – this time as many as the stars in the heavens. This is a number that cannot be counted, especially with the naked eye.

At this point, the Scriptures record that Abram "believed" in YHWH and it was counted as righteousness. The word "believe" is "aman" (אמן) in

modern Hebrew or ᔯᔮᐊ in Ancient Hebrew. This is an indication that it is righteousness to believe the promises of YHWH. YHWH again promised land, and Abram asks how he will know that he possesses it. In other words, where is the proof of the promise – the covenant.

So far, he had a promise and he acted upon the promise, but the deal had not yet been sealed. Abram first had to go to the land, but he was still a stranger in a land not his own. He clearly had to believe the promise and in order to enter into covenant there was further action required. Abram had to gather the sacrifices and slaughter them. This was a lot of work. In fact, based upon the time indications provided in the text, it probably took all day.

This is an example of a very elaborate blood covenant. By the end of the day Abram had slaughtered the animals and divided them in two, excluding the birds. So we see eight pieces total, displayed parallel to one another with a path of blood running between them. According to the ancient blood covenant tradition, the parties to the covenant would walk between the pieces, in the blood.

Interestingly, this did not happen. The Scriptures record that when the sun was going down, "a deep sleep fell upon Abram." This should immediately bring to mind the incident involving Hawah being birthed from Adam. The word is the same - "tardemah" (ᔯᔮᐊᔮX). As a result, we should be thinking of this Covenant in the context of a marriage covenant.

It was when Abram was in this "deep sleep," which was a picture of death, that Abram was told about his seed and when they would inherit the land. Then, after the sun went down and it was dark, the Covenant was executed. It is important to recognize that the sun setting and darkness indicated a new day.[36]

A key point in this Covenant was the fact that all of the parties did not pass between the pieces. The Scriptures record that "a smoking furnace and a burning torch" passed between the pieces. Abram did not pass through the pieces. In a typical blood covenant, both of the participants would literally walk between the pieces of the covenant, which was drenched with the blood of the slaughtered animal. The parties to the Covenant would both have the blood of the covenant upon them. This entire process symbolized the severity of breaking the covenant – bloodshed and death.

At Beresheet 15:17 we are told to "behold," which is "hineh" (הנה) in modern Hebrew or ᓬ ᕁ ᓬ in ancient Hebrew. The ancient language is particularly interesting in this instance because the character surrounded by each hey (ᓬ) is a nun (ᕁ) which means: "continue" or "perpetuate." It is specifically pointing to the "seed" continuing through this Covenant, which is made while one of the participants is virtually "dead."

A "smoking furnace" and a "burning torch" passed through the cuttings as a demonstration that YHWH would bear the responsibility for both of the parties. The words for "smoking furnace" are תנור עשן. These words can also mean a "smoking firepot." The words for "burning torch" are לפיד אש, literally a "fire flame." Just how exactly these two things appeared is a mystery, but judging from the combined meanings of the words one thing is for sure, there was a lot of fire.

This should immediately direct us back to the beginning. Remember that the word "beresheet" (בראשית) was the word "fire" (אש) surrounded by the

"covenant" (ברית). We know that the Covenant contained fire, which was clearly demonstrated here with Abram. So from the very beginning this event was foretold, and as a result, we should pay close attention.

This was none other than the Word of YHWH passing through the pieces. It meant that the Word of YHWH would pay the price – remember He said that He was the shield and the sakar. He would protect Abram and be the reward as well as the payment if the Covenant was broken. The only requirement on the part of Abram was to believe. His belief was demonstrated by his actions, and this was counted as righteousness.

So this was a Covenant made between Abram and YHWH. The Word of YHWH was the party responsible for keeping the promises and paying the penalty. This Covenant was essentially about the Land grant as was specifically declared after the Covenant was executed.

The Scriptures provide: "*In that same day YHWH made a Covenant with Abram saying To your seed I have given this Land . . .*" Now it is important to understand that this was a very large piece of Land from the Nile River as the western boundary to the Euphrates River as the eastern boundary. While it contained the land of Canaan, it went well beyond the Canaanite territory.

After receiving these great promises and entering into Covenant, Abram eventually awoke. This was a picture of resurrection from his former state of death. Abram entered into Covenant while "dead" and through this Covenant he was given life. So we see that through the Covenant, which he will not pay the penalty for breaking, he would pass from death to life. These promises would flow through his seed.

Up to this point, Sarai had not born any children to Abram. This was, no doubt, quite frustrating to both of them. A woman's stature and worth to her family and community was often dependent on her ability to provide children to her husband, especially sons.

Sarai was surely pained by her inability to provide children to her husband. Abram was obviously frustrated because he was already willing to name Eliezer as his heir. He apparently had resigned himself to the fact that Sarai would not bear him any children.

His faith must have been renewed and refreshed by this Covenant, and the promises provided through the process. He now clearly understood that his seed would come from his flesh, although at this point, Sarai's unique role was not necessarily understood. As a result, we see Sarai actually giving her servant, Hagar, to Abram for the sake of fulfilling this promise. Some look at this act as a hasty or presumptuous decision, but I believe that it ended up providing an important pattern.

While Hagar was the female servant of Sarai, Abram actually married her so they became husband and wife. The Scriptures record that Hagar became his "woman" – aishah (אשה) in Hebrew. Hagar was Egyptian, and she likely came out of Egypt with Abram and Sarai after the plagues upon Pharaoh. She is actually a very interesting and important individual.

The name Hagar contains a mystery that is often overlooked, but it carries a very profound message. In modern Hebrew Hagar is spelled hey (ה), gimel (ג), resh (ר) – הגר. In Ancient Hebrew it appears as ᐞᑎᐞ. The name literally means: "the ger." The word "ger" means: "foreigner, stranger, temporary dweller, newcomer, proselyte or convert."[37] Hagar was actually HaGeR – "the

stranger."

So Abram, who entered Egypt as a ger, experienced an exodus from Egypt with his bride Sarai, and another bride - a foreigner who he would later marry. Hagar came out of Egypt, representing the stranger who became a "convert" by joining into the household of Abram. She was a servant who later became a wife.

After becoming the wife of Abram, Hagar conceived and bore Abram a son named Ishmael, better known as Yishmael. This was now seed from the body of Abram that went into "the ger." Abram was 86 years old when Yishmael was born. It would appear that the problem was solved. Abram now had an heir from his own body through which the promises of YHWH could be fulfilled.

Thirteen (13) years passed. Abram was 99 years old when YHWH again appeared to him in order to enter into Covenant with him.

"*1* *When Abram was ninety-nine years old, YHWH appeared to him and said, 'I Am El Almighty; walk before Me and be blameless.* *2* *I will make (give) My Covenant between Me and you and will greatly increase your numbers.'* *3* *Abram fell facedown, and Elohim said to him,* *4* *'As for Me, this is My Covenant with you: You will be the father of many nations.* *5* *No longer will you be called Abram; your name will be Abraham, for I have made you a father of many nations.* *6* *I will make you very fruitful; I will make nations of you, and kings will come from you.* *7* *I will establish My Covenant as an everlasting Covenant between Me and you and your seed after you for the generations to come, to be your Elohim and the Elohim* of your seed after you. [8] <u>The whole land of Canaan, where you are now an alien, I will give as an everlasting possession to you and your descendants after you; and I will be their Elohim.</u>' [9] Then Elohim said to Abraham, 'As for you, you must <u>keep</u> My Covenant, you and your descendants after you for the generations to come. [10] This is My Covenant with you and your descendants after you, the Covenant you are to <u>keep</u>: Every male among you shall be circumcised. [11] You are to undergo circumcision, and it will be the sign of the Covenant between Me and you. [12] For the generations to come every male among you who is eight (8) days old must be circumcised, including those born in your household or bought with money from a foreigner - those who are not your offspring. [13] Whether born in your household or bought with your money, they must be circumcised. My Covenant in your flesh is to be an everlasting Covenant. [14] Any uncircumcised male, who has not been circumcised in the flesh, will be cut off from his people; he has broken my covenant.' [15] Elohim also said to Abraham, 'As for Sarai your wife, you are no longer to call her Sarai; her name will be Sarah. [16] I will bless her and will surely give you a son by her. I will bless her so that she will be the mother of nations; kings of peoples will come from her.' [17] Abraham fell facedown; he laughed and said to himself, 'Will a son be born to a man a hundred years old? Will Sarah bear a child at the age of ninety.' [18] And Abraham said to Elohim, 'If only Yishmael might live under your blessing!' [19] Then Elohim said, 'Yes, but your wife Sarah will bear you a son, and you will call him Isaac (Yitshaq). I will establish My Covenant with him as an everlasting Covenant for his

descendants after him. ²⁰ *And as for Yishmael, I have heard you: I will surely bless him; I will make him fruitful and will greatly increase his numbers. He will be the father of twelve rulers, and I will make him into a great nation.* ²¹ But My Covenant I will establish (confirm) with Isaac (Yitshaq), whom Sarah will bear to you by this time next year.' ²² When He had finished speaking with Abraham, Elohim went up from him." Beresheet 17:1-22.

Here again we read about a Covenant made with YHWH, and eight (8) times it is referred to as "My Covenant." This time the Covenant is made with Abraham, not Abram. Abram is told to "walk" (halak) before YHWH, and be perfect (tamiym). These are the same words used to describe Noah, the prior individual chosen to covenant with YHWH. His name is then changed to Abraham.

By now, the pattern should be clear. YHWH is looking for certain traits in individuals with whom He will enter into relationship. He wants them to be "clean" by walking in His ways, according to His instructions. The same instructions that were given to Adam and that have always existed – the instructions of the Torah.

This was a different Covenant made with a "different" man. This time YHWH told Abraham that he would be the father of many nations. So significant is this element of the Covenant that it was repeated three (3) times. His seed will not only be numerous, they will also be nations and kings – not just one kingdom. This is a royal Covenant.

It is significant to note that the Land grant associated with this Covenant was only the land of Cannan. This differs from the previous Covenant made with Abram, which spanned from the Nile to the Euphrates. Also, this Covenant was not simply made with one man, it was made with the man and his seed.

Although Abram now had seed, as promised by YHWH, he was informed that Yishmael was not the seed that these promises would flow through. YHWH had another seed in mind.

Abram surely loved his son Yishmael and attempted to intervene on his behalf. YHWH said he would bless Yishmael, who was Abram's seed, but it would be the promised son Yitshaq, who would continue the Covenant with YHWH. Yitshaq would come from Abraham, not Abram. Just as YHWH chose a specific man to establish His Covenant, He would choose a specific seed from that man to continue the Covenant as a perpetual Covenant. Only this time, it would be through the changed man Abraham.[38]

This name change is significant for several reasons. Many attempt to explain the change by stating that Abram simply meant "exalted father," while the name Abraham meant "father of multitudes." This may be true, but does not necessarily make etymological sense. If we look to the ancient script we can glean more information.

The name Abram in the Ancient Script is: 𐤌𐤓𐤁𐤀. As with Adam, the name begins with an aleph (𐤀) and ends with a mem (𐤌). So, once again we see "am" (𐤌𐤀) surrounding the name. The Hebrew word "am" (𐤌𐤀) means: "nations, peoples or womb." In the midst of the name we see "bar" (𐤓𐤁) which means: "son." Remember that with Adam we saw the "dalet" (𐤃), "the door," in the midst of the peoples. Now with Abram we see "the son" equated with "the door."

When his name was changed, a hey (𐤄) was added, and we see something even more profound. His name became Abraham (𐤌𐤄𐤓𐤁𐤀), and it was still surrounded by am (𐤌𐤀), only now there was a new word in the center. In the midst of this new name we have the word "brah" (𐤄𐤓𐤁) which means: "to cut a covenant." So at the heart of this new name we see the cutting of the Covenant, and it is at this point that the Covenant literally is cut in the man – the Covenant of Circumcision.

There is now a pattern developing with the people. We see that the door involves a son of the cutting – the Covenant of Circumcision. Abraham would now be like Adam, he would be the "womb" of this new nation of peoples. We see seed (peoples and nations) coming from Abram, and we see seed (peoples and nations) coming from Abraham.

The important distinction between the two different seeds – Yishmael and Yitshaq - was where they came from, and where they were planted. Yishmael was the seed of Abram, while Yitshaq would be from Abraham. The name change was closely associated with the Covenant of circumcision then established by YHWH. Abraham would now shed his own blood in Covenant with YHWH. While Abram would become a great nation (Beresheet 12:2), from Abraham would come nations and kings (Beresheet 17:6).

The seed - Yishmael - passed through the uncircumcised organ of Abram, while the seed of Yitshaq would pass through the cutting of Abraham. The seed of Yitshaq would literally pass through the cutting of the Covenant made with Abraham. By passing through the cutting, the seed would now be bearing the responsibilities of the Covenant.

Just as the Word of YHWH would bear the penalty of the Covenant with Abram, Abraham and his seed would bear the punishment of breaking the Covenant. This Covenant of circumcision was not just made with Abraham, it was also made with his seed.

Another important distinction between Yishmael and Yitshaq involved where the seed was deposited. In the case of Yishmael, the seed entered into the womb of Abram's wife Hagar – "the stranger." With Yitshaq, the seed would enter into the womb of Abraham's wife, whose name was changed from Sarai to Sarah.

This time, Sarah was a specific and critical part of the Covenant. She had previously received seed from the uncircumcised Abram, but that seed would not bear fruit in her womb. It was only after Abraham was circumcised, and their names were changed, that she could receive the seed and bear a son. Through that seed, which passed through the cutting of the Covenant, she would be the mother of kings. We now have Kingdom language associated with this new man Abraham and this new woman Sarah. YHWH was now establishing a royal family for this promised kingdom.

The Covenant of Circumcision was built upon the prior Covenant, but it was unique in the sense that it was established differently. It involved cutting all the males presently in the household of Abraham – thus by doing so they would be joining into the Covenant.

The Hebrew word for "circumcise" is "namal" (ℓⴄ4). It literally means: "to become clipped" or "to cut off." Circumcision involved cutting the foreskin of the male. Just how much flesh was removed is the subject of debate. There is a belief that the circumcision procedure

today is far more extensive than the ancient tradition.

Regardless of how much flesh was removed, blood was surely shed, and that was the primary point of this particular Covenant, and it is the final distinction between Yishmael and Yitshaq. Yishmael was circumcised when he was 13 years old, while Yitshaq would be circumcised on the 8th day, as would all future generations born into the Covenant. This Covenant too involved shedding blood, but this time it would not be the blood of animals, it would be the blood of men. This was pointing to a future fulfillment of the Covenant.

The circumcision was actually the mark of the Covenant. It was a sign of the Covenant made with Abraham and his seed through Yitshaq, just as the bow was the sign of the Covenant made with Noah. It was a mark that was to be carried on the person of every male. It was a visible reminder of the Covenant.

The location of the mark was particularly significant, because it was intimately associated with the seed. It was inscribed upon an organ that actually pierces the veil of the hymen of a woman, which in turn caused her to shed blood. So in the context of a marriage the symbolism is highly significant.

As mentioned, YHWH also changed the name of Abraham's wife from Sarai to Sara<u>h</u>. He added a hey (ﬡ) to her name also. (Beresheet 17:15). This reveals that the Covenant would pass from the seed of Abraham through the cutting - brit - into the womb of Sarah.

Their very names provide a prophetic picture of this Covenant involving a man and a woman. This was a sort of re-creation. Through the name Abraham we see the "father" (ﬡﬡ) as the source of the seed, passing through the cutting of the Covenant (ﬡﬡﬡ), into the water of the womb (𐤟). Sarah as that womb and her name represents spiritual royalty. A royal family filled with the Spirit.

Just as Hawah was a bride for Adam - YHWH is showing us that through Abraham and Sarah - He was preparing a Bride for Himself. Interestingly, we see two heys (𐤄) added to this union, and we find the hey (𐤄) two times in the Name of YHWH (𐤄𐤅𐤄𐤉).[39]

Abraham was instructed to circumcise himself, and <u>every male in His household</u> - not just his physical seed. This is a very critical point to understand - Abraham had a very large household that traveled with him. They were not all his physical seed, but they were part of his household and they dwelled within his tents. Therefore, the Covenant was made with him and included all of his household - just as the rainbow was the sign of the Covenant made previously with Noah and all of his household in perpetuity.

The significance of the circumcision was that Abraham's seed would pass through the cutting of the Covenant, and then the promises of the Covenant would pass through with the seed. The male child would then be circumcised on the eighth day, and when that child grew up to become a man - his seed would in turn pass through the cutting of the Covenant and so on - it was an everlasting, perpetual Covenant.

There is a distinct connection between the eight (8) pieces of flesh involved in the Covenant with Abram, and the eighth day circumcision of the Covenant established with Abraham, when the flesh of the male is cut. The number eight (8) typically signifies a "new beginning" after the completion of the Scriptural cycle. The fact that Abram and Sarai were both given new

names at the establishment of this Covenant only reinforces that fact.

Remember the number eight is the same as the letter het (ח) in Hebrew, which means: "a fence" or "separation." This concept is evident in the ancient Hebrew script - "ᕼ". Therefore, from this Covenant we can see that the physical descendants of Abraham, and those in his household who were circumcised, were to be set apart.

They were to be surrounded by the hedge of the Torah – just as we saw in the Garden. This is very clear in the Scriptures. In fact, here is what YHWH said about Abraham in Beresheet 18:19: *"For I have known him, in order that he may command his children and his household after him, that they **keep** the Way of YHWH, to do righteousness and justice, that YHWH may bring to Abraham what He has spoken to him."*

We read in the Hebrew text the word "shamar" (שמר) that has been translated as "keep." Abraham was charged to watch and keep the hedge around his children and his entire household - all those who dwelled with him. (Beresheet 17:9). This is the same command given to Adam. Abraham instructed all those who dwelled in his tents in the Way - which is the Torah. Abraham had joined with YHWH, and his household represented the House of YHWH – a people in Covenant with the Creator.

The purpose of this Covenant with Abraham was to prepare a people who could be restored to their Creator. They needed to know and obey the ways of YHWH, and their faith, demonstrated by their conduct, would be counted toward righteousness.

This is an important point to understand.

YHWH demonstrated that He alone would suffer the penalty for the Covenant with Abram. Nevertheless, those in the Covenant of Circumcision walk in the ways of YHWH, just as Abram, and later Abraham, had walked out his faith.

If Abram had not gone from Ur as instructed, he never would have seen the Promised Land. He never would have entered into Covenant with YHWH. His obedience was important to get him to the place where he could be in Covenant with YHWH. His continued obedience was then required to keep him within the hedge of the Covenant – in a place where he could be blessed.

There was still a problem that plagued all of mankind since the garden – death. All the good works in the world would not overcome this barrier that prevents mankind from dwelling with the Living Elohim. This is the underlying purpose of these Covenants made in the life of Abraham – that Abraham, and all those who keep faith with YHWH Elohim, will live with Him.

Abram lived in a pagan society and he needed to come out of that old life and express belief in YHWH. By doing so, the Word of YHWH would make atonement for him. Once this atonement was provided, Abram could then become a new creation. The "hey" (ﬡ) or "breath of the spirit" could then be breathed into him and his mate, just as it had been in Adam and Hawah. These two could then join together and, through the Covenant of Circumcision, become restored to YHWH and walk and be clean.

This is where the pattern of the promised son of the Covenant becomes so important to understand. The promised son was specifically to come from this union

between Abraham and Sarah. This chosen son was named by YHWH Himself and would be called Yitshaq (יצחק).

This promise of a child was given at a specific time - next year at *"the Appointed Time."* Beresheet 18:14.[40] This is important to recognize, because these words were spoken immediately prior to the judgment that was about to befall Sodom and Gomorrah.

Since we are provided some hints that Lot was eating unleavened bread (Beresheet 19:3), Yitshaq's birth likely occurred at the time that we now refer to as Passover.[41] Just as the righteous were delivered from Egypt hundreds of years later, Lot and his family were delivered from judgment during Unleavened Bread.

After Yitshaq was born and grown, Elohim said to Abraham: *"Take your son, your only son, Yitshaq, whom you love, and go to the region of Moriah. Sacrifice him there as a burnt offering on one of the mountains I will tell you about."* Beresheet 22:2.

Imagine! This promised son was a miracle child who was given to Abraham and Sarah in their old age in order to fulfill the promises of great multitudes of descendents. YHWH was now telling Abraham to sacrifice him as a burnt offering. This would involve slaughtering him, by shedding his blood and then burning him by fire.

I doubt that Abraham told Sarah. Instead, early the next morning he arose and took Yitshaq and two servants. On the third day[42] they arrived in the land of Moriah. Abraham told the two servants, "stay here with the donkey, the young man

and I will go yonder and worship, and we will come back to you." Abraham placed the wood of the sacrifice on the shoulders of Yitshaq. Abraham took the fire for the burnt offering and a knife.

Yitshaq must have known that something was amiss. Abraham was probably not himself as he struggled to obey this difficult command. They typically would have brought their sacrifice with them, leading Yitshaq to ask the question: *"We have the fire and the wood. Where is the lamb?"* Abraham's response was: *"Elohim Himself will provide the lamb for the burnt offering, my son."* Beresheet 22:8. A direct translation from the Hebrew reads: *"Elohim will provide Himself a lamb."*

When they came to the place where YHWH had told Abraham to make the offering,  he built an altar and laid out the wood on the altar. Abraham then bound Yitshaq and laid him on the altar to sacrifice him. It is important to note that there is nothing to indicate that Yitshaq struggled or protested. He was a grown man while Abraham was quite old. According to the Book of Yasher, Yitshaq was 37 years old, so he likely could have escaped, but it appears that he willingly laid down his life. (Yasher 22:41,53).[43]

As Abraham was about to slaughter his son, he was stopped by the Messenger of YHWH and told not to touch his son. The Messenger then went on to state: *"Now I know that you fear Elohim, because you have not withheld from me your son, your only son."*

There was a sacrifice made that day, only it was not Yitshaq. It was a ram caught in a thicket by his

horns. This ram in the thicket was then slaughtered and offered as a burnt offering by fire. This was the provision of YHWH, and the entire event provided a picture of how the Covenant with Abraham would culminate. Abraham called the place "YHWH Yireh" as it is said to this day: "In the Mountain of YHWH it shall be seen." The question any reader should ask is: What shall be seen?

This moment was revealing how YHWH would provide the redemption and restoration of Creation through the Covenant with Abraham. It actually brings us back to the former Covenant, and makes the connection between the Word of YHWH and the Lamb of Elohim. This picture of the restoration provided by YHWH repeatedly emphasizes: "your son, your only son." Obviously, Abram had a son named Yishmael, but the "only son" referred to by YHWH was Yitshaq. This distinction is critical.

There is so much more going on in this passage than we can possibly see by simply reading the English. On the surface we see a great promise that "the seed" of Abraham will be incredibly numerous and powerful and all the nations of the earth would be blessed because of the seed.

As with many Scripture passages, we can only understand the profound depth of the text by reading and studying the original Hebrew. For instance, this entire passage is filled with the Aleph Taw (𐤗𐤊), which is a clear indication that it is a Messianic reference.

There are three times that Yitshaq is referred to as, "*your son, your only son.*" In each of those three references there are three occurrences of the untranslated Aleph Taw (𐤗𐤊). In Beresheet 22:9, the passage where it describes Abraham as laying the wood on the altar and binding Yitshaq, there are three occurrences of the untranslated Aleph Taw (✗✗). Also in the following passage when Abraham was prepared to slay Yitshaq there are three occurrences of the untranslated Aleph Taw (✗✗).

It could not be any clearer that this incident, often referred to as "the Akeda," was a shadow picture of the fact that Elohim would provide a Lamb, His only Son. Some believe that Abraham simply obeyed and was willing to kill his son out of pure obedience – in a robotic fashion.

This is neither a fair nor a complete understanding of the faith and righteousness expressed by Abraham, for it is equally clear that Abraham must have believed that his "only son" would be resurrected. Since the Covenant was promised to pass through the son, it was imperative that this "only son" live, even if he was offered as a sacrifice.

Therefore, the faith of Abraham was not so much that he was willing to kill his promised son, pagans regularly offered their children to their gods. The faith of Abraham was more fully expressed by his belief in the resurrection of his son. He specifically told the servants, "we will come back to you." He fully expected Yitshaq to live <u>after</u> being slaughtered.

The Lamb of Elohim would be slain, and the promise to Abraham that *"all nations would be blessed"* would extend through this Lamb. This is powerful information and it can only fully be seen in the Hebrew text.[44]

Many fail to recognize the Messianic significance of this Covenant made with Abraham, which was

proclaimed immediately after he offered his son. A substitute sacrifice was made, just as had been done for Adam and Hawah. YHWH had provided His Lamb in place of the Covenant Son.

"*[15] The messenger of YHWH called to Abraham from heaven a second time [16] and said, "I swear by Myself, declares YHWH, that because you have done* X⟨ *this thing* X⟨ *and have not withheld your son,* X⟨ *your only son,* [17] *that in blessing I will bless and in multiplying I will multiply your* X⟨ *seed as numerous as the stars in the heavens and as the sand on the seashore, and shall possess, your seed,* X⟨ *the gates of their enemies,* [18] *and through your seed all nations on earth will be blessed, because you have obeyed Me."* Beresheet 22:15-18.

The message could not be any clearer. The Covenant Son would receive atonement by the shed blood of the Lamb of Elohim. To confirm this point, in this passage of Scripture, the word "son" is couched between two instances of the untranslated Aleph Taw (X⟨). Likewise, when the Messenger refers to the seed, there are two occasions when the untranslated Aleph Taw (X⟨) is right next to the word "seed."

This is a clear Messianic reference and it is interesting to note that the word "seed" (O⟨⟨) is a singular subject noun, it is not plural. While the seed of Abraham is often interpreted to mean his descendants, the text can also refer to one Seed. This is the same Seed described in Beresheet 3:15, as the promised Seed of Hawah that would crush the head of the nachash.[45]

So we see from this example in the Covenant with Abraham that YHWH would offer up the Lamb of Elohim - His only Son. This offering would be specifically related to the Covenant. That is why

Abraham called the place YHWH Yireh, because "*On the mountain of YHWH it will be seen.*" Beresheet 22:14. On the mountain of YHWH it would be seen how the Lamb of Elohim would be provided.

While tradition holds that this is the same location that the House of YHWH was later erected by Solomon, it is also very possible that this was on the Mount of Olives where the Red Heifer was sacrificed on what is called the Miphkad Altar.[46] The location provided in the Scriptures is the general location "in the land of Moriah," not Mount Moriah specifically.

"In the Jewish tradition, the Binding of [Yitshaq] is also remembered on Passover. The *Akeda* is interpreted as a historical precedent with regard to the miracles associated with the holiday. Because [Yitshaq] was Abraham's first-born son, it is believed that [Elohim] spared the first-born Israelites over the first-born Egyptians because he remembered the Binding of [Yitshaq]. Similarly, there is an idea that the reason the blood of the lamb was spread over the door was to remember that just as the ram was sacrificed in the place of [Yitshaq], the lamb is being sacrificed to save the first-born Israelites. This idea comes from the *Mekhilta of Rabbi Ishmael*, which said " And when I see the blood, I will pass over you. I see the blood of the Binding of [Yitshaq]."[47]

After Abraham had offered the ram, in place of Yitshaq, we read the following: "*[15] The Messenger of YHWH called to Abraham from heaven a second time [16] and said, I swear by Myself, declares YHWH, that because you have done this and have not withheld your son, your only son, [17] I will surely bless you and make your descendants as numerous as the stars in the sky and as the sand on the seashore. Your*

descendants will take possession of the cities of their enemies, [18] and through your offspring all nations on earth will be blessed, because you have obeyed me. [19] Then Abraham returned to his servants, and they set off together for Beersheva. And Abraham stayed in Beersheva." Beresheet 22:15-19.

This was a sort of merging of the Covenants made with Abram and Abraham. Previously, YHWH had promised seed as numerous as the dust of the Earth, prior to Abram entering into the Land. Later, when YHWH entered into Covenant with Abram, He promised seed as numerous as the stars of the heavens. Now after offering up His only son, the promise was elevated to include numbers as great as the stars in the heavens <u>and</u> the sand on the seashore. This is a promise not to be taken lightly, and the significance will become clearer as this discussion continues.

It is important to point out that the Scriptures only describe Abraham coming down from the mountain, even though Abraham indicated to his servants that both he and his son would return. This begs the question: "Where was Yitshaq?"

Some use this passage to assert the position that Yitshaq actually was sacrificed, and was later resurrected. The text simply does not support such a notion. Rather, he may have stayed on the mountain.

Yitshaq was likely alive, but the absence of him returning with Abraham, and then his sudden appearance years later when Abraham decides to find him a bride, makes an interesting metaphorical death and resurrection. This, of course, is consistent with the pattern provided by the event, and the faith demonstrated by Abraham that his "only son" would be resurrected.[48]

Notice, once again, that this was a sacrifice with a fire, which connects with the message provided from the beginning – Beresheet (Χ𝟤𝐖𐤊𝟫𝟬). Remember that there was fire – "esh" (𝐖𐤊) in the midst of the brit (Χ𝟤𝟫𝟬). Remember also that during the Covenant made with Abram, the Word of YHWH passed between the cuttings, in the blood of the Covenant. The Word of YHWH is therefore directly connected to the Promised Son – The Lamb of Elohim. There is blood and fire associated with this Covenant of YHWH.

The Covenant made with Abraham is an everlasting Covenant. It is still in existence. That Covenant did not belong to Abraham or his seed. It always belonged to YHWH, but it was confirmed, or rather, established through the line of Yitshaq, not through the line of Yishmael.

That does not mean that Yishmael was never in Covenant with YHWH. When he was circumcised with his father, and when he dwelled in the Tents of his father, he was indeed in Covenant with YHWH. Whether he would remain in Covenant is yet to be seen, but there was another level of fulfillment that would occur through the promised son Yitshaq and his seed.

The Covenant involving the land of Canaan was made with Abraham's seed through Sarah, not Hagar. This has resulted in a deep-seeded sibling rivalry for the blessing of YHWH, which has continued for 4,000 years.

It is important to remember that YHWH promised to make Abraham the "father of many nations." He made this point very clear that the Covenant people would consist of many nations. YHWH also indicated that Sarah would be the mother of nations. Therefore, as we look upon the earth today

we see that the seed of Abram and Hagar, as well as the seed of Abraham and Sarah have been spread throughout the earth becoming many nations. Not one nation or two, but many nations with numerous kings.

If you serve the same Elohim as Abraham, then you must learn from and follow the spiritual journey blazed by Abraham. The Covenant cycles that he lived out are patterns for us to learn from as we too enter into the Covenant of YHWH.

Abram came out of a pagan culture and was the first recorded Hebrew. He "crossed over" from a foreign land to the Land promised to him by YHWH. He believed YHWH, and that belief was counted as righteousness.

He entered into Covenant with YHWH while he was uncircumcised. He walked with YHWH, and he guarded the instructions. He did not just believe in his heart, his belief was expressed through his actions – through his walk. He then entered into the Covenant of circumcision. He was cut, his blood was shed, and he bore the sign of the Covenant. Through this process Abram was given a new name, he became a new man.

It is critical to understand that YHWH entered into Covenant with Abram, and later entered into Covenant with Abraham. While he was the same being, he was a changed man. The man Abram was uncircumcised, while Abraham was circumcised. This is a pattern and would appear to point to a future progression that his seed must make as they cross over from death to life, from goy to Hebrew. To a time when they too would need to become circumcised as Abraham was circumcised.

The Covenant made through Abraham is critical

to understand. Up to Abraham, we saw glimpses of the plan of YHWH. Through the life of that man and his seed, and the Covenant process involving them all, YHWH revealed His plan for the restoration of mankind.

The promises given to Abraham were not all fulfilled during his life, nor the life of the promised son and his direct descendents. Abraham had to trust YHWH, even beyond his life to fulfill those promises.

5

Israel

From the Covenant made with Abraham we see a clear picture of the promised Son, the Messiah. The Son Who will come from the line of Abraham through Yitshaq. Remember that Yitshaq was considered to be "the only son" of Abraham. This is because Yishmael came from the uncircumcised Abram.

Yishmael was not the promised son of the Covenant of circumcision made with Abram, because he did not pass through the cutting of the Covenant. He did not come from Sarah, and he was not circumcised on the 8th day. The promised son is a son of the Covenant, and YHWH made it clear that the seed must also enter the ordained womb, just like a seed must be planted in the right soil.

This does not mean that people outside of this line could not be in the Covenant. Anyone who was circumcised and followed the Torah, the instructions of YHWH, could join into the Covenant. YHWH was simply revealing a deeper fulfillment of the Covenant through the promised son. Yitshaq would reveal how the Son would pass through the Covenant, and how the Son would be offered up as the Lamb of Elohim.

Abraham now understood that it was not only important where the seed came from, but also where it was planted. Yitshaq was the first son of the Covenant that passed through the cutting of Abraham, and he was circumcised on the 8th day. Accordingly, it was critical that the seed that passed from Yitshaq also be planted in the proper womb.

As a result of his special status, Abraham did not want Yitshaq to intermarry with those who dwelled in the Land of Canaan. Even though this was the Land that his seed would eventually inherit, the people of the Land were polluted, and it was important that his son marry from within his clan.

It is important to note that Yitshaq did not leave the Land to seek out a bride. Rather, the servant went out and found a bride and brought her back to the Land. The bride was brought to Yitshaq from a far off land by Abraham's servant Eliezer. This was the same Eliezer who Abraham thought might be his heir.

Eliezer means: "El is my helper" or "El is my protector." He left the Promised Land to search out a bride for Yitshaq, after swearing an oath to Abraham not to take Yitshaq with him back to Haran. Many Scriptures record that he made the oath by placing his hand "under the thigh" of Abraham, but it was much more explicit. Eliezer actually placed his hand on the circumcision of Abraham while swearing this oath because this act of finding a bride for Yitshaq was an integral part of the Covenant that, in turn, was linked with the promised son and the Promised Land.

That circumcision represented all of the promises made by YHWH to this new man Abraham. It was the actual sign of the Covenant. Eliezer also carried this sign, since he remained in the household of Abraham. Therefore, he too was joined in the Covenant. This may

seem a strange event, but probably not to these two men who had both been circumcised in their old age, and who understood the solemn importance of the Covenant with YHWH.

Their circumcisions were not inward decisions made in some quiet, private solemn ceremony. Rather they were bloody, painful and messy, likely requiring the assistance of others to actually cut the flesh of their very intimate private parts. These two men had seen a lot together, and they had been through a lot together. In fact, it is very probable that they circumcised each other.

As a result, Eliezer knew the significance of this sign, he had felt the pain and shed the blood of that same Covenant. He was the one who Abraham originally intended to inherit, but that decision was trumped by the very Covenant that he had entered into. It was through that very cutting that the promised son was given. It was therefore imperative that Yitshaq and his Bride be married in the Promised Land.

The servant travelled back to the land of Abram and sought a wife for his master's son. Eliezer went to the land of Mesopotamia, and after praying, he found Ribkah. He gave her gifts: a nose ring and two bracelets of gold weighing ten sheqels. After negotiating the bride price and giving gifts to her family, Eliezer transported Ribkah along with her maids and Abraham's servants on ten (10) camels.

When Yitshaq first met Ribkah, we read in the Scriptures that he took her into his mother's tent and "married" her. The Hebrew is more to the point as it states: "he took ✗𐤊 Ribkah and she became his wife, and he loved her." Beresheet 24:67. This was no ordinary "church wedding" as Yitshaq apparently skipped the nuptials and consummated their relationship without delay. It is significant that he took her into Sarah's tent. Sarah was dead, but her tent would now become the dwelling place of Ribkah, which means that the Covenant seed would pass into her, as it had with Sarah.

In the passage we have a clear Messianic reference as can plainly be seen in the Hebrew text. Between the words "took" and "Ribkah" is the Aleph Taw (𐤀𐤕), which represents the Messiah, as the promised Covenant Son, consummating the marriage Covenant with the Bride of the Covenant in the Covenant Land. Notice that the Bride was brought into the Land from far off – out of Babylon. This is an important pattern.

The Scriptures record that "²⁰ *Yitshaq was forty (40) years old when he took Ribkah as wife, the daughter of Bethuel the Armite of Padan Aram, the sister of Laban the Aramite.* ²¹ *Now Yitshaq pleaded with YHWH for his wife, because she was barren; and YHWH granted his plea, and Ribkah his wife conceived.* ²² *But the children struggled together within her; and she said, 'If all is well, why am I like this?' So she went to inquire of YHWH.* ²³ *And YHWH said to her: 'two nations are in your womb, two peoples shall be separated from your body; one people shall be stronger than the other, and the older shall serve the younger.'* ²⁴ *So when her days were fulfilled for her to give birth, indeed there were twins in her womb.* ²⁵ *And the first came out red. He was like a hairy garment all over; so they called his name Esau.* ²⁶ *Afterward his brother came out, and his hand took hold of Esau's heel; so his name was called Jacob. Yitshaq was sixty (60) years old when she bore them.* ²⁷ *So the boys grew. And Esau was a skillful hunter, a man of the field; but Jacob was a mild man, dwelling in tents.* ²⁸ *And Yitshaq loved Esau because*

he ate of his game, but Ribkah loved Jacob." Beresheet 25:19-
28.

The number forty (40) has deep Messianic
significance,[49] and though this Covenant son married his
bride when he was forty (40), she did not conceive until
he was sixty (60) years old. It turns out that Ribkah was
initially barren, as was Sarai. Only through prayer was
she eventually able to conceive two children who would
eventually become two nations.

Her older son was named Esau and her younger
son was named Jacob. Ribkah was told that the older
would serve the younger, which was not the norm. So we
know that the Covenant promise would pass through the
younger son, although that was not immediately
apparent to their father Yitshaq, or the older son Esau,
who fully expected all the rights and privileges of the
first born son.

The life of Jacob is filled with much deception
and intrigue. He was a twin who wrestled with life, even
inside the womb. We read from the account of his birth
how he struggled to be the firstborn, and came out of the
womb grasping his brother Esau's heel. Thus the name
Jacob, which is Yaakob (יעקב) in Hebrew, means
"supplanter."

From his birth it appears that Yaakob desired the
firstborn status. He was reminded daily, through his
name, just how close he was to having it. After he was
grown we read how his brother Esau sold his birthright
for a bowl of stew.

After this event, we read that Esau "despised his
birthright." Essentially, he despised the Covenant.
(Beresheet 25:34). The Scriptures then describe a famine
in the land "beside the first famine that was in the days

of Abraham." YHWH then appeared to Yitshaq and specifically instructed him not to go to Egypt. Typically, Egypt was a place of refuge and provision during periods of famine and persecution. Once again, we see that Yitshaq was not to leave the Covenant Land.

During the meeting, the Covenant promise is declared to Yitshaq: "*3 Sojourn in this land, and I will be with you, and will bless you, for unto you and unto your seed I will give all these countries and I will perform the oath that I swore with Abraham your father. 4 And I will make your seed to multiply as the stars of heaven and will give unto your seed all these countries, and in your seed all the nations of the earth will be blessed. 5 Because that Abraham obeyed (shema) My voice and kept (shamar) My charge, My commandments, My statutes and My instructions (torah).*" Beresheet 26:3-5.

Notice the emphasis on "My." Again, this Covenant belonged to YHWH. Abraham was allowed to participate because he listened, obeyed and kept the terms of the Covenant. For Yitshaq to receive the blessings, he needed to do the same. Yitshaq indeed stayed in the land of Gerar. He was truly blessed by YHWH. The Scriptures record that: "*12 Yitshaq sowed in that land and received in the same year an hundred fold, and YHWH blessed him. 13 And the man waxed great and went forward and grew until he became very great.*" Beresheet 26:12.

Yitshaq then went about opening the wells of Abraham that the Philistines had stopped up. He also dug new wells and was repeatedly in conflict with the herdsmen of Gerar. He finally received a respite when he dug a well and was at peace. He named the well Rehoboth. He then moved to Beersheba where YHWH again appeared to him. He was again given the promise

of the Abrahamic Covenant. YHWH said the He would bless Yitshaq and multiply his seed. Then Yitshaq built an altar, called upon the name of YHWH, pitched his tent and dug a well, called Shebah.

When Esau was forty (40), he married two (2) Hittite women. This demonstrates that he was living in rebellion, outside the Covenant. This grieved his parents, and the time was now ripe for Yaakob to "seal the deal" concerning the birthright. When Yitshaq was old and his eyes were dim, Yaakob, with the assistance of his mother, deceived his father Yitshaq. By pretending to be Esau, Yaakob received the blessing of Esau.

We read in the Scriptures how Yitshaq, almost reluctantly, blessed Yaakob. It appears that Yitshaq suspected something was afoul. Regardless, he blessed Yitshaq with the blessing of the firstborn - an act which apparently could not be undone.

After he had actually "officially" lost the blessing, Esau was filled with anguish and rage. This prompted Yaakob to flee the Land that his fathers were promised, and find safe haven with his Uncle Laban, Ribkah's brother. His departure was also based upon the concern of his father and mother that he not marry "*the daughters of the land.*" Beresheet 27:46.

This was the same concern expressed by Abraham for Yitshaq. Therefore, Yaakob was sent to the family of Ribkah to find a bride. So while Yitshaq remained in the Land while a bride was brought to him, Yaakob fled the Land in search of his bride.

Before Yaakob left, his father spoke a blessing over him. Interestingly, this was after he was deceived, so he was apparently resigned to the fact that Yaakob was to receive the blessing. It is possible that he knew all along, and had merely been testing Yaakob.

In any event, we now read that Yitshaq freely spoke a blessing over Yaakob, and charged him as follows: "*¹ You shall not take a wife from the daughters of Canaan. ² Arise, go to Padan Aram, to the house of Bethuel your mother's father; and take yourself a wife from there of the daughters of Laban your mother's brother. ³ May Elohim Almighty bless you, and make you fruitful and multiply you, that you may be an assembly of peoples; ⁴ And give you the blessing of Abraham, to you and your descendants with you, that you may inherit the Land in which you are a stranger which Elohim gave to Abraham. ⁵ So Yitshaq sent Yaakob away, and he went to Padan Aram, to Laban the son of Bethuel the Syrian, the brother of Ribkah, the mother of Yaakob and Esau.*" Beresheet 28:1-5.

On his way from Beersheba to Haran, Yaakob stopped to rest. "*¹¹ When he reached a certain place, he stopped for the night because the sun had set. Taking one of the stones there, he put it under his head and lay down to sleep. ¹² He had a dream in which he saw a ladder resting on the earth, with its top reaching to heaven, and the messengers of Elohim were ascending and descending on it. ¹³ There above it stood YHWH, and he said: 'I am YHWH, the Elohim of your father Abraham and the Elohim of Yitshaq. I will give you and your descendants the land on which you are lying. ¹⁴ Your descendants will be like the dust of the earth, and you will spread out to the west and to the east, to the north and to the south. All peoples on earth will be blessed through you and your offspring. ¹⁵ I am with you and will watch over you wherever you go, and I will bring you back to this Land. I will not leave you until I have done what I have promised you.' ¹⁶ When Yaakob awoke from his sleep, he thought, "Surely YHWH is in this place, and I was not aware of it." ¹⁷ He was afraid and*

said, *How awesome is this place! This is none other than the house of Elohim; this is the gate of heaven."* Beresheet 28:11-17.

When Yaakob awoke, he called the place called Bethel or rather Beit El. Beit means: "house" and El is the short form of Elohim. Thus the place was called "House of El." It was here, after he had received the blessing of his father, that he happened upon the House of Elohim, where he would meet YHWH. It was here that he understood the Covenant promise was now to flow through him and his seed.

One cannot ignore the parallels from the Covenant with Abram. Remember Abram was at Bethel when Lot left him – Lot the son of Haran. Now Yaakob was at this same place, on his way to Haran. It was at this place that Abram built an altar and called on the Name of YHWH.

It was here that the following words were spoken to Abram: *"¹⁴ Lift up your eyes from where you are and look north and south, east and west. ¹⁵ All the land that you see I will give to you and your offspringᵃ forever. ¹⁶ I will make your offspring like the dust of the earth, so that if anyone could count the dust, then your offspring could be counted. ¹⁷ Go, walk through the length and breadth of the land, for I am giving it to you."* Beresheet 13:14-17.

So the promise of a multitude of seed as the "dust of the earth" was given to Abram at Bethel, as he was given the Land and told to walk throughout the Land. Yaakob was given the same promise at Bethel, after sunset. He was told that his seed would fill the Land. Like Abram, he had no seed at the time that the promise was given. Unlike Abram, he was on his way out of the Land, and did not know when he would return.

Early in the morning, at the dawning of the day, "¹⁸ . . . Yaakob took ✕𝐊 the stone he had placed under his head and set it up as a pillar and poured oil on top of it. ¹⁹ He called ✕𝐊 the name of that place Bethel, though the city used to be called Luz. ²⁰ Then vowed Yaakob a vow, saying, If Elohim will be with me and will watch over me on this journey I am taking and will give me food to eat and clothes to wear ²¹ so that I return safely to my father's house, then YHWH will be my Elohim ²² and this stone that I have set up as a pillar will be Elohim's house, and of all that you give me I will give you a tenth." Beresheet 28:18-22.

He set up the stone that he rested his head upon, as a pillar or a memorial stone, and poured oil upon the "head" of it at the dawning of the day. It is highly significant to note that this stone, which was literally lying down, used as his pillow while he slept, was raised up at the dawning of the day. He literally "anointed" this stone with oil which, in the Hebrew text, is closely linked with ✕𝐊. This act of "anointing" the stone should draw attention to the stone, particularly in the Hebrew.

The word for stone is "aben" (𝟒𝟗𝐊) in Hebrew. It begins with "ab" (𝟗𝐊), which means: "father" and ends with "ben" (𝟒𝟗), which means: "son, branch or shoot." The letter that connects these two together is the bet (𝟗) – the house. Recall the enlarged bet (𝟗), at the very beginning.

The house was emphasized at the beginning of the Scriptures and now we see this anointed stone at Bethel – the House of YHWH. This is an incredibly important event because it reaffirms the father/son aspect of the Covenant, connected in the House. Our full attention is now directed to the Messiah, the Anointed

Son, standing in the House - the place where Abram had built an altar to YHWH. This was a place where blood was shed, and this was a place of the Covenant – the House of Elohim.

Yaakob made a vow to Elohim essentially promising that if YHWH would protect him and take care of his physical needs, then YHWH would be his Elohim. He declared that the stone that he anointed would be YHWH's House, and that he would give a tenth of all that he had to YHWH. This was the same tithe that Abram had given to Melchizedik, and the reference here seems to connect the concepts with the Covenant. Remember, this is a great picture being painted by the Master. As we read the Scriptures we gradually see His plan, through the Covenant, come together.

After the event at Bethel, Yaakob then departed in peace. He went on to prosper in the household of Laban, although things did not go exactly as planned. Just as he had deceived his father, he too was deceived into marrying Laban's oldest daughter Leah when he thought it was Rachel.

While outside the Land he had eleven sons by his two wives, Leah and Rachel, and two concubines, Bilhah and Zilpah. His sons were Reuben, Simeon, Levi, Judah, Dan, Naphtali, Gad, Asher, Issachar, Zebulun and Joseph. This is important, because things are coming full circle. Remember the path that Abram took, through this very land into the Land of promise, into Egypt and then back to the land of Canaan. As far as we know, the first son of the Covenant, the only son of Abram never left the Land. Now we see this son of the Covenant fleeing the Land and having eleven (11) sons outside the Land –

the last and youngest being Joseph.

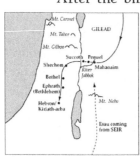

After the birth of Joseph, and twenty (20) years after he began working for Laban, Yaakob departed from the household of Laban and returned to the Land of his fathers. Yaakob then turned his attention to confronting his brother Esau, who he thought might want to kill him after the deception concerning the birthright.

On his way home, he saw two messengers and called the place "mahanaim" which means "two camps" in Hebrew. This is significant because it explains what Yaakob does next. When he was informed that Esau was coming to meet him, he divided his family – his tribe – into two camps or two households. (Beresheet 32:8). He apparently did this to protect them in the event that Esau attacked - believing that if one were attacked the other could escape. This was actually a prophetic picture of a future event, a future division of the Children of Yisrael who were destined to become many nations.

In preparation of the impending conflict, Yaakob sent gifts ahead of him. He sent his family and possessions to the other side of the ford of Yabbok until he was alone. It is there, when he was alone, that he wrestled with a man until the break of day. This was the dawning of the day, which is a very special time of day that has great Messianic significance.[50]

The man touched the "socket of his hip" which was wrenched. Regardless of this inflicted injury, Yaakob would not let go until he received a blessing. The man told him: "*Your name will no longer be Yaakob, but am*

(אֵל) Yisrael, *because you have struggled with Elohim and with men and have overcome.*" Beresheet 32:28. He then blessed Yaakob, but he would not tell him his name.

This change of name is quite significant, as with every name change that we read about in the Scriptures. His name was changed from Yaakob to Yisrael (יִשְׂרָאֵל), which is quite a significant change. Often a name change would involve adding a letter, but in this case the new name was drastically different.

It should immediately make one think of Yishmael (יִשְׁמָעֵאל), the son of Abram. Interestingly, these two names are remarkably similar, yet there are some very important differences.

The name Yishmael is often translated "El will hear." This translation is due to the fact that the word "shema" (שָׁמַע) is located in the middle of the name. Shema, also rendered sh'ma, actually means: "hear and obey." We hear and obey El, thus the name Yishmael. Remember that Yishmael was a loved son of Abram and he was, in fact, circumcised and entered into the Covenant.

We can learn that those who desire to be in the Covenant must "hear and obey El" which is what Abram did, in order to get into a place where he could walk in the fullness of the Covenant. This is the first step in the Covenant walk. We then look to Yisrael for the next step, or cycle, in the Covenant.

Yisrael (יִשְׂרָאֵל) is often translated to mean: "he will rule as El." This is because the name actually contains the root of the name of Sarah – sar (שַׂר). "Sar" means: "ruler or prince." Interestingly, we can break the name Yisrael (𐤋𐤀𐤓𐤔𐤉) down further in the Ancient Script, which provides even more detail. We could define the word as "the possession (W𝟐) of El (𝓛𝓴) with El in the center, as the head (𝟒)." The root "yisr" (𝟒W𝟐) means: "straight." So Yisrael could mean "those who belong to El, who follow El and walk straight in His path."

Names are often an important part of understanding the Scriptures, and the names of these two seed tell us much concerning the Covenant path. The lives of these two seed are also remarkably similar. We already read how Yishmael would have twelve (12) sons, called princes, who would become a great people. (Beresheet 17:21). We shall soon see that Yisrael also will have twelve (12) sons.

Despite the similarities, there were also some very important and distinct differences. While Yishmael was the eldest son, he came from the uncircumcised Abram. He was not the promised son that would be given to Abraham through Sarah, nor was he circumcised on the 8th day as was Yitshaq. Yisrael, did not come directly from Abraham, but rather, he came from the circumcised "promised son" – the one who represented the Messiah as the Lamb of Elohim.

Therefore, the similarity in their names and lives is intended to draw our attention to them, and actually highlight the differences. Those differences reveal a pattern. Yishmael represents one born in an uncircumcised state who later enters into Covenant with Elohim. This one came from the womb of HaGer – the stranger.

While Abram was uncircumcised, he heard and obeyed (shema) the voice of Elohim. In this uncircumcised condition he entered into Covenant with Elohim – the Word of YHWH. Because of his

obedience, he was given an even greater promise. Yisrael represents the next level in the Covenant where, through the Promised Son - the Lamb of Elohim - we enter into the Kingdom of Elohim as nobility (sar).

These Covenant promises are actually playing out in history through the physical seed, but their spiritual fulfillment points to a Kingdom Family that will fill the House of Elohim.

In that regard, there is another very interesting item in the passage describing the name change. If you were simply reading a translation you would miss it completely. In the Hebrew text the word "am" (𐤏𐤌) appears right next to the name Yisrael. This was the "am" (𐤏𐤌) that we discussed earlier, and it was signifying that the Covenant points to Yisrael. The people of Yisrael are the Covenant people promised from the beginning. They are the noble family that would be in the Kingdom.

As a Covenant people, Yisrael returned with his twelve (12) children, eleven (11) sons and one (1) daughter, to the Covenant Land - Land of Canaan. Interestingly, the text continues to call him Yaakob. The first place that they lived was Succot. Yaakob built a house (beit) and succas for his animals – thus the name of the place. This is a very significant place, and as we shall see, it is also a time. This subject will be discussed further on in the text.

After leaving Succot, they then moved to the region of Shechem, another very significant place, where Yaakob bought some land and built an altar. In the Hebrew, it says that he came to "Shalem, a city of Shechem" a distinction often overlooked in translations.

Remember that Abram broke bread and drank

wine with Melchizedek, the King of Shalem, who was a priest of El Eloyon (El Most High). Beresheet 14:18. Amazingly, Yaakob built an altar and called it El Elohe Yisrael, which means: "The Mighty El of Yisrael." Yaakob was using his new name and connecting it directly with Elohim. He was acting in the capacity of Melchizedek, a king and priest of El.

After an incident involving his daughter Dina, and certain sons deceiving and slaughtering the men of Shechem, Yaakob decided to move his family. There were problems and they needed to get cleaned up. The Scriptures record that: "*⁴ So they gave Yaakob all the foreign gods they had and the rings in their ears, and Yaakob buried them under the oak at Shechem. ⁵ Then they set out, and the terror of Elohim fell upon the towns all around them so that no one pursued them.*" Beresheet 35:4-5.

He returned to the place where his journey began – Beit El – the House of Elohim. He built an altar and called it El Beit El, because it was there that Elohim revealed Himself to Yaakob. It was here at this special place that he had another encounter with Elohim.

"*⁹ After Yaakob returned from Paddan Aram, Elohim appeared to him again and blessed him. ¹⁰ Elohim said to him, 'Your name is Yaakob, but you will no longer be called Yaakob; your name will be* 𐤅𐤀 *Yisrael.' So He called* 𐤗𐤀 *his name Yisrael. ¹¹ And Elohim said to him, 'I am Elohim Almighty; be fruitful and increase in number. <u>A nation and a community of nations will come from you, and kings will come from your body</u>. ¹² The Land I gave to Abraham and Yitshaq I also give to you, and I will give this Land to your descendants after you. ¹³ Then Elohim went up from him at the place where he had talked with him. ¹⁴ Yaakob set up a standing stone* (𐤉𐤏𐤀) *at the place where Elohim had talked with him, and*

he poured out a drink offering on it; he also poured oil on it.[15] Yaakob called the Name of the place where Elohim had talked with him Elohim Beit El." Beresheet 35:9-15.

This event completed a cycle which began and ended at The House of Elohim. It began there when Yaakov was fleeing the Land. He was awestruck by the vision he had seen, and declared to be the House of Elohim – the very door to the Heavens. He set up a standing "stone" (𐤀𐤁𐤍) and poured oil over it. He also made an oath to Elohim.

The cycle ended with a confirmation of the Covenant, which included "a nation and a community of nations . . . and kings." It also involved the Land promised to Abraham and Yitshaq – the Land of Canaan. He, once again, set up a standing "stone" (𐤀𐤁𐤍), only this time he poured a libation offering and oil upon the stone. We see in the Hebrew similar language to that used to anoint a king. This stone, pronounced "aben" (𐤀𐤁𐤍), standing in the House of Elohim represented the anointed King. The King Who would come through the Covenant. This is powerful imagery which cannot be ignored

Yaakob had fled the Land promised to his fathers and lived in exile – a veritable slave to his father-in-law. He returned a different man – a man with direction and purpose – a man in Covenant with YHWH. This "new man" was given a new name, 𐤀𐤋 Yisrael, signifying that he was not the same person as the last time he was there. He was now representing a community of people in Covenant with YHWH. He was remembering his vow and walking in the Covenant way.

After leaving Bethel we read that Rachel gave birth to Benjamin, his twelfth son, just outside of

Bethlehem. Rachel was also the mother of Joseph, who was the youngest son when they lived outside the Land. Interestingly, Joseph was the last in the procession to enter and dwell in the Land when Yisrael divided his household. Benjamin, on the other hand, was the only child to be born in the Land, and he remained the youngest of the sons of Yisrael. Sadly, Rachel died while giving birth to Benjamin.

Very interestingly, it is after the birth of Benjamin that the Scriptures briefly refer to Yaakob by his new name Yisrael. It appears that Benjamin brought a completion to the Community of Yisrael. The birth of Benjamin must have been  bittersweet for Yisrael, as his favored wife, Rachel, was now dead. Yisrael eventually returned to his father Yitshaq who was living in Hebron. It was there that he saw his father die when he was 180 years old. Both Esau and Yisrael buried Yitshaq there, a very significant place where Abraham and Sarah were also buried.

As the twelve (12) sons of Yisrael grew up in the Land, we read of a conflict that arose between Joseph and the rest of his brothers. The Scriptures record that Joseph was the favored son of Yisrael. "*Yisrael loved* ✗✗ *Joseph more than his other children.*" Beresheet 37:3. Notice the ✗✗ attached to Joseph. This is a clue that the life of Joseph has great Messianic significance. Yisrael made Joseph "a richly ornamented robe" or a "coat of many colors." This coat was a visible demonstration of the favored status given to Joseph and it has been the subject of much confusion.

In the Hebrew it is described as "kethonet pasim," which is כתנת פסים in modern Hebrew and 𐤌𐤉𐤎𐤐 𐤕𐤍𐤕𐤊 in ancient Hebrew. The word "kethonet" is typically translated as a "coat or robe." In the basic sense it was a "covering." The confusion primarily comes from the word passim, which can mean "wide, long, broad, colored, ornamented."

We actually get a definition of this garment from a later Scripture passage. In 2 Shemuel 13:18-19 we read about the virgin Tamar who was raped by her brother Amnon. "*[18] She was wearing a richly ornamented robe (פסים כתנה), for this was the kind of garment the virgin daughters of the king wore. [19] Tamar put ashes on her head and tore the ornamented robe (כתנה פסים) she was wearing.*"

This helps us better understand that the robe of Joseph represented both royalty and purity. It was a picture of a pure, virgin bride. Joseph was treated as the firstborn son due to the sin of his brothers. He was chosen to be a prince in this Covenant assembly, and this robe represented his position. Joseph even had dreams of his entire family bowing down to him, which confirmed the fact that he was above all in Yisrael, including his parents.

This is a very important concept to understand – Joseph was given the blessings of the firstborn and would be exalted over the Covenant people. He was representing the Bride that YHWH was preparing through the Covenant. As a result, his brothers were extremely jealous of him and grew to hate him. Their deep seeded jealousy led to their desire to kill him.

The brothers went to feed their flocks in, none other than, Shechem. Yisrael told Joseph to go to Shechem. Joseph went from Hebron to Shechem, and a man found him wandering in a field. This mysterious man asked Joseph what he was looking for and told him that his brothers had gone to Dotayanah.

When his brothers saw him coming, they conspired to kill him and throw him into a pit. Reuben convinced them to throw him into the pit, and not to kill Joseph. He planned to return later and pull Joseph out. Upon Joseph's arrival, instead of being greeted by a band of loving brothers, he was assaulted by an angry mob. The Scriptures record: "[23] *So it came to pass, when Joseph had come to his brothers, that they stripped* 𐤀𐤕 *Joseph* 𐤀𐤕 *of his robe,* 𐤀𐤕 *the ornamented robe that was on him.* [24] *Then they took him and cast him into a pit. And the pit was empty; there was no water in it.*" Beresheet 37:23-24.

Notice how the untranslated Alep Taw (𐤀𐤕) is intimately connected to Joseph and his symbol of royalty. This is a Messianic pattern that will be discussed further in the text. It reveals Joseph as a suffering servant, stripped of his royal robes by his brothers and "cast into the pit" – a metaphorical death.

It is interesting that his brothers were compelled to strip him of this royal garment (𐤊𐤕𐤍𐤕 𐤐𐤎𐤉𐤌). That coat apparently bothered them so much that they had to get it off him immediately. They hated the fact that he was favored, and their jealousy was eating away at them.

They threw him into a pit naked. This pit, known as a "habor" (𐤄𐤁𐤓), was a well or cistern without any water. This dark, empty hole in the ground represented his grave, because he was really supposed to be dead. Joseph would have been killed if Reuben had not intervened with the idea to throw him in the pit. The brothers then sat down to eat, and they saw a caravan of

Yishmaelites.

At the suggestion of Judah, they decided to sell Joseph instead of kill him. It is interesting that they were willing to sell their brother to distant relatives through Abraham. This event directly connects the Covenant with Abram, and the Covenant with Abraham. The seed of Abraham was being sold to the seed of Abram. The agreed upon price was twenty (20) pieces of silver.

Many translations indicate that his brothers pulled him out of the pit, but that is not so clear from the text. Here is an accurate rendering of the event. *"Then there passed by Midianite merchant men and they drew and lifted up* ✗✗ *Joseph out of the pit and sold* ✗✗ *Joseph to the Yishmaelites for twenty pieces of silver and they brought* ✗✗ *Joseph to Egypt."* Beresheet 37:28.

This incident contains three instances of the Aleph Taw (✗✗), and describes how Joseph was ultimately sold to Yishmaelites for twenty (20) pieces of silver. Interestingly, this was the value of a male, between the ages of 5 and 20, dedicated to YHWH by a vow. That is, if pieces are the same as shekels, which is often thought to be the case. (Vayiqra 27:5).

After Joseph was taken to Egypt, his brothers had unfinished business with that royal robe. *"[31] So they took* ✗✗ *Joseph's robe, killed a kid of the goats, and dipped* ✗✗ *the robe in the blood. [32] Then they sent* ✗✗*the ornamented robe, and they brought it to their father and said, 'We have found this. Do you know whether it is your son's robe or not?' [33] And he recognized it and said, 'It is my son's robe. A wild beast has devoured him. Without doubt Joseph is torn to pieces.' [34] Then Yaakob tore his clothes, put sackcloth on his waist, and mourned for his son many days. [35] And all his sons and all his daughters arose to comfort him; but he refused to*

be comforted, and he said, 'For I shall go down into the grave to my son in mourning.' Thus his father wept for him." Beresheet 37:31-35.

Notice how his brothers killed a kid of the goats. This was from the flock that they were supposed to be tending and guarding. They were not only wreaking havoc on Joseph, their father's son, they were also killing from their father's herd to cover up their actions. They then lied to their father and caused him incredible grief. All of their actions were completely self-centered, and showed a disregard and disrespect for their father. It did not appear that they loved their father.

There is much to be gleaned from this passage. Just as Abraham slaughtered a male animal, so too these brothers selected a male goat. The passage describing the slaughter of the goat includes three (3) instances of the untranslated Aleph Taw (✗✗), which is another clue that this is likely a prophetic picture of the Messiah. The coat was ripped and dipped in blood, but not Joseph's blood.

It is believed that both of these events speak of atonement, and are intimately linked with the Appointed Times. The Book of Jubilees 34:12 says the sons of Yaakob slaughtered a kid, dipped the coat of Joseph in the blood, and sent it to Yaakob their father on the tenth day of the seventh month on Yom Kippur. The brothers told Yaakob that Joseph had been killed and for all intents and purposes, Joseph was dead. Yisrael was now divided and incomplete, thus we see Yaakob being referenced instead of Yisrael.

Joseph was actually sold into slavery in Egypt and then thrown into prison, but he always received favor from YHWH. Through his interpretations of Pharaoh's

dreams, he was responsible for saving Egypt and the surrounding nations from famine and starvation. Through Joseph's actions, Pharaoh increased in wealth and power.

As a result of these actions, Joseph rose to the level of viceroy in the Egyptian kingdom, second only to Pharaoh. While in Egypt he married  the daughter of a pagan priest who gave birth to two children, Manasheh and Ephraim. His brothers and father later came to Egypt during a time of famine. Remember that Joseph's father Yaakob came to Egypt just as his great grandfather Abram had done in a time of famine, but Joseph's grandfather Yitshaq was told by YHWH not to go to Egypt during a famine.

Because of their need for food, Yaakob and his extended family were reunited and restored with Joseph who fed them. To his father, it was as if Joseph had come back from the dead. At the point where Yaakob heard and finally understood that Joseph was alive and not dead, he is again referred to as Yisrael in the Scriptures. (see Beresheet 45:27-28). Essentially, Yaakob is only referred to as Yisrael when the community is complete. When the community is fractured or divided, we read about Yaakob. This is an important distinction to remember.

The symbolism found in the life of Joseph is profound. It is full of Messianic patterns from which there is much to learn. Before he died, Yisrael blessed his children and something very profound occurred relative to Joseph and his two sons. Here is the account as it is

stated in the Torah:

"*13 And Joseph took both of them, Ephraim on his right toward Yisrael's left hand and Manasheh on his left toward Yisrael's right hand, and brought them close to him. 14 But Yisrael reached out his right hand and put it on Ephraim's head, though he was the younger, and crossing his arms, he put his left hand on Manasheh's head, even though Manasheh was the firstborn. 15 Then he blessed Joseph and said, 'May the Elohim before whom my fathers Abraham and Yitshaq walked, the Elohim who has been my Shepherd all my life to this day, 16 the Messenger who has delivered me from all harm - may He bless these boys. <u>May they be called by my name and the names of my fathers Abraham and Yitshaq, and may they increase greatly upon the earth.</u>' 17 When Joseph saw his father placing his right hand on Ephraim's head he was displeased; so he took hold of his father's hand to move it from Ephraim's head to Manasheh's head. 18 Joseph said to him, 'No, my father, this one is the firstborn; put your right hand on his head.' 19 But his father refused and said, 'I know, my son, I know. He too will become a people, and he too will become great. <u>Nevertheless, his younger brother will be greater than he, and his descendants will become a group of nations.</u>' 20 He blessed them that day and said, 'In your name will Yisrael pronounce this blessing: May Elohim make you like Ephraim and Manasheh.' <u>So he put Ephraim ahead of Manasheh.</u>*" Beresheet 48:13-20.

What happened here is quite significant. Yisrael actually adopted the children of Joseph as his own. These two boys were born in Egypt to an Egyptian mother who was the daughter of a pagan priest. They had Egyptian

blood and they were the only children of Yisrael that were adopted. They were not only adopted, Ephraim, the youngest, was elevated to firstborn status of all of the children of Yisrael. The great promise of the Covenant was spoken over him – Ephraim would become "a group of nations." This event has great prophetic significance, as we shall examine later in this text.

After speaking the blessings over Ephraim and Manasheh, Yisrael then went on to call his remaining sons and spoke to them as follows:

"*2 Assemble and listen, sons of Yaakob; listen to your father Yisrael. 3 Reuben, you are my firstborn, my might, the first sign of my strength, excelling in honor, excelling in power. 4 Turbulent as the waters, you will no longer excel, for you went up onto your father's bed, onto my couch and defiled it. 5 Simeon and Levi are brothers - their swords are weapons of violence. 6 Let me not enter their council, let me not join their assembly, for they have killed men in their anger and hamstrung oxen as they pleased. 7 Cursed be their anger, so fierce, and their fury, so cruel! I will scatter them in Yaakob and disperse them in Yisrael. 8 Judah, your brothers will praise you; your hand will be on the neck of your enemies; your father's sons will bow down to you. 9 You are a lion's cub, O Judah; you return from the prey, my son. Like a lion he crouches and lies down, like a lioness - who dares to rouse him? 10 The scepter will not depart from Judah, nor a lawgiver from between his feet, until Shiloh; and unto Him shall the gathering of the people be. 11 He will* tether his donkey to a vine, his colt to the choicest branch; he will wash his garments in wine, his robes in the blood of grapes. [12] His eyes will be darker than wine, his teeth whiter than milk. [13] Zebulun will live by the seashore and become a haven for ships; his border will extend toward Sidon. [14] Issachar is a strong donkey lying down between two burdens. [15] When he sees how good is his resting place and how pleasant is his land, he will bend his shoulder to the burden and submit to the task. [16] Dan will provide justice for his people as one of the tribes of Yisrael. [17] Dan will be a serpent by the roadside, a viper along the path, that bites the horse's heels so that its rider tumbles backward. [18] I look for your deliverance, O YHWH. [19] Gad will be attacked by a band of raiders, but he will attack them at their heels. [20] Asher's food will be rich; he will provide delicacies fit for a king. [21] Naphtali is a doe set free that bears beautiful fawns. [22] Joseph is a fruitful vine, a fruitful vine near a spring, whose branches climb over a wall. [23] With bitterness archers attacked him; they shot at him with hostility. [24] But his bow remained steady, his strong arms stayed limber, because of the Hand of the Mighty One of Yaakob, because of the Shepherd, the Rock of Yisrael, [25] because of your father's Elohim, who helps you, because of the Almighty, who blesses you with blessings of the heavens above, blessings of the deep that lies below, blessings of the breast and womb. [26] Your father's blessings are greater

than the blessings of the ancient mountains, than the bounty of the age-old hills. Let all these rest on the head of Joseph, on the brow of the prince among his brothers. [27] *Benjamin is a ravenous wolf; in the morning he devours the prey, in the evening he divides the plunder.* [28] *All these are the twelve tribes of Yisrael, and this is what their father said to them when he blessed them, giving each the blessing appropriate to him."* Beresheet 49:2-28.

While these words are called blessings, it should be evident that most of the brothers did not walk away feeling blessed that day. Only two brothers really stand out – Judah and Joseph. Interestingly, it is these two who are emphasized during the life of Yisrael, after he returns to the Land. We read about the enslavement and elevation of Joseph which was, by far, the dominant story in the text. We also read an interlude involving Judah and his daughter-in-law  Tamar, which led to the birth of twin sons, Peretz and Zerah, which points to the lineage of Messiah. (see Beresheet 38:1-30).

In fact, aside from the Messianic prophecies flowing through Judah, this was Joseph's day to be sure. Joseph was directly and intimately tied with the Elohim of the Covenant. The word "bless" is used emphatically toward Joseph. No doubt, Joseph was receiving the abundant blessings, far beyond that of his brothers. As if to make the point irrefutable, Joseph was referred to as

Prince among his brothers. Joseph was royalty in Yisrael, as well as in Egypt.

Yisrael began as a man who inherited the promises of his fathers. This man originally named Yaakob eventually became Yisrael whose children were divided into tribes, soon to become a nation. His son Joseph inherited the birthright while Judah received the kingship. This is an important distinction with much significance which must be recognized and understood

After blessing his children, Yisrael died. His body was brought back to Hebron and buried with his fathers in the Covenant Land. We know that the number of descendents who went to Egypt was seventy (70). (see Shemot 1:1-5). This number is significant, because numerically it represents "the nations." These people remained in the Land of Egypt after the death of Yisrael so that the promise made to Abram could be fulfilled. (see Beresheet 15:13-16).

What began as twelve (12) sons of a man who wrestled with life, and with his Creator, soon became twelve (12) tribes that grew into a nation within the nation of Egypt. The Scriptures tell us: *"⁶ Now Joseph and all his brothers and all that generation died, ⁷ but the Yisraelites were fruitful and multiplied greatly and became exceedingly numerous, so that the land was filled with them."* Exodus (Shemot) 1:6-7.[51]

6

Moses

Joseph had originally entered Egypt as a slave, but ultimately he became a great ruler. Quite the opposite occurred with his brethren. While the seventy (70) descendents of Yisrael freely entered Egypt, there came a time when the status of their descendants changed. A future Pharaoh would eventually forget Joseph and the favor bestowed upon him. The Yisraelites had arrived in Egypt as free men, escaping famine, but they ended up becoming slaves.

Egypt was the land inhabited by the descendants of Mitsrayim the son of Ham. In Hebrew, the word Mitsrayim has come to be likened with "bondage."[52] The Yisraelites grew into a nation while in Egypt until the specified time had elapsed. This, of course, was all part of the pattern and the plan foretold to Abram by YHWH.

When YHWH entered into the Covenant with Abram He stated: *"[13] Know for certain that your descendants will be strangers in a country not their own, and they will be enslaved and mistreated four hundred years. [14] But I will punish the nation they serve as slaves, and afterward they will come out with great possessions."* Beresheet 15:13-14.

When this period of captivity was concluded, YHWH chose another man named Moses (Mosheh)[53] to help deliver them out of bondage. The irony is that

Mosheh was raised in the household of Pharaoh. Just as Joseph had been grafted into the Egyptian power structure to bring Yisrael into Egypt, now Mosheh was grafted into the Egyptian power structure to lead the nation of Yisrael out. This was accomplished in a very unique and interesting fashion.

The Scriptures describe a time when the Pharaoh of Egypt instructed two Hebrew midwives to kill males that were born to Hebrew women. The midwives refused to obey. They revered Elohim over Pharaoh and they were blessed while the Yisraelites prospered. Later the Scriptures record: "*So Pharaoh commanded all his people, saying, 'Every son who is born you shall cast into the river, and every daughter you shall save alive.'*" Shemot 1:22.

A reasonable person might question why Pharaoh would do such a thing. Maybe he was cognizant of the fact that someone important was about to be born. Could it be that he was aware of the promise made to Abraham? After all, Abraham had contacts with Egypt.

Apparently, Pharaoh saw the Hebrews as a threat and sought to weaken them by killing their male offspring. There was a reason that Pharaoh had the children thrown into the Nile River. These children were an offering to the river god Hapi. Therefore, it was by no coincidence that YHWH sent a deliverer from those very waters.

Here is the account from the Scriptures. "*¹ And a man of the house of Levi went and took* ✗⚒ *a daughter of Levi. ² So the woman conceived and bore a son. And when she saw* ✗⚒ *that he was a beautiful child, she hid him three months. ³ But when she could no longer hide him, she took an ark of bulrushes for him, daubed it with*

asphalt and pitch, put therein ✕✗ *the child, and laid it in the reeds by the river's bank.*" Shemot 2:1-3. Interestingly, in this passage which first describes the baby, there are three instances of the untranslated Aleph Taw (✕✗).

The Scriptures proceed to describe how this child was spared from the death sentence issued by Pharaoh. "[5] *Then the daughter of Pharaoh came down to bathe at the river. And her maidens walked along the riverside; and when she saw* ✕✗ *the ark among the reeds, she sent* ✕✗ *her maid to get it.* [6] *And when she opened it, she saw* ✕✗ *the child, and behold, the baby wept. So she had compassion on him, and said, 'This is one of the Hebrews' children.'*" Shemot 2:5-6.

This passage also includes three instances of the untranslated Aleph Taw (✕✗) so by now a person reading the Hebrew text would begin to realize that this baby was quite special. There are many others that follow in the subsequent text as it describes how Pharaoh's daughter proceeds to adopt the child and name him Mosheh.[54]

It was truly a miracle that this child was saved and adopted by the same family that was set to kill him. Pharaoh's daughter instantly knew that he was one of the Hebrews, because he was circumcised – he was a son of the Covenant.

There are two important questions that anyone would reasonably ask. First, Why did the mother of Mosheh choose this method of getting her child into the hands of Egyptian royalty? The second is: Why would the daughter of Pharaoh adopt a slave baby that was supposed to be killed?

The answer to both questions is better understood when you realize why Pharaoh's daughter was likely bathing in the Nile. We are talking about a River that is

generally heavy laden with silt and filled with crocodiles. Not a very inviting place to take a bath. The princess could surely have had a nice, clean relaxing bath in the safety and security of the palace.

Some speculate that she was not taking a bath, but rather that she was immersing herself in the sacred River because she was barren. She was immersing herself in the hope that Hapi, the fertility god, would give her a child. Under these circumstances, you can imagine that the baby would have been considered to be an answer to prayer – a miracle child straight from the gods.

It is possible that Mosheh's mother was hoping for just that response. Any other way would have likely led to Mosheh being killed, along with the other Hebrew babies. How ironic, since the method of disposing of the Hebrew children was to throw them into the Nile as an offering. Mosheh's mother surely knew the story of Noah being protected from the waters of judgment. Therefore, she made an ark for her son to escape Pharaoh's judgment.

As with Noah – this Ark was intimately connected with the Covenant. It pointed to the fact that the man in this "Covenant House" would be used by YHWH as a mediator for His Covenant plan. This child was a son of the Covenant – circumcised on the 8th day no doubt. He was being prepared to lead the seed of Abraham into their inheritance.

This is where it gets really interesting, because it was Abram who was told that his seed would go into bondage. When that Covenant was made, Abram was uncircumcised, and he did not pass through the cuttings. It would be through their captivity in Egypt that the seed of Abraham would mix with the nations, representing

the uncircumcised, and an incredible pattern will emerge. Through this promise, the nations would be brought out of Egypt and gathered to YHWH.

In order for this to occur, YHWH would raise up a deliverer to represent Him through the process. So we see this child, Mosheh, who was born to a Hebrew slave from the Tribe of Levi, and then placed into an ark. He was put into the Nile River, the very place where the other Hebrew children were being thrown to their death. He survived Pharaoh's judgment and was adopted into the royal family of Egypt.

Mosheh was actually a prince of Egypt. He was apparently adopted by Sobekhotep IV Khaneferre, of the 13th Dynasty, whose wife was named 'Merris' according to ancient Jewish historian Artaponus.[55] Other texts describe the daughter of Pharaoh as Bathia or Bithia.[56]

According to extra-Scriptural Book of Yasher, after murdering an Egyptian at eighteen, Mosheh went to live with the Cushites for nine years. After nine years with the Cushites, Mosheh was made King of the Cushites at the age of twenty seven.[57] He remained their King for forty years and at the age of sixty seven he fled to Midian where he met Zipporah at the well.[58]

Zipporah's father Jethro (Yithro) was described as the priest of Midian. He imprisoned Mosheh for a period of ten years.[59] However, at the end of ten years Mosheh was released and married Zipporah when he was seventy six years old.[60] Mosheh had two sons with Zipporah when he was between seventy six and seventy eight, two years before the Exodus.

While in Midian he returned to the heritage of his ancestors and became a shepherd of flocks. This life in Midian was quite different than in Egypt. It must have been a humbling experience since shepherding was a lowly profession in Egyptian society. This was important training as he was preparing to lead the flock of Yisrael.

When Mosheh was seventy seven years old, three years before the Exodus, he saw a bush that burned with fire, but was not consumed. It is important to note that this event occurred on Mt. Horeb, described as the Mountain of Elohim. The Messenger of YHWH appeared in "a flame of fire" out of the midst of a bush. (Shemot 3:1-2). In Hebrew "a flame of fire" is "b'labat ash" (W𐤊 ×𐤙𐤋𐤙).

Also, the Hebrew for bush is "senah" (𐤙𐤉𐤊𐤕) which means "thorn, prick or bramble." Remember that Abraham took the ram from the thicket or thorn bush. He specifically said: "It shall be seen on the Mountain of YHWH." Was this what he was talking about?

Here we have fire - fire in a thorn bush. This was the same fire that passed through the pieces when Abram was "dead" during the Covenant process. Now this fire was in a thorn bush, just as the ram provided by YHWH was in a thorn bush. The connection between the fire and the ram is clear. This should immediately make us think about the Covenant, and this event is all about the Covenant with Abraham.

Mosheh then proclaimed: "*I will turn aside now and see* ×𐤊 *this great appearance (phenomenon)*." Shemot 3:3. Mosheh turned to see the Aleph Taw, which also is connected with the fire and the ram. The implication is that Mosheh actually met with the Messiah, functioning as the Messenger of YHWH. The Scriptures record that YHWH saw him turn aside and Elohim called from the bush. We now see a direct connection between Elohim,

the fire, the ram and the Messiah in this event. Mosheh was told to take off his sandals for where he stood was holy – set apart – because the presence of YHWH was manifested in that space.

The Scriptures record: "² *Elohim also said to Mosheh, 'I Am YHWH. ³ I appeared to Abraham, to Yitshaq and to Yaakob as El Shaddai, but by My Name YHWH was I not known to them. ⁴ I also established* ✕𐤊 *My Covenant with them to give them* ✕𐤊 *the Land of Canaan,* ✕𐤊 *where they lived as aliens. ⁵ Moreover, I have heard* ✕𐤊 *the groaning of the Yisraelites, whom the Egyptians are enslaving, and I have remembered* ✕𐤊 *My Covenant. ⁶ Therefore, say to the Yisraelites: 'I Am YHWH, and I will bring you out from under the yoke of the Egyptians. I will free you from being slaves to them, and I will redeem you with an outstretched arm and with mighty acts of judgment. ⁷ I will take you as My own people, and I will be your Elohim. Then you will know that I Am YHWH your Elohim, who brought you out from under the yoke of the Egyptians. ⁸ And I will bring you to the Land I swore with uplifted hand to give to Abraham, to Yitshaq and to Yaakob. I will give it to you as a possession. I Am YHWH.'"* Shemot 6:2-8.

Mosheh was told that YHWH saw the suffering of the Yisraelites. YHWH then charged Mosheh to return to Egypt and deliver His people and gather His sheep out of bondage. This encounter was directly linked to the Covenant with Abraham and the Land of Canaan. YHWH remembered His Covenant with the offspring of Abraham and was ready to fulfill His promise. In that passage we see numerous instances of the Aleph Taw (✕𐤊).

Shemot 6:2 is interesting as it says, "I appeared to Abraham, Yitshaq and Yaakob as El Shaddai, but by My

Name YHWH was I not known to them?" The entire meaning of the sentence can vary depending upon whether a question mark is inserted at the end of the sentence, and this is a matter of interpretation. Either YHWH is asking a rhetorical question, or He is making a definitive statement to Mosheh.

The Name of YHWH first appears in Beresheet 2:4 and is used 14 times before it is used in Beresheet 3:9 when YHWH asks Adam, "Where are you?" YHWH talked to Noah in Beresheet 7:1.

When YHWH first spoke to Abram in Beresheet 12:1, it was the 50th time the Name of YHWH appeared in the Scriptures. Between Beresheet 12:1, and Beresheet 25:8 when Abraham died, the Name of YHWH appears 78 times [including 18:3, 18:27, 18:30, 18:32, 19:18 and 20:4 where the sopherim changed YHWH to Adonai]. The point is that Abram knew YHWH, that is why he is called a friend of Elohim in 2 Chronicles 20:7 and James 2:23. It would be very difficult for Abram to be a friend of Elohim if he did not know that His Name was YHWH. And for this reason it seems certain that Shemot 6:2 is a rhetorical question.

The Scriptures make it very clear that Abram knew YHWH, that YHWH appeared to Abram, that Abram built an altar to YHWH and that Abram called on the name of YHWH.

"^{7} Then YHWH appeared to Abram and said, "To your descendants I will give this land." And there he built an altar to YHWH, who had appeared to him. ^{8} And he moved from there to the mountain east of Bethel, and he pitched his tent with Bethel on the west and Ai on the east; there he built an altar to YHWH and called on the name of YHWH." Beresheet 12:7-8.

This is important to understand for anyone claiming to be of the faith of Abraham. For in order to believe and obey the One Who Abraham did, one must call on the Name of YHWH and believe and obey Him. Abraham was on a "first name basis" with YHWH. Regarding the Covenant that YHWH made with Abram, the plan was always that all of the families of the earth would be blessed (Beresheet 12:3). And this plan was for Abram's descendants to have the most intimate relationship with YHWH possible – Marriage.

In fact, YHWH said He would "take" the Yisraelites to be His own people and He would be their Elohim. The Hebrew word for "take" is "laqach" (𐤄𐤒𐤋) which can mean: "to take in marriage." This relationship language, repeated throughout the Scriptures, describing YHWH as their Elohim, and Yisrael as His people, refers to the marital relationship accomplished through the Marriage Covenant.

Mosheh was apparently overwhelmed with the great task assigned to him. He immediately begged YHWH not to make him speak as he was instructed. He indicated that he was slow of speech and tongue. Amazingly, this prince of Egypt, personally chosen by YHWH Himself, was shy and afraid. This once strong and bold man was now unsure of himself and his ability to speak so YHWH instructed Mosheh to use his brother Aaron (Aharon)[61] as his mouthpiece.

Mosheh and Aharon approached Pharaoh and attempted to obtain his permission to let the Yisraelites go into the desert to hold a festival to YHWH. The Scriptures detail the confrontation: *"¹ Afterward Mosheh and Aharon went to Pharaoh and said, This is what YHWH, the Elohim of Yisrael, says: 'Let My people go, so that they* may hold a festival to Me in the desert.' ² Pharaoh said, 'Who is YHWH, that I should obey Him and let Yisrael go? I do not know YHWH and I will not let Yisrael go.' ³ Then they said, 'The Elohim of the Hebrews has met with us. Now let us take a three-day journey into the desert to offer sacrifices to YHWH our Elohim, or He may strike us with plagues or with the sword.'" Shemot 5:1-3.

It is quite interesting to note that Pharaoh, the ruler of a large portion of the civilized world, did not know the Name of the Elohim of a large part of his population. That was about to change because YHWH prepared a great deliverance for His people so that the whole world would thereafter know his Name.

These people, who were in Covenant with YHWH were known as Hebrews, and they were part of an assembly called Yisrael. While there was a tribe called Yahudah, members of which were later referred to as Jews, the Covenant people were Hebrews and YHWH is the Elohim of the Hebrews.

"¹³ Then YHWH said to Mosheh, Get up early in the morning, confront Pharaoh and say to him, This is what YHWH, the Elohim of the Hebrews, says: 'Let My people go, so that they may worship Me, ¹⁴ or this time I will send the full force of My plagues against you and against your officials and your people, so you may know that there is no one like Me in all the earth. ¹⁵ For by now I could have stretched out My Hand and struck you and your people with a plague that would have wiped you off the earth. ¹⁶ But I have raised you up for this very purpose, that I might show you My power and that My Name might be proclaimed in all the earth." Shemot 9:13-17.

Notice again that YHWH identified Himself as "The Elohim of the Hebrews." Abram, being the first person called a Hebrew, represented a people who

followed YHWH. In the Paleo script the word Hebrew is depicted as: 𐤏𐤓𐤁𐤏. A mechanical translation is "eye – house – head – hand." Could it be that a Hebrew is one who sees the house and knows and does the commandments? There are many possible expansions and translations of this very important word and Abram is the model for this word. We actually looc to his life for the definition and it did not stop with Abram.

Abram was later circumcised, and his name was changed to Abraham. So a Hebrew is one who enters into the household of YHWH by hearing and obeying – Shema. The Hebrew then enters into the blood Covenant and becomes transformed into a new being. The Covenant of Circumcision leads one into the community of Yisrael (𐤉𐤔𐤓𐤀𐤋). When you take the mark of circumcision, you are acknowledging that you belong to the royal family of El, that you walk straight in His path and He is your head. Therefore, Yisrael is essentially a community of Hebrews.

The household of Abram, and later Abraham, consisted of many people who were not his direct offspring. If they lived under his tent – they too were Hebrews if they followed his Elohim - YHWH. Therefore, it was YHWH, the Elohim of the Hebrews, the individual beings in the nation of Egypt Who had sent a representative to collect His people. It was now time for the Name of YHWH to be proclaimed in all the earth.

After Pharaoh resisted, YHWH decimated this powerful nation through a series of plagues. He eventually killed all of the firstborn of Egypt, who were not covered by the blood of the lamb, during the Passover, known as "Pesach" (𐤐𐤎𐤇). This was in direct retaliation for what Pharaoh had done to the Hebrews.

It is important to note that the Yisraelites were not harmed by those plagues because they were set apart from the Egyptians. The Passover was specifically orchestrated to provide them protection from the tenth and final plague – the death of the firstborn.

The Passover was a critical part of the deliverance of the Hebrews and it was all about the Covenant made with Abraham. Here is the Command given to Mosheh concerning the Passover. "*³ Speak to all the congregation of Yisrael, saying: 'On the tenth of this month every man shall take for himself a lamb, according to the house of his father, a lamb for a household. ⁴ And if the household is too small for the lamb, let him and his neighbor next to his house take it according to the number of the persons; according to each man's need you shall make your count for the lamb. ⁵ Your lamb shall be without blemish, a male of the "first" (𐤉𐤔) year. You may take it from the sheep or from the goats. ⁶ Now you shall keep it until the fourteenth day of the same month. Then the whole assembly of the congregation of Yisrael shall kill it at twilight. ⁷ And they shall take some of the blood and put it on the two doorposts and on the lintel of the houses where they eat it. ⁸ Then they shall eat the flesh on that night; roasted in fire, with unleavened bread and with bitter herbs they shall eat it. ⁹ Do not eat it raw, nor boiled at all with water, but roasted in fire - its head with its legs and its entrails. ¹⁰ You shall let none of it remain until morning, and what remains of it until morning you shall burn with fire. ¹¹ And thus you shall eat it: with a belt on your waist, your sandals on your feet, and your staff in your hand. So you shall eat it in haste. It is YHWH's Passover.*" Shemot 12:3-11.

Clearly the message behind Passover is the protective covering of the blood of the lamb, and the

Passover is closely related to the Covenant. In fact, in Shemot 12:13 YHWH specifically states that the blood was a "sign" which demonstrates that it is a Covenant event. It was this shedding of blood that would "mark" the next phase in this Covenant journey involving the seed of Abraham.

From Abraham we saw that YHWH would provide His Lamb and it would be His "only Son." Prior to the Passover, the people were to select a lamb and bring it into their home on the tenth day of the first month. Interestingly, we read that the lamb is to be of the "first" year. In the Hebrew we read ben (**ン ソ**), which means "son."

This lamb was to be a son. It would reside in their home for four (4) days and become part of their family before it is slain. As with the number forty (40), the number four (4) is also linked to the Messiah. After four (4) days, on Day 14 of Month 1, the lamb was slaughtered, and the blood was placed on the doorposts of the house.

The doorway was the way in and out of the house. It represented the authority, ownership and control of the house. Many people place their names and street numbers on or near the entrance to their home to identify their ownership.

A doorway without a door would be meaningless. The door provides protection for the occupants of the house. It provides a separation and keeps those unwanted outside. Only members of the house and invited guests are supposed to pass through the door. As a result, the blood on the doorposts symbolizes that YHWH lays claim to the inhabitants.[62] Those inside are part of His family.

Remember that the Hebrew pictograph "dalet" (◁) means "door." This is the dalet (◁) that we originally saw in the midst of the am (𝑌𝐾) in the name Adam (𝑌◁𝐾). So the Lamb of Elohim is the door for the people of Elohim. The blood on the door represented that the occupants of the house were the am (𝑌𝐾) – the people of Elohim. This was the message provided from the very beginning. Through this rehearsal, the Hebrews were getting a vivid picture of how the restoration of mankind would be accomplished through the Covenant.

This lamb, which was a son, was killed and eaten by families in their homes. The flesh became food that was ingested and gave life, while the blood provided protection from death for those who dwelt in the home – specifically the first born. From the Passover we learn that the Lamb of YHWH must be killed, but that the blood of the Lamb would provide a covering for those households that had it on their doorposts. Only those first born in the homes of those who diligently obeyed this commandment of YHWH were spared. So it required obedience of the Covenant participants, but it was the blood that protected them.

The Passover was a meal eaten in haste. You were to wear your outer garments with your sandals on your feet and your walking stick or rod in your hand. All were to keep vigil that night. (Shemot 12:42). A picture that we might envision in this age is that they were fully clothed with their shoes on their feet, their bags packed, the keys were in the ignition, the gas tank was full and the car was running. They were ready to leave.

This particular Feast is all about leaving slavery and going to freedom, which is life with YHWH. The freedom comes not just from leaving slavery though. It

primarily involves going somewhere special – to the Land of promise – the Covenant Land.[63]

Now we do not know precisely who obeyed and who did not obey. There was clearly a distinction made between Yisrael and Egypt on that night. The Yisraelites were those who obeyed the instructions of YHWH delivered through Mosheh and Aharon, and the Egyptians were those who did not obey. The primary distinction was not where you were born, they were all born in Egypt – thus they were technically all Egyptians by birth. The real question was whether or not they were in Covenant with YHWH. Those who are in Covenant with YHWH become citizens of the Kingdom of YHWH.

All the males who obeyed were circumcised, and every one who was part of Yisrael ate of the lamb. (Shemot 12:43-49). All had to be within the Covenant of Circumcision which involved, not only the act of circumcision, but also belief in the promises of YHWH.

Every individual had to demonstrate that belief by following the instructions, called the Torah. YHWH was very specific about the fact that: *"the same Torah applies to the native-born and to the alien living among you."* Shemot 12:49. There were not different rules for different people. Just as with the tents of Abraham, if you wanted to dwell within the Covenant, you obeyed the same rules of the house – no exceptions and no differences.

As a result, everyone who participated in the Passover was am Yisrael – the people of Yisrael. The firstborn of am Yisrael were delivered from death, while the firstborn of the Egyptians were killed.[64] The households of all who obeyed - all that were protected by the blood of the Lamb - were delivered from death. But there was more to the promise than mere salvation from physical death of the firstborn. There was still much more to be completed at the Mountain of YHWH.

Just as Adam was connected to YHWH, and that connection was broken through disobedience, YHWH had plans to reconnect that relationship through the union of marriage with those who obeyed. This pattern was seen through the life of Abraham.

After the meal and the night of death, the Children of Yisrael plundered the Egyptians and departed in a calm and organized fashion. They were loaded with gold and silver. These people had overnight become free and rich!

It is critical to point out that the children of Yisrael were miraculously delivered from Egypt, not by themselves, but along with a mixed multitude of people. According to Shemot 12:37-38: "*37 The children of Yisrael journeyed from Rameses to Succot, about six hundred thousand men on foot, besides children. 38 A mixed multitude went up with them also, and flocks and herds - a great deal of livestock.*"

This is a very important and often overlooked. Remember that as a result of Joseph and his leadership Egypt owned much land and possessions. People had come from all over the world seeking food and many sold themselves into servitude. The children of Yisrael were probably not the only slaves in Mitsrayim. This is how the unique Covenants made with Abram and Abraham would be combined. It is a pattern of how the nations would be joined, through the shedding of blood, with Yisrael.

I imagine that if you were a slave, and just witnessed your master decimated by a Mighty Elohim,

you would probably leave if you had the chance. This is not to say that everyone that went with Yisrael was a slave. There were likely a variety of people from every level of Egyptian society. This mixed multitude consisted of a diversity of people from a range of cultures and languages.

It was the children of Yisrael, along with this mixed multitude, who were redeemed. It is at this point in the Scriptures that we begin to see the redemption plan of YHWH unfold. In ancient days, the process of redemption typically involved purchasing something that used to belong to you or a kinsman. It might be land, property or even a person.

The Exodus from Egypt was an act of redemption, and this concept of redemption is essential to understand. It implies either ownership, right or title to something or someone. It was because of this relationship, through the Covenant established with Abraham, that the Hebrews were redeemed and the price of redemption was the blood of the Lamb which was demonstrated through the Passover. This redemption was for a reason higher than merely freeing slaves. The redemption was meant to restore that which had been lost in Eden.

After this great troop of people marched out of Egypt as a conquering army, the Scriptures record that they camped at a place called Succot. It is no coincidence that the first place that they camped was Succot, just as their father Yisrael had first camped at Succot when he returned to the Land.[65]

These were not the same physical locations, but they obviously are meant to tell us something. Succot, as it turns out, is more than just a place – it is also a time. It

is a very important Appointed Time when all who are in Covenant with YHWH are to meet with Him and dwell in Succas, which are temporary dwellings.

All who follow YHWH are supposed to celebrate Succot every year as a remembrance, and as a rehearsal for a future event. It is an Appointed Time of YHWH - not a Jewish Holiday as some incorrectly believe. It is a time for everyone in Covenant with YHWH to obey, and some day the entire planet will be observing this Feast.[66]

After leaving Succot, the Yisraelites then proceeded to different camps led by YHWH, Who appeared as "a pillar of fire" by night and "a pillar of cloud" by day. This imagery should continue to remind the reader of when the smoking furnace and the lamp of fire passed through the cuttings of the Covenant made with Abram. This fire and cloud was YHWH fulfilling His promise. This was a Covenant procession.

Again, notice that just as the household of Abraham had originally contained numerous individuals who were not his physical descendants, so too this great assembly included the physical offspring of Yisrael as well as a mixed multitude of people.

The Scriptures record that the assembly was led to the edge of the Red Sea where they found themselves trapped between water and the army of Pharaoh. *"Then Mosheh stretched out* X✗ *his hand over the sea; and YHWH caused* X✗ *the sea to go back by a strong east wind all that night, and made* X✗ *the sea into dry land, and the waters were divided."* Shemot 14:21. In this passage there are three instances of the Aleph Taw (X✗) related directly to the waters of the sea.

The waters have always symbolized judgment

and cleansing. When YHWH previously flooded the planet, He was judging the people for their sin, while cleansing the planet from that sin. When the Yisraelites passed through the parted waters of the Red Sea, they literally passed through judgment and were cleansed. The very same waters that were used to cleanse this people were then used to judge Egypt. This act of passing through the waters was symbolic immersion or "mikvah."[67]

Remember, they were on their way to the Land promised to Abraham. These people were like a bride preparing to be married to YHWH. Their journey was symbolic of the preparations for wedding. As the Bride of YHWH they first needed to be separated from the abominations of the Egyptians and then they needed to be cleansed. Once this occurred, they needed to prepare themselves for the wedding ceremony.

Prior to a Hebrew wedding the bride immerses herself, which represents that she is pure for her husband. This was the purpose of the waters of the Red Sea. This multitude received cleansing through these divided waters while the Egyptians received judgment. The symbolism with the Covenant established with Abram is profound. The fire was there protecting the Hebrews, as a shield. The waters of this "red" sea actually symbolized the blood of the Covenant.

The interesting thing that must be pointed out is that within this dual Covenant, there is individual responsibility, and community responsibility. The people must obey individually, and they must obey as a community. They were washed as a community, but they would still need to cleanse themselves individually.

The Scriptures record that the Children of Yisrael

were led into the Desert of Shur. For three days they travelled without finding water, and they grumbled against Mosheh. They had just been passed over from death, freed from slavery, given great wealth and miraculously saved from the army of Pharaoh, and it only took them three days to start complaining.

Mosheh cried out to YHWH and YHWH showed him a piece of wood that, when thrown into the water, made it sweet. The people were being tested and they were given a very specific and powerful promise. *"If you listen carefully to the voice of YHWH your Elohim and do what is right in His eyes, if you pay attention to His commands and keep all His decrees, I will not bring on you any of the diseases I brought on the Egyptians, for I AM YHWH Who heals you."* Shemot 15:26.

Just as He instructed Abraham to walk perfect before Him, YHWH was telling these people to do the same. In other words, in order to avoid the judgments that the Egyptians had just experienced – walk perfect. This perfect walk then led them to a veritable oasis called Elim, which contained twelve (12) springs and seventy (70) palm trees. One cannot ignore the significance of these numbers.[68]

After leaving Elim they travelled to the desert of Sin. On the 15th day of the second month, the whole community grumbled against Mosheh and Aharon. This time they were complaining about the food. They alleged that Mosheh and Aharon brought them out into the wilderness to starve to death. Notwithstanding the fact that they came out of Egypt with their cattle, YHWH provided them with quail in the evening and manna in the morning. They were not to keep any manna overnight. They were to gather it for six days, but not

the seventh, which was the Sabbath.

YHWH, once again, gave them very specific instructions to test them. He wanted to see if they would diligently obey His commandments. Many would not.

When they left Sin, they journeyed to Rephidim where there was no water. Again, they were being tested and they quarreled with Mosheh. This time Mosheh was instructed to take some of the elders, along with the rod that he used to strike the Nile. He struck the rock at Horeb at the place he called Massah and Meribah. Water poured forth from the rock for all the people to drink.

Sadly, the people had been tested and they failed. They still had a slave mentality and needed a serious attitude adjustment. In order to be Covenant people they needed to trust the One Who they were in Covenant with. They needed to believe as their father Abraham believed.

Later, when they fought the Amalekites, they were victorious as long as Mosheh kept his arms raised to YHWH. The point was crystal clear – Yisrael was to look to YHWH. They needed to have faith and give Him worship and praise. He would provide for their every need. He would even fight with them in their battles.

The people eventually moved on from Rephidim to the desert of Sinai where they camped in front of Mount Sinai. When they arrived at the mountain we read the following passage. "*³ Then Mosheh went up to Elohim, and YHWH called to him from the mountain and said, This is what you are to say to the house of Yaakob and what you are to tell the people of Yisrael: ⁴ You yourselves have seen what I did to Egypt, and how I carried you on eagles' wings and brought you to Myself. ⁵ Now if you obey me fully and keep My Covenant, then out of all nations you will be My treasured possession. Although the whole earth is mine, ⁶ you will be for Me a kingdom of priests and a set apart nation. These are the words you are to speak to the Yisraelites.*" Shemot 19:3-6.

Notice the distinction between "the house of Yaakob" and "the people of Yisrael." The house of Yaakob was referring to all of the direct descendants of Yaakob, and the people of Yisrael were all those in Covenant with YHWH. Yaakob was the name of Yisrael before he entered into the fullness of the Covenant. Yisrael is the name representing the people in Covenant with YHWH.

<u>Your inherited genetics do not dictate your Covenant status – it is your heart.</u> We shall soon see that the Covenant of Circumcision that began in the male organ ultimately extends to the heart. Our willingness to obey is often a good representation of our hearts.

Here is the mandate for these people – keep (shamar) the Covenant. Guard it and protect it, just as Adam was to have done and as Abraham had done. They needed to obey YHWH fully, not partially or half-heartedly. If they did this, then they would be a kingdom of priests, set apart from all other nations.

This was essentially a marriage proposal which Mosheh then brought to the elders and the people.

Their response was unequivocal – "We will do everything YHWH has said." In other words – "I do." They accepted the proposal and were all told to get cleaned up for the ceremony. Even though they were part of a community, as individuals they all had to wash their clothes, wash their bodies – consecrate themselves like a bride preparing for her wedding. The ceremony would take place "on the third day." Then YHWH would come down from the mountain in the sight of all the people.

YHWH was in the process of fulfilling the marriage Covenant aspect of the Abrahamic Covenant. Included within that Covenant were those who dwelled together in the community known as Yisrael. They would know Him by His Name - YHWH - just as Abram did. They did not know Him as Adonai, HaShem, Allah, the LORD or God. They knew Him as YHWH. The instructions, known as the Torah,  remained at the center of the Covenant - like a Ketubah or a written marriage contract between a husband and a wife.[69]

When a bride and groom entered into their marriage relationship they would traditionally stand underneath a Huppa, which consists of the four-cornered garment of the husband, known as a tallit. This symbolized the protection or the covering of YHWH over the relationship. When YHWH prepared to marry Yisrael, His Huppa of smoke descended over them. They then camped at the base of Mount Sinai and preparations were made for the wedding ceremony.

Remember, this was the Mountain of YHWH

where Mosheh originally received instructions from the fire in the thicket bush. This is where the fullness of the Covenant was going to be revealed to the seed of Abraham.

As YHWH began to speak the terms of the Covenant, the people began to experience the awesome presence of YHWH and became afraid. *"[18] Now all the people saw X✗ the thunderings and X✗ the lightning flashes and X✗ the voice (sound) of the shofar, and X✗ the mountain smoking; and when the people saw it, they trembled and stood afar off. [19] Then they said to Mosheh, You speak with us, and we will hear; but let not Elohim speak with us, lest we die."* Shemot 20:18-19.

After Elohim had spoken what are referred to as the Ten Commandments, or Ten Words, the people could not take anymore. They were afraid of what they saw. They even saw the sound. They asked Mosheh to listen to the commandments and then relay them to the people. This is very important because they are asking Mosheh to represent YHWH in their marital relationship. They are asking a man to stand between them in their relationship with YHWH.

YHWH agreed to this request. So Mosheh, as the mediator of the Covenant, drew near the thick darkness where Elohim was. He would then transmit the Words to the people.

While the instructions had been revealed to mankind from the beginning, something different was happening at Mount Sinai - just like something different happened with Abraham. It was another step in the process of restoring mankind with the Creator. It was another phase in the Covenant cycle. This time the Torah was written and incorporated into a Covenant

with a nation of people called Yisrael.

YHWH had told Abram that his seed would be afflicted for 400 years.[70] When the time was up - the promise was fulfilled through the seed of Abraham that passed through Yitshaq to Yaakob - whose name was changed to Yisrael.

At Sinai, YHWH was consummating the marriage Covenant, and included within that Covenant were those who dwelled with Yisrael. You see, anybody could sojourn with Yisrael as long as they agreed to obey YHWH Elohim the Holy One of Yisrael. This was what we saw with Abraham. Anyone could live with Abraham and enter into the Covenant if they were circumcised and followed the ways of YHWH.

The Torah was for all mankind, as it was from the beginning. Remember, Adam was not a Hebrew, a Yisraelite, a Jew or a Christian - he was a man created in the Image of YHWH. In order to live in the "house" of Elohim he had to obey the rules of the House – the Torah. After the sin of Adam and Hawah, it was then necessary to restore individuals and mankind back into a right relationship and standing before the Creator. Anyone who desires to reside with YHWH must follow His ways – not just some exclusive group or elite religion.

YHWH was always concerned about the individual, and when He established Yisrael as a nation, it did not mean that He forgot about those who came prior to Yisrael, nor does it mean that He was not concerned about the other nations that inhabited the planet. In fact, He established Yisrael to reveal Himself to those very nations.[71] Yisrael was supposed to be the conduit for the Messiah, Who would ultimately draw mankind back to the Creator through the pattern revealed in the Abrahamic Covenant.

Therefore, anyone who wanted to enter into this Covenant relationship with the Creator could do so, provided that they observed the terms of the Covenant - which was the Torah. This is specifically stated in Vayiqra 19:33-34: "*33 And if a stranger dwells with you in your Land, you shall not mistreat him. 34 The stranger who dwells among you shall be to you as one born among you, and you shall love him as yourself; for you were strangers in the land of Egypt: I am YHWH your Elohim.*"

After Mosheh received the Words of YHWH, he was given a very interesting promise. "*20 Behold, I send a messenger before you to keep you in the way and to bring you into the place which I have prepared. 21 Beware of him and obey his voice; do not provoke him, for he will not pardon your transgressions; for My Name is in him. 22 But if you indeed obey his voice and do all that I speak, then I will be an enemy to your enemies and an adversary to your adversaries. 23 For My messenger will go before you and bring you in to the Amorites and the Hittites and the Perizzites and the Canaanites and the Hivites and the Jebusites; and I will cut them off.*" Shemot 23:20-24.

Some texts translate "messenger" as "angel." The Hebrew word is "malak" (𐤄𐤊𐤋𐤌) and generally means: "a messenger, priest, prophet or teacher." So YHWH would provide a messenger Who carried His Name and His authority. He would lead Yisrael in the way and they were to obey his voice. This was a great promise of guidance, protection and victory – provided that they obeyed his voice.

YHWH then described how He would remove the inhabitants from the Land, as well as the boundaries

of the Land – the same boundaries promised to the seed of Abraham. "*²⁷ I will send My fear before you, I will cause confusion among all the people to whom you come, and will make all your enemies turn their backs to you. ²⁸ And I will send hornets before you, which shall drive out the Hivite, the Canaanite, and the Hittite from before you. ²⁹ I will not drive them out from before you in one year, lest the land become desolate and the beasts of the field become too numerous for you. ³⁰ Little by little I will drive them out from before you, until you have increased, and you inherit the land. ³¹ And I will set your bounds from the Red Sea to the sea, Philistia, and from the desert to the River. For I will deliver the inhabitants of the land into your hand, and you shall drive them out before you. ³² You shall make no covenant with them, nor with their gods. ³³ They shall not dwell in your land, lest they make you sin against Me. For if you serve their gods, it will surely be a snare to you."* Shemot 23:27-33.

After these Covenant promises were made to the people of YHWH, a wedding feast was held. "*¹ Then He said to Mosheh, 'Come up to YHWH, you and Aharon, Nadab and Abihu, and seventy (70) of the elders of Yisrael. You are to worship at a distance, ² but Mosheh alone is to approach YHWH; the others must not come near. And the people may not come up with him. ³ <u>When Mosheh went and told the people all YHWH's words and right-rulings, they responded with one voice, 'Everything YHWH has said we will do.' ⁴ Mosheh then wrote down everything YHWH had said.</u> He got up early the next morning and built an altar at the foot of the mountain and set up twelve stone pillars representing the twelve tribes of Yisrael. ⁵ Then he sent young Yisraelite men, and they offered burnt offerings and sacrificed young bulls as fellowship offerings to YHWH. ⁶ Mosheh took half of the blood and put it in bowls, and the other half he* sprinkled on the altar. *⁷ Then he took the Scroll of the Covenant and read it to the people. They responded, 'We will do everything YHWH has said; we will obey.' ⁸ Mosheh then took the blood, sprinkled it on the people and said, 'This is the blood of the Covenant that YHWH has made with you in accordance with all these words.'"* Shemot 24:1-8.

Notice that Mosheh first spoke all the Words that YHWH told him and the people agreed to do everything YHWH said. Mosheh then wrote everything down. He then set up twelve (12) stone pillars as Yaakob, and later Yisrael, had each set up a pillar at the House of Elohim (Beit El). This represented Yisrael being part of the House of Elohim once they agreed to obey the rules of the House.

Young men then prepared offerings. Half of the blood was put in bowls while the other half was sprinkled on the altar. Mosheh then read the Words from the Scroll, the terms of the Covenant – the Ketubah. The people responded that they would do everything – they would obey. Mosheh then sprinkled the blood in the bowls upon them.

Here we see blood being shed. This was the Abrahamic Covenant being affirmed with his seed. It was by no means the complete fulfillment of the Covenant. The Land still remained unclaimed. This was a cycle of fulfillment of the Marriage Covenant portion, which now meant that a promised son would be produced from this relationship. The Promised Son that would complete the pattern of Yitshaq, and be the Lamb of Elohim that would pay the price for the breaking of the Covenant.

The blood was sprinkled on the people and (12) twelve standing stones were erected, representing the

twelve (12) Tribes of Yisrael. Remember that there was a mixed multitude with Yisrael, but there was no separate "tribe of the nations" or "tribe of the mixed multitude." They were grafted into Yisrael through the twelve (12) tribes and became part of Yisrael. They too were sprinkled by the blood, and were therefore included within this Covenant.

After this blood covenant ritual, which consummated the relationship, we then read about the wedding banquet. "⁹ *Mosheh and Aharon, Nadab and Abihu, and the seventy (70) elders of Yisrael went up* ¹⁰ *and saw the Elohim of Yisrael. Under His feet was something like a pavement made of sapphire, clear as the sky itself.* ¹¹ *But Elohim did not raise His Hand against these leaders of the Yisraelites; they saw Elohim, and they ate and drank.*" Shemot 24:9-11.

Interestingly, there were not twelve (12) elders of Yisrael, rather there were seventy (70). Mosheh and Aharon in their combined role represented the Messiah, and when we add Nadab and Abihu to the seventy (70) we have six (6) representatives from each tribe – six (6) being the number of man. So we have a very interesting picture of a wedding feast on the mountain.

It is important to recognize the emphasis on the number seventy (70) during this process. Once again seventy (70) represents the nations of the world, and this new nation of priests were meant to be priests to YHWH on behalf of the nations. We can see a future fulfillment of this Covenant pattern as the Messiah brings together the nations through Yisrael.

Just as seventy (70) beings went into Egypt, these seventy (70) represented the beings who came out and Covenanted with YHWH. They ate with Elohim, and they saw Elohim on the mountain. This is what

Abraham meant when he proclaimed <u>YHWH Yireh</u> on the mountain of Moriah.

After this, Mosheh was called up the mountain with his servant Joshua. The elders remained and were told to wait for them to return. Mosheh was then given very detailed instructions for building a house for YHWH. Interestingly, this House was a tent, or succa, often referred to as The Tabernacle. It was a temporary dwelling that was meant to be portable.

When all of the instructions were given, YHWH then provided Mosheh with two (2) tablets of the Witness, tablets of stone, written with the finger of Elohim. This cycle was now almost complete, although Mosheh and Joshua had been up on the mountain for some time. The people grew impatient and did not want to wait for this man who they had specifically asked to mediate for them.

"[1] Now when the people saw that Mosheh delayed coming down from the mountain, the people gathered together to Aharon, and said to him, Come, make us an elohim that shall go before us; for as for this Mosheh, the man who brought us up out of the land of Egypt, we do not know what has become of him. [2] And Aharon said to them, Break off the golden earrings which are in the ears of your wives, your sons, and your daughters, and bring them to me. [3] So all the people broke off the golden earrings which were in their ears, and brought them to Aharon. [4] And he received the gold from their hand, and he fashioned it with an engraving tool, and made a molded calf. Then they said, 'These are your Elohika, O Yisrael, that brought you out of the land of Egypt!' [5] So when Aharon saw it, he built an altar before it. And Aharon made a proclamation and said, 'Tomorrow is a Feast to YHWH.' [6] Then they rose early on the next day, offered burnt offerings, and brought

peace offerings; and the people sat down to eat and drink, and rose up to play." Shemot 32:1-6.

The problem with growing up in a pagan society is that it is hard to stay set apart from all of the pagan elements that impact your day to day life. A casual observer might ask: Why on earth would they construct a golden calf? It seems ridiculous, until you realize that they were doing what was familiar to them. They were worshipping "god" the way that the gods had been worshipped in Egypt.

You see, pagan societies such as Egypt did not worship one god - they worshipped many gods. There were a multitude of gods and goddesses that symbolized different things on the earth and in the spirit realm. One of the major cults in Egypt was the worship of Hathor.

Hathor was originally considered to be the mother of Horus, the falcon god. That title eventually went to Isis and Hathor was in later times regarded as his wife. Hathor was associated with love, fertility, sexuality, music, dance and alcohol. Who better to invite to a party - at least that is what the Yisraelites thought.

"She was sometimes represented entirely anthropomorphically, in the form of a cow, or as a woman with cow's ears. When in human form, her headdress could be one of cow's horns with a solar disc, or a falcon on a perch. She was also a sky goddess, and was regarded as a vast cow who straddled the heavens, with her four legs marking the four cardinal points."[72] She was honored as the "Lady of Byblos," the source of the word "Bible."[73]

 The Yisraelites declared a Feast to YHWH which was not a feast prescribed or ordained by YHWH.[74] They built an altar and made an idol in the manner that they had learned while in Egypt. The golden calf was the child of Hathor and Apis. Thus we see an example of a pagan trinity - father, mother, child worship which is predominate in pagan systems and derives from Babylon.[75]

The people took what they were used to doing in a pagan society and began doing it to YHWH. The only problem was that it was an abomination to YHWH. They were supposed to be a "holy" people. The English word "holy" is "qadosh" (קדש) in Hebrew and means: "set apart." They were not supposed to be doing pagan things and saying that they were doing them to YHWH. They were mixing abominations in their worship - that is strictly prohibited. Sadly, this error was continually repeated by Yisrael.[76]

There is no reason to think that only the non-native Yisraelites worshipped false gods. In fact, their readiness to worship false gods only weeks after witnessing the miraculous deliverance from Egypt only strengthens the position that many of the Yisraelites had fallen into pagan worship while enslaved in Egypt. After all, they were surrounded by these gods and goddesses that pervaded every aspect of the Egyptian culture.

These gods and goddesses had names, faces and temples where they could be worshipped. They had carved and painted images, statues and idols that could be seen and touched - they appeared real to those who

worshipped them. In this pagan environment, Yisrael may have forgotten or neglected the Elohim of their father Abraham because He was invisible.

Sadly, their act of "idolatry" constituted "adultery." The marriage process was not even completed and they were already proving themselves to be unfaithful. While Mosheh was on the Mountain receiving the Ketubah, "*two tablets of the witness, tablets of stone written with the finger of Elohim*" (Shemot 31:18), Yisrael was down below playing the harlot.

YHWH had provided tablets to Mosheh with the instructions written upon them – inscribed by the very finger of Elohim. The Hebrew word is "katab" (**𐤊𐤕𐤁**) which means: "to write" or "to inscribe" and it is where we derive the word Ketubah. How incredible that the literal meaning of these symbols is " **𐤁** - Hand" " **𐤕** - Covenant" " **𐤊** - House." By the very Hand of Elohim He would write and lead the way through the Covenant and into the House.

In the meantime, the people persuaded Aharon to make a golden calf. YHWH told Mosheh to go down as the people had corrupted themselves. YHWH indicated that He was going to destroy the people, but Mosheh once again intervened. He actually negotiated with YHWH as Abraham had once done for the people of Sodom.

Mosheh then reminded YHWH of the Covenant. "*Remember Your servants Abraham, Yitshaq and Yisrael, to whom You swore by Your Own Self: 'I will make your seed as numerous as the stars in the sky and I will give your seed all this Land I promised them, and it will be their inheritance throughout the ages.'*" Shemot 32:13.

After remembering the Covenant, YHWH

relented and did not destroy the people. Mosheh then started to go down the mountain to the people with the tablets in his hands. These tablets are specifically described in the Scriptures. *"15 . . . The tablets were written on both sides; on the one side and on the other they were written. 16 Now the tablets were the work of Elohim, and the writing was the writing of Elohim engraved on the tablets."* Shemot 32:15-16.

So these tablets were very special – they were the work of Elohim, and they had writing on both sides. The writing was in the Paleo Hebrew script, not modern Hebrew or Roman numerals as is often depicted.

When Mosheh returned from atop of the mountain with the tablets in hand, he was enraged by what he observed. He threw the tablets and broke them. This vividly symbolized the fact that the Covenant was essentially broken.

Mosheh had previously intervened and stopped YHWH from destroying the people, but he now called those who were with YHWH to stand with him. The Levites came to Mosheh and slew their friends, sons and relatives – about 3,000 total. As a result of their actions they were ordained for YHWH and blessed on that day. (Shemot 32:29).

Mosheh then returned up the mountain and sought to atone for their sins. He asked YHWH to forgive them, but if not, *"blot me out of Your Scroll You have written."* Shemot 32:32. Mosheh, as the intermediary between YHWH and Yisrael, was looking to be the atonement for their sins. Being blotted out of the book was death – eternal death. This is an important pattern because YHWH responds, *"Whoever has sinned against Me, I blot him out of My Scroll."* (Shemot 32:33).

He then told Mosheh to lead the people to the place that He designated, and His messenger would go before him. He then plagued the people, *"because they made the calf which Aharon made."* (Shemot 32:35). We see here that people are responsible for their actions. Those who sinned would be blotted out of the Scroll of YHWH. Through their actions they demonstrated an unwillingness to be faithful to YHWH.

After the plague, YHWH tells Mosheh to leave and speaks of the Covenant again. *"¹ Leave this place, you and the people you brought up out of Egypt, and go up to the Land I promised on oath to Abraham, Yitshaq and Yaakob, saying, 'I will give it to your descendants.' ² I will send a messenger before you and drive out the Canaanites, Amorites, Hittites, Perizzites, Hivites and Jebusites. ³ Go up to the land flowing with milk and honey. But I will not go with you, because you are a stiff-necked people and I might destroy you on the way."* Shemot 33:1-3.

We see that YHWH was willing to continue to bring them into the Covenant promises, although things had changed. YHWH indicated that He would not go in their midst, because they were a "stiff necked people." They were rebellious and stubborn, refusing to yield to the yoke of YHWH and follow His guidance. This, of course was an essential part of being a Covenant people.

So what was YHWH to do with the seed of Abraham who were supposed to be numerous, but refused to stay on His path and walk "perfect" before Him?

We now see the people at Mount Horeb. Things had changed and the people were quite somber. YHWH would not dwell in their midst, but rather He would meet outside the camp of the people, "far from the camp" at the Tent of Meeting. It was there that the column of cloud would descend and meet with Mosheh. It was there YHWH would speak to Mosheh face to face, "as a man speaks to his friend." The servant of Mosheh, Joshua, would not leave the Tent when Mosheh returned to the people.

After a very interesting encounter, Mosheh is told that he found favor in the eyes of YHWH, and he is allowed to see the esteem of YHWH. Let us take a moment to examine what happened, because this event is quite telling.

"*19 And YHWH said, I will cause all My goodness to pass in front of you, and I will proclaim My Name, YHWH, in your presence. I will have mercy on whom I will have mercy, and I will have compassion on whom I will have compassion. 20 But, He said, you cannot see My face, for no one may see Me and live. 21 Then YHWH said, There is a place near Me where you may stand on a rock. 22 When My splendor passes by, I will put you in a cleft in the rock and cover you with My Hand until I have passed by. 23 Then I will remove My ✗≮ Hand and you will see My ✗≮ back parts; but My face must not be seen."* Shemot 33:19-23.

Mosheh was placed in a fissure in a rock, and the Hand of YHWH covered him. When the Hand was removed Mosheh saw the Hand and the "back parts" of YHWH. Interestingly, both the Hand and the back parts of YHWH are directly connected with the Aleph Taw (✗≮), and these are the two parts of YHWH that Mosheh saw. This provides a very important connection with the Messiah.

After this great event, Mosheh is then instructed to cut two tablets of stone "like the first ones," so that YHWH could write the same Words on these tablets

that He wrote on the first tablets which were broken.

Mosheh had to carve out two new tablets and carry them up Mt. Sinai. Mosheh was once again, on the mountain for forty (40) days and forty (40) nights. This was done to make a very important point. YHWH surely could have spoken the Words to Mosheh within minutes or hours. Mosheh was on the mountain for forty (40) days and forty (40) nights, without eating or drinking, to make a distinct connection with Noah and the Messiah.[77]

It is important to recognize that this was a renewal of the marriage Covenant previously made with Yisrael, only now it was done through a man. A man had to cut the tablets and carry them up the mountain to present them before YHWH. YHWH wrote the Ten Words on the tablets cut by man, and this time Mosheh had to write the Words. (Shemot 34:27-28).

This provides a pattern for renewal of the Covenant when it is broken. For YHWH would later take the form of a man as the Messiah. The Messiah, as the Son of Elohim, would actually come down to earth and renew the Covenant in His own blood before ascending to the Father.

YHWH next directed Mosheh to build his House – the Tabernacle, along with all of the furnishings. The picture provided through the Tabernacle and the sacrificial system surrounding it is critical to understanding the Covenant path.

The Tabernacle represented the House of YHWH, which the people dwelled around – not in. So we see that the Covenant was not yet fully accomplished. Mankind was still not yet permitted back in the Garden to fellowship directly with the Creator. Rather, an elaborate system of sacrifices was implemented to demonstrate how YHWH would fulfill His Covenant.

The sacrificial system was not new, there was and remains a Melchizedek priesthood that has served mankind before YHWH since the beginning. Now YHWH established a separate priesthood for Yisrael and their service was provided to reveal the path back into the House.

These priests, consisting of the Tribe of Levi, were taken as YHWH's and they represented firstborn sons. (See Bemidbar 3:11-12 and Shemot 13). They were essentially adopted as firstborn sons into the service of the House of YHWH. They were substitutes for all of the firstborn males from the other Tribes of Yisrael. The message was clear, you have to be a child of YHWH to dwell and serve in His House.

The Tabernacle, which was essentially a large tent, has many levels of teaching. As the House of YHWH, it revealed the path into fellowship with Him. Those who desired entry first needed to wash at the Brazen Laver. There needed to be a blood atonement at the Altar before entry could be made. Once in the House there was a table set with bread and wine. This table contained (12) twelve loaves of bread, which were enough to feed all of Yisrael at that table.

The room was lit with the light of the Menorah, which represented the seven Spirits of YHWH. (Yeshayahu 11:1). It was also filled with worship, represented by The Altar of Incense. There was another room, separated by a veil. The Most Set Apart Place was a place where the presence of YHWH was seated on the Ark of the Covenant – the Mercy Seat. It was the place where intimate relations took place. Only the High

Priest was allowed access to this place once each year, and he had to bring blood with him.

As we can see from the example, this was a pattern, but it was not a completion. There was still more that needed to be done before the Covenant was fully revealed and fulfilled. The relationship had to be elevated to another level. Nowhere in the Scriptures is this better revealed than in the command referred to as the Shema.

The Shema is found in Debarim 6:4 and a typical English rendering is as follows: "*Hear, O Yisrael YHWH our Elohim, YHWH is one!*" This could also be translated "*Hear O Yisrael YHWH our Elohim, YHWH is unified.*" It is interesting that the Name YHWH appears twice in the passage with Elohim in the middle. In the modern Hebrew text we see:

שְׁמַע ישראל יהוה אלהינו יהוה אחד

Notice the enlarged ayin (עַ) in the word "shema" (שמע) and the enlarged dalet (ד) in the word "echad" (אחד). The ayin means: "eye" which can be better seen in the ancient script (⊙). The dalet means: "door" and the door to a tent is pictured in the ancient script (◁). So the enlarged letters are telling us to "see the door" within the Shema. The door is obviously the entrance to the House of YHWH. This door is made open by the blood of the Lamb of Elohim.

The next sentence in the Shema commands those in Covenant. "*You shall love YHWH your Elohim with all your heart, with all your soul, and with all your strength.*" Debarim 6:5. Only those who love YHWH with all of their hearts and all of their strength and all of their being

can enter through the door. This is a complete love being referred to – loving YHWH with every part of your being. We demonstrate our love by obeying His Commandments.

This level of intimacy is also seen by the very structure of the Tabernacle that, on another deeper level, represents a body. When you read the description (Shemot 26) it is easy to see the symbolism of a person including the skeleton, the skin, the flesh and blood (bread and wine) and the Spirit.

The essence of this picture is the Spirit of YHWH residing inside of the person. When YHWH and His Bride become one (echad), as a man and woman become one, that is when the Covenant will be fulfilled. Until that time, we continue to move in cycles of righteousness through time, which will lead to that ultimate fulfillment.

It should be plain to see that this was not a new Covenant. Some call this the Sinai Covenant, but it was really the same Covenant made with Abram, and later Abraham, continued through the seed of Abraham. It is another cycle in the everlasting Covenant.

While we see a refreshed, or renewed, relationship between YHWH and His Covenant people, they still are not residing in the Covenant Land, which represents the marital residence. That would be the next step – the next cycle. After the wedding, the bride and the groom move into their new home to dwell together. For this people to become a Nation, they needed Land – in this case the Covenant Land – The Land of Canaan.

7

Joshua

Interestingly, up to this point we have read about Joshua, the servant of Mosheh. It is only when it came time to explore the Promised Land that we learn Mosheh had changed Joshua's name. The list of the men chosen to go ahead of the people cites: "*Hoshea son of Nun from the Tribe of Ephraim.*" (Bemidbar 13:8). It is at the end of the list that we are provided with the following information- "*And Mosheh called Hoshea the son of Nun Joshua.*" (Bemidbar 13:16).

The name commonly translated as Joshua is spelled יהושע in modern Hebrew, and 𐤉𐤄𐤅𐤔𐤏 in ancient Hebrew. The name is properly transliterated as Yahushua or Yahusha. We do not know exactly when his name was changed from Hoshea to Yahushua, but there can be no doubt that the timing of this mention is of great significance.

Immediately prior to him entering the Land we are told of his name change. In other words, his name was changed before he entered into the Land, just as Yaakob's name was changed before he entered the Land. This is significant and should alert us to pay close attention to this man.

Yahushua was chosen, along with eleven other representatives, to explore the Land and bring back a report. Before the twelve (12) representatives set out on the reconnaissance mission they were given specific instructions by Mosheh.

"*[17] When Mosheh sent them to explore Canaan, he said, 'Go up through the Negev and on into the hill country. [18] See what the land is like and whether the people who live there are strong or weak, few or many. [19] What kind of land do they live in? Is it good or bad? What kind of towns do they live in? Are they unwalled or fortified? [20] How is the soil? Is it fertile or poor? Are there trees on it or not? Do your best to bring back some of the fruit of the land.' (It was the season for the first ripe grapes.)*" Bemidbar 13:17-20.

The twelve (12) spied out the Land for forty (40) days and came back with their report along with some grapes, pomegranates and figs. Again, we see the number forty (40), which points to a Messianic pattern. The spies set out on Day 29 of Month 3 according to Seder Olam B, and returned on Day 9 of Month 5 according to Taanit 26B. These facts become important when examining the future implications of these patterns.

The Land was clearly good, and the fruit was apparently plentiful and enormous. Sadly, the report given to the people was less than positive, and certainly not unanimous.

"*[26] They came back to Mosheh and Aharon and the whole Yisraelite community at Kadesh in the Desert of Paran. There they reported to them and to the whole assembly and showed them the fruit of the land. [27] They gave Mosheh this account: 'We went into the land to which you sent us, and it does flow with milk and honey! Here is its fruit. [28] But the people who live there are powerful, and the cities are fortified and very large. We even saw descendants of Anak there. [29] The Amalekites live in the Negev; the Hittites, Jebusites and*

Amorites live in the hill country; and the Canaanites live near the sea and along the Jordan.' *³⁰* Then Caleb silenced the people before Mosheh and said, 'We should go up and take possession of the land, for we can certainly do it.' *³¹* But the men who had gone up with him said, 'We can't attack those people; they are stronger than we are.' *³²* And they spread among the Yisraelites a bad report about the land they had explored. They said, 'The land we explored devours those living in it. All the people we saw there are of great size. *³³* We saw the Nephilim there (the descendants of Anak come from the Nephilim). We seemed like grasshoppers in our own eyes, and we looked the same to them." Bemidbar 13:26-33.

So the Land was good, but the Yisraelites feared the inhabitants. Those who gave a bad report did not trust the fact that YHWH would help them defeat the inhabitants. We see here Caleb giving a good report to no avail. He was outnumbered by negative reports from ten others and the people believed the ten.

"*¹* That night all the people of the community raised their voices and wept aloud. *²* All the Yisraelites grumbled against Mosheh and Aharon, and the whole assembly said to them, 'If only we had died in Egypt! Or in this desert! *³* Why is YHWH bringing us to this land only to let us fall by the sword? Our wives and children will be taken as plunder. Wouldn't it be better for us to go back to Egypt?' *⁴* And they said to each other, 'We should choose a leader and go back to Egypt.' *⁵* Then Mosheh and Aharon fell facedown in front of the whole Yisraelite assembly gathered there. *⁶* Yahushua son of Nun and Caleb son of Jephunneh, who were among those who had explored the land, tore their clothes *⁷* and said to the entire Yisraelite assembly, 'The land we passed through and explored is exceedingly good. *⁸* If YHWH is pleased with us, He will lead us into that land, a land flowing with milk and *honey, and will give it to us.⁹ Only do not rebel against YHWH. And do not be afraid of the people of the land, because we will swallow them up. Their protection is gone, but YHWH is with us. Do not be afraid of them.' ¹⁰ But the whole assembly talked about stoning them."* Bemidbar 14:1-10.

The words of Yahushua and Caleb fell on deaf ears, which displayed the fact that the people's hearts were uncircumcised. There is a direct connection between what we are willing to hear, and what we are willing to obey. (Jeremiah 6:10). This is the essence of the word "shema."

The people refused to hear the good report. They did not want to continue on their walk with YHWH. This was pure rebellion on the part of the Assembly. The people wanted to kill the leadership chosen by YHWH and then choose their own leaders. They wanted to return to Egypt where they were slaves instead of entering in to the Covenant Land. This was a rejection of YHWH and His Covenant.

Remember that this was the Land repeatedly promised to Abraham. It was an essential part of the Covenant. It was the new dwelling place for this Bride, Yisrael, and it was unquestionably a good Land.

The problem was not the Land, it was fear of the inhabitants of the Land. The Yisraelites were afraid of what they heard. All twelve "spies" saw the same thing, yet ten (10) gave a bad report. Two (2) saw the promise and trusted in YHWH while ten (10) succumbed to fear. The people then inclined toward the majority, despite the fact that the ten (10) were wrong. The Covenant way is not a democracy - it does not operate by the will of the majority.

The people had just recently witnessed YHWH miraculously decimate the Nation of Egypt and the Egyptian army. He had already demonstrated His power and His willingness to protect and defend them. He even promised that the Messenger of YHWH would go before them, but apparently it was not good enough for the people. They apparently did not trust or believe in the promises. So essentially we see this bride rejecting the marital residence as well as her Husband.

It was Yahushua and Caleb who brought back a good report and desired to take the Land. It was likely these two individuals who carried out the large cluster of grapes as proof of the bounty of the Land. Regardless of what the people saw, it was what they ended up hearing that decided their fate. They believed the bad report, not the good report, and by doing so they rejected YHWH. As a result of their continued rebellion, YHWH was ready to destroy the people, but once again Mosheh intervened.

"²⁰ YHWH replied, I have forgiven them, as you asked. ²¹ Nevertheless, as surely as I live and as surely as the glory of YHWH fills the whole earth, ²² not one of the men who saw My glory and the miraculous signs I performed in Egypt and in the desert, but who disobeyed Me and tested Me ten (10) times, ²³ not one of them will ever see the Land I promised on oath to their forefathers. No one who has treated Me with contempt will ever see it. ²⁴ But because My servant Caleb has a different spirit and follows Me wholeheartedly, I will bring him into the Land he went to, and his descendants will inherit it. ²⁵ Since the Amalekites and Canaanites are living in the valleys, turn back tomorrow and set out toward the desert along the route to the Red Sea. ²⁶ YHWH said to Mosheh and Aharon: ²⁷ How long will this wicked community grumble against Me? I have heard the complaints of these grumbling Yisraelites. [28] So tell them, As surely as I live, declares YHWH, I will do to you the very things I heard you say: [29] *In this desert your bodies will fall - every one of you twenty years old or more who was counted in the census and who has grumbled against Me. [30] Not one of you will enter the Land I swore with uplifted Hand to make your home, except Caleb son of Jephunneh and Yahushua son of Nun. [31]* As for your children that you said would be taken as plunder, I will bring them in to enjoy the land you have rejected. [32] But you - your bodies will fall in this desert. [33] *Your children will be shepherds here for forty (40) years, suffering for your unfaithfulness, until the last of your bodies lies in the desert.* [34] *For forty (40) years - one year for each of the forty (40) days you explored the land - you will suffer for your sins and know what it is like to have Me against you.* [35] I, YHWH, have spoken, and I will surely do these things to this whole wicked community, which has banded together against Me. They will meet their end in this desert; here they will die." Bemidbar 14:20-35.

Day 9 of Month 5 was supposed to be one of the happiest days in history. It was the day that Yisrael was to receive the Promised Land as a gift from YHWH. He had already promised it, and the day the 12 spies returned was the day they were to receive it. However, Yisrael rejected this gift through unbelief. As Yisrael seemed bent on turning a happy day into a sad day, YHWH gave them the desire of their heart. He made sure that Day 9 of Month 5 would be remembered as the most miserable day in the history of Yisrael.

Both the First Temple and the Second Temple were destroyed on Day 9 of Month 5. The Judeans were expelled more than once from foreign lands on this very

day. Pogroms also took place on this day later in Yisrael's history. There is even a historical tradition regarding the generation that received the bad report from the 10 spies. The Scriptures make it clear that everyone counted in the census died in the wilderness, but for Joshua and Caleb. The historical tradition is, that during the wilderness wanderings, large numbers of Yisraelites died every year on Day 9 of Month 5 until they were all dead.

This rebellious generation that rejected the Land was allowed to live. They were forgiven, but they were still going to be punished by wandering in the wilderness for forty (40) years – a year for a day. Once again, we see the prominence of the number forty (40). This form of punishment is similar to another punishment that will be meted out in the future.[78]

This event should make us recollect the fate of Adam and Hawah who disobeyed and were expelled from the Land – the Garden. They were not immediately killed for their offense. They were still permitted to live out their lives, but not in the place intended. Even in punishment YHWH is merciful. In fact, during this period of time, their garments and sandals did not wear out. (Debarim 29:5). They were also provided with food – manna.[79]

Nevertheless, they were not allowed entrance into the House. This is a critical point to understand. In order to dwell with YHWH you need to be in Covenant with Him, which involves obeying the terms of the Covenant.

During this forty (40) year period, they did not drink wine nor did they eat bread. They were not circumcising their males, which meant they were not partaking of the Covenant meal – the Passover. Why would they - after all, they had rejected the Covenant. The next generation would now have to wait their turn at the expiration of the forty (40) year sentence.

Remember that the number forty (40) is intimately linked with the Messiah. It was the duration of a generation and would now be the duration for a new generation to enter in. It was during this time that new leadership was prepared for the next generation – namely Yahushua.

An important point to recognize is that only two adults from the generation that left Egypt in the Exodus actually crossed over into the Promised Land: Yahushua and Caleb - two of the twelve who previously explored the land. They were the two who gave a good report to the people, and encouraged them to enter into the Land - despite the presence of giants. They also likely took the trouble to haul out a cluster of grapes as proof of the bounty that awaited them. (Bemidbar 13:23).

The reason why these two individuals were different is specifically detailed in the Scriptures: *"not one except Caleb son of Yephunneh the Kenizzite and Yahushua son of Nun, for they followed YHWH wholeheartedly."* Bemidbar 32:12.

Notice that Caleb was not a native Yisraelite. The Scriptures record that his father was a Kenizzite, yet his family became part of Yisrael. Despite the fact that his father was from a foreign land, the Scriptures list Caleb as being part of the Tribe of Judah. This means that at

some point his family was "grafted in" to the tribe of Judah, properly known as Yahudah.[80]

This is how it worked when Yisrael camped after the Exodus. They divided into tribes and they camped around the Tabernacle. There was no "Tribe of the Mixed Multitude" - no "Tribe of the Nations." The mixed multitude was not separated from the other tribes, they became part of Yisrael, just as Caleb's family joined Yisrael through the Tribe of Yahudah. Anyone who entered into Covenant with YHWH joined Yisrael, and was ultimately "grafted in" through a tribe.

Now look at Yahushua son of Nun. His name was changed from Hoshea which, means "salvation," to Yahushua which means: "Yah is salvation." Yah is the short form of YHWH, so the name is 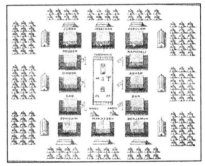 a declaration that it is YHWH Who saves.

As with Abram and Sarai, a letter was added to his name, and he was given a new name. The Hebrew letter yud (ʼ) was added to his name. The yud (ﭏ) represents an "arm" in the Ancient Hebrew Script. The yud is also the first letter in the Name of YHWH (ﭏﭏﭏﭏ).

So as we saw with Abraham and Sarah - the Marriage Covenant revealed through the Covenant - we now saw a man acting as the Arm of YHWH, bringing about a fulfillment of the Covenant.[81]

Yahushua was from the Tribe of Ephraim. The Tribe of Ephraim is extremely interesting, because the name itself means: "doubly fruitful." Remember that Ephraim was the son of Joseph and he was born in Egypt along with his brother Manashah. Their mother Asenath was an Egyptian - the daughter of a pagan priest - just as Mosheh's wife was the daughter of a pagan priest.[82]

Ephraim and Manashah were of mixed descent. They were Egyptian, because that is where they were born. They had been mixed into the Egyptian people, but their seed passed through the cutting of Joseph, the royal son of Yisrael. Yisrael has always been mixed with the other nations, and these two boys were no exception.

Interestingly, today these boys would not be accepted into the modern State of Israel, because their mother was not "Jewish."[83] Something amazing occurred which took away any doubt that they belonged in the Covenant. Yisrael very specifically placed his hands upon these two boys and blessed them. He not only blessed them – he adopted them.

Ephraim was the youngest son of Joseph, yet he received the blessing and birthright of a firstborn son. He was adopted by his grandfather Yisrael, and elevated as the firstborn son of Yisrael. So we have this powerful picture of a child born into a pagan culture, and Yisrael then adopting him into the family, making him a tribe and blessing him - as a firstborn son! (Beresheet 48).

Therefore, we see the two men - Caleb and Yahushua - representing Yahudah and Ephraim, both of whom were adopted into Yisrael in different ways. These were the only two individuls who would enter into the Land from their generation. How profound and encouraging for anyone born into paganism, finding themselves outside of the Covenant. There is room for everyone in Yisrael – all who are willing to believe in the

promises and obey the commandments.

When the forty (40) year period in the wilderness had expired, it was time to enter in to the Land with Yahushua leading this new generation. Mosheh was not permitted to enter in because he did not diligently obey the instructions of YHWH.[84] Before his death, Mosheh, along with Yahushua, renewed the Covenant with the next generation while they were in Moab – the land just east of the Jordan River Valley.

We read in Debarim 29:1 *"These words of the Covenant commanded YHWH* ✕𐤊 *Mosheh to make* ✕𐤊 *the children of Yisrael in the land of Moab, beside (𐤃𐤉𐤋𐤌) the Covenant He had made with them at Horeb."* The translation is more mechanical in order to place each Aleph Taw (✕𐤊) in its proper place. This is an interesting verse because many translations imply that this was an additional Covenant, which it was not. The word for "beside" is "milbad" (𐤃𐤉𐤋𐤌), and it portrays a picture of walking through waters (𐤌) led by a shepherd with a staff (𐤋) into the house (𐤉) through the door (𐤃). This was the long awaited moment to finally move in to the House. They were getting a Covenant refresher course before they moved in.

All of Yisrael was assembled, including sojourners (ger) in the midst of the assembly, to hear the words of the renewed Covenant.

"[2] Now Mosheh called all Yisrael and said to them: 'You have seen all that YHWH did before your eyes in the land of Egypt, to Pharaoh and to all his servants and to all his land [3] the great trials which your eyes have seen, the signs, and those great wonders. [4] Yet YHWH has not given you a heart to perceive and eyes to see and ears to hear, to this very day.[5] And I have led you forty (40) years in the wilderness. Your

clothes have not worn out on you, and your sandals have not worn out on your feet.[6] You have not eaten bread, nor have you drunk wine or similar drink, that you may know that I am your Elohim.[7] And when you came to this place, Sihon king of Heshbon and Og king of Bashan came out against us to battle, and we conquered them. [8] We took their land and gave it as an inheritance to the Reubenites, to the Gadites, and to half the tribe of Manasseh. [9] Therefore keep the Words of this Covenant, and do them, that you may prosper in all that you do. [10] 'All of you stand today before YHWH your Elohim: your leaders and your tribes and your elders and your officers, all the men of Yisrael, [11] your little ones and your wives - also the sojourner (ger) who is in your camp, from the one who cuts your wood to the one who draws your water [12] that you may enter into Covenant with YHWH your Elohim, and into His oath, which your Elohim makes with you today, [13] that He may establish you today as a people for Himself, and that He may be Elohim to you, just as He has spoken to you, and just as He has sworn to your fathers, to Abraham, Yitshaq and Yaakob. [14] I make this Covenant and this oath, not with you alone, [15] but with him who stands here with us today before YHWH our Elohim, as well as with him who is not here with us today [16] (for you know that we dwelt in the land of Egypt and that we came through the nations which you passed by, [17] and you saw their abominations and their idols which were among them - wood and stone and silver and gold); [18] so that there may not be among you man or woman or family or tribe, whose heart turns away today from our Elohim, to go and serve the gods of these nations, and that there may not be among you a root bearing bitterness or wormwood; [19] and so it may not happen, when he hears the words of this curse, that he blesses himself in his heart, saying, 'I shall have peace, even though I follow the dictates of my heart' - as though the drunkard could be included

with the sober. [20] YHWH would not spare him; for then the anger of YHWH and His jealousy would burn against that man, and every curse that is written in this Scroll would settle on him, and YHWH would blot out his name from under heaven.[21] And YHWH would separate him from all the tribes of Yisrael for adversity, according to all the curses of the Covenant that are written in this Scroll of the Torah, [22] so that the coming generation of your children who rise up after you, and the foreigner who comes from a far land, would say, when they see the plagues of that land and the sicknesses which YHWH has laid on it." Debarim 29:1-22.

The Covenant was renewed with that new generation as well as with those who were not there. This points to a future people who would enter into the same Covenant - which would again be renewed.[85]

Notice that YHWH is establishing this Covenant with the Children of Yisrael *and with the sojourner* who is in the camp. Some translations define the Hebrew word "ger" (ﭏ‎ﭏ) as "convert." In the ancient script we see a vivid illustration of the meaning. The "gimel" (ﭏ) represents the camel and the "resh" (ﭏ) represents a man. So we see a man and a camel – a wanderer. The word represents a person without a home.

The conversion would involve turning away from their pagan practices, and joining into the Covenant by following YHWH. Since the Covenant promises Land and a House, the person is no longer a sojourner. We know that Yisrael came out of Egypt with Egyptians, as a mixed multitude. It is known that Caananites also joined with Yisrael in the days of Mosheh, and Gibeonites joined with Yisrael in the days of Yahushua.[86]

Therefore, if anyone wanted to follow and serve

YHWH, they joined with Yisrael and entered into the Covenant. Emphasis was specifically provided that these ger (ᔕᑊ) were included in the Covenant. Notice also that the Covenant was a perpetual Covenant. It is not only made with those who stood there that day, but also with those who were not present.

In other words, this Covenant was extended to future parties in perpetuity. It is clear that YHWH intends for future generations to obey His Torah. For YHWH says He will blot out the names of the disobedient from under heaven.

After declaring the blessings associated with obeying the Covenant, and the curses associated with disobeying, Mosheh said something very interesting. *"¹ When all these blessings and curses I have set before you come upon you and you take them to heart wherever YHWH your Elohim disperses you among the nations, ² and when you and your children return to YHWH your Elohim and obey Him with all your heart and with all your soul according to everything I command you today, ³ then YHWH your Elohim will restore your fortunes and have compassion on you and gather you again from all the nations where He scattered you. ⁴ Even if you have been banished to the most distant land under the heavens, from there YHWH your Elohim will gather you and bring you back. ⁵ He will bring you to the Land that belonged to your fathers, and you will take possession of it. He will make you more prosperous and numerous than your fathers. ⁶ YHWH your Elohim will circumcise your hearts and the hearts of your descendants, so that you may love Him with all your heart and with all your soul, and live. ⁷ YHWH your Elohim will put all these curses on your enemies who hate and persecute you. ⁸ You will again obey YHWH and follow all His commands I am giving you today. ⁹ Then YHWH your*

Elohim will make you most prosperous in all the work of your hands and in the fruit of your womb, the young of your livestock and the crops of your land. YHWH will again delight in you and make you prosperous, just as He delighted in your fathers, ¹⁰ if you obey YHWH your Elohim and keep His commands and decrees that are written in this Scroll of the Torah and turn to YHWH your Elohim with all your heart and with all your soul." Debarim 30:1-10.

This is particularly interesting because it is at a time when they are getting ready to finally enter into the Promised Land, and Mosheh is telling them what will happen when they are scattered. He talked about "when" they would be cursed, and "when" they would be disbursed – not "if." He essentially was telling them that they would disobey, be punished and be scattered, but if they turned to YHWH they would return.

The good news was that they would be restored when they repented (returned), and obeyed YHWH with all their heart and all their being. Mosheh stated that they would not only be restored to the Land, but YHWH would also circumcise their hearts. So now we see that this Covenant of Circumcision was intended to go beyond merely cutting the flesh, it was supposed to penetrate the heart. This is physically represented by the focus on the circumcised male organ. It not only joins the man and woman as one (echad), it is also the conduit for the seed that passes from the male to the female during procreation.

Ultimately, the commands that were etched in stone would be written on their hearts and in their minds. Through that process, the people could truly turn to YHWH with all their heart and with all their being – this is the ultimate fulfillment of the Covenant cycles.

Before entering into the Promised Land, the assembly of Yisrael was specifically commanded not to worship false gods. *"You shall not bow down to their gods or serve them or do after their works; but you shall utterly overthrow them and break down their pillars and images."* Shemot 23:24.

They were also instructed not to set up poles and pillars in order to worship false gods. *"²¹ You shall not plant for yourself any tree, as a wooden image, near the altar which you build for yourself to YHWH your Elohim. ²² You shall not set up a sacred pillar, which YHWH your Elohim hates."* Debarim 16:21-22.

The Yisraelites were supposed to live holy, set apart, lives according to the Torah – their wedding contract. They were supposed to stay true to their Husband YHWH and not commit spiritual idolatry with other gods, which would constitute adultery, as they did at Sinai.

In other words, as the Bride of YHWH, if they wanted to live in His House – the Land – then they needed to remain faithful to Him and His ways. This, after all, was the essence of the Abrahamic Covenant that was being fulfilled. Abraham demonstrated his faith and trust in YHWH through his obedience. He was instructed to walk perfect before YHWH, and the Scriptures confirm that he obeyed the voice of YHWH, kept (shamar) His charge – mishmeret (משמרת), His commandments – mitzvot (מצוה), His statutes – chuqah (חקה) and His instructions - torah (תורה). (Beresheet 26:5).

This way of living was nothing new, and Mosheh specifically stated that this was not too difficult for the Bride. *"¹¹ Now what I am commanding you today is not too*

difficult for you or beyond your reach. *¹² It is not up in heaven, so that you have to ask, 'Who will ascend into heaven to get it and proclaim it to us so we may obey it?' ¹³ Nor is it beyond the sea, so that you have to ask, 'Who will cross the sea to get it and proclaim it to us so we may obey it?' ¹⁴ No, the word is very near you; it is in your mouth and in your heart so you may obey it."* Debarim 30:11-14.

Many believe that Yisrael was given "the Law" which was a harsh set of rules, too difficult for them to obey. This would insinuate that YHWH was a cruel Husband, and that Mosheh was a liar.

To the contrary, YHWH is continually described as: *"merciful and gracious, slow to anger, and abounding in steadfast love and faithfulness, keeping steadfast love for thousands, forgiving iniquity and transgression and sin . . ."* (Shemot 34:5-7). The terms of the Covenant were no harder than that of a faithful spouse. Yisrael was to stay true to her Husband YHWH, and keep a "clean" unpolluted House – it was not too difficult. It was only later, when men started toying with those simple instructions and created "laws," that Yisrael fell under oppression.

Through the leadership of Yahushua, Yisrael was finally permitted to enter into the Land, which would now be divided up into "different rooms" between the tribes. Before entering into the Land, Yahushua secretly sent only two spies. From past experience, two witnesses was the way to go, and I am sure he chose those two very carefully. This time they both returned with a good report. *"They said to Yahushua, 'YHWH has surely given the whole Land into our hands; all the people are melting in fear because of us.'"* Yahushua 2:24. The theme of the two witnesses also appears in Revelation Chapter 11.

To emphasize that this entrance into the Land was part of the Covenant, the first thing that they did was pass through the waters of the Jordan carrying the Ark of the Covenant. When the priests carrying the Ark entered the water, it piled up so that the Assembly of Yisrael could cross on dry ground.

This crossing was like a corporate mikvah, and resembled the previous crossing - only this time they were heading into the Land, rather than the wilderness. The symbolism was specifically meant to direct people back to the crossing out of Egypt. In fact, when they crossed over, they chose twelve stones from the middle of the Jordan to set up as a remembrance. They were supposed to connect this event directly with the Red Sea crossing, because this was all part of the same Covenant that brought them out of Egypt. (Yahushua 4:21-24).

To emphasize this point, the Scriptures indicate that it was on Day 10 of Month 1 that they went from the Jordan to Gilgal. This was a very significant day – it was "lamb selection day" leading up to the Passover. Because this was all about the Covenant of Circumcision, they needed to be circumcised in order to partake in the Passover meal, and that is exactly what they did. None of the males had been circumcised in the wilderness, so Yahushua made knives of flint and circumcised all of the males.

"*¹⁰ On the evening of the fourteenth day of the month, while camped at Gilgal on the plains of Jericho, the Yisraelites celebrated the Passover. ¹¹ The day after the Passover, that very day, they ate some of the produce of the Land: unleavened bread and roasted grain. ¹² The manna stopped the day after they ate this food from the Land; there*

was no longer any manna for the Yisraelites, but that year they ate of the produce of Canaan." Yahushua 5:10-12.

How appropriate that this event would occur at the end of their captivity in Egypt, and at the beginning of their entrance into the Land. It is as if the Passover had bracketed the wilderness experience which expressed the dual nature of this Appointed Time – deliverance and restoration. The Passover is and was, after all, the Covenant meal. In order to move into the Covenant Land with all of the associated blessings, you must be joined into the Covenant. This new generation had agreed to the Covenant in Moab, but now they had to "cross over" and enter in.

After miraculously defeating the walled city of Jericho, and then burning the city of Ai, they then went on to Shechem. Again, this was where Abraham first erected an altar to YHWH. It is also where the man Yisrael built an altar went when he returned to the Land. Shechem was the unifying place of this ancient Covenant. It was a place where the cycles of the Covenant would return, and therefore it was there that the assembly would journey to confirm the Covenant once they entered into the Land.

As a result, Yahushua built an altar on Mount Ebal in 1394 BCE. *"³⁰ Then Yahushua built on Mount Ebal an altar to YHWH, the Elohim of Yisrael, ³¹ as Mosheh the servant of YHWH had commanded the Yisraelites. He built it according to what is written in the Scroll of the Torah of Mosheh - an altar of uncut stones, on which no iron tool had been used. On it they offered to YHWH burnt offerings and sacrificed fellowship offerings. ³² There, in the presence of the Yisraelites, Yahushua copied on stones the Torah of Mosheh, which he had written. ³³ And all Yisrael, the sojourner (ger) as* well as the native born, and their elders, officials and judges, stood on either side of the Ark before the priests the Levites, which bare the Ark of the Covenant of YHWH. Half of the people stood in front of Mount Gerizim and half of them in front of Mount Ebal, as Mosheh the servant of YHWH had formerly commanded when he gave instructions to bless the people of Yisrael. [34] Afterward, Yahushua read all the words of the Torah - the blessings and the curses - just as it is written in the Scroll of the Torah. [35] There was not a word of all that Mosheh had commanded that Yahushua did not read to the whole assembly of Yisrael, including the women and children, and the sojourners (ger) who lived among them." Yahushua 8:30-35.

Notice the prominence of the Ark, often referred to as the Ark of the Covenant. It carried the tablets – the Marriage Ketubah. It was placed right in the center of Yisrael, which demonstrated that the Covenant was at the very heart of this ceremony. Also notice the emphasis of the sojourner (ger) when it mentions the Ark of the Covenant. Once again, the Covenant was available to the nations, but joining the Covenant meant joining the assembly of Yisrael.

Before Mosheh died, YHWH had commanded Yisrael to set up stones with the instructions of the Torah inscribed on them on the day they crossed the Jordan. Here is what was supposed to occur. "[2] And it shall be when you have crossed the Jordan into the Land YHWH your Elohim is giving you, set up some large stones and coat them with plaster. [3] Write on them all the Words of this Torah when you have crossed over to enter the Land YHWH your Elohim is giving you, a Land flowing with milk and honey, just as YHWH, the Elohim of your fathers, promised you. [4] And when you have crossed the Jordan, set up

these stones on Mount Ebal, as I command you today, and coat them with plaster. *⁵ Build there an altar to YHWH your Elohim, an altar of stones. Do not use any iron tool upon them. ⁶ Build the altar of YHWH your Elohim with fieldstones and offer burnt offerings on it to YHWH your Elohim. ⁷ Sacrifice fellowship offerings there, eating them and rejoicing in the presence of YHWH your Elohim. ⁸ And you shall write very clearly all the Words of this Torah on these stones you have set up."* Debarim 27:2-8.

Yisrael crossed the Jordan on Day 10 of Month 1 on Yom Shishi, which is the sixth day of the week, in 1397 BCE. Yahushua later renewed the Covenant on Day 21 of Month 7 on Yom Shishi, which is the sixth day of the week, at Mount Ebal in 1394 BCE.* And so Yisrael set up the stones on the day they crossed over the Jordan – on Yom Shishi.

Previously, in Moab they were told about the blessings and the curses, now they actually participated in the reading of those blessings and curses. This was what they were commanded to do at Shechem "between the shoulders" of Gerezim and Ebal. It is a very long passage, but essential to understand the terms of the Covenant.

"¹² When you have crossed the Jordan, these tribes shall stand on Mount Gerizim to bless the people: Simeon, Levi, Yahudah, Issachar, Joseph and Benjamin. ¹³ And these tribes shall stand on Mount Ebal to pronounce curses: Reuben, Gad, Asher, Zebulun, Dan and Naphtali. ¹⁴ The Levites shall recite to all the people of Yisrael in a loud voice: ¹⁵ 'Cursed is the man who carves an image or casts an idol - a thing detestable to YHWH, the work of the

craftsman's hands - and sets it up in secret.' Then all the people shall say, 'Amen!' [16] 'Cursed is the man who dishonors his father or his mother.' Then all the people shall say, 'Amen!' [17] 'Cursed is the man who moves his neighbor's boundary stone.' Then all the people shall say, 'Amen!' [18] 'Cursed is the man who leads the blind astray on the road.' Then all the people shall say, 'Amen!' [19] 'Cursed is the man who withholds justice from the sojourner (ger), the fatherless or the widow.' Then all the people shall say, 'Amen!' [20] 'Cursed is the man who sleeps with his father's wife, for he dishonors his father's bed.' Then all the people shall say, 'Amen!' [21] 'Cursed is the man who has sexual relations with any animal.' Then all the people shall say, 'Amen!' [22] 'Cursed is the man who sleeps with his sister, the daughter of his father or the daughter of his mother.' Then all the people shall say, 'Amen!' [23] 'Cursed is the man who sleeps with his mother-in-law.' Then all the people shall say, 'Amen!' [24] 'Cursed is the man who kills his neighbor secretly.' Then all the people shall say, 'Amen!' [25] 'Cursed is the man who accepts a bribe to kill an innocent person.' Then all the people shall say, 'Amen!' [26] 'Cursed is the man who does not uphold the words of this Torah by carrying them out.' Then all the people shall say, 'Amen!' [28:1] _If you fully obey YHWH your Elohim and carefully follow all His commands I give you today, YHWH your Elohim will set you high above all the nations on earth._ [2] _All_

these blessings will come upon you and
accompany you if you obey YHWH your
Elohim: ³ You will be blessed in the city and
blessed in the country. ⁴ The fruit of your
womb will be blessed, and the crops of your
land and the young of your livestock - the
calves of your herds and the lambs of your
flocks. ⁵ Your basket and your kneading trough
will be blessed. ⁶ You will be blessed when you
come in and blessed when you go out. ⁷
YHWH will grant that the enemies who rise
up against you will be defeated before you.
They will come at you from one direction but
flee from you in seven. ⁸ YHWH will send a
blessing on your barns and on everything you
put your hand to. YHWH your Elohim will
bless you in the Land He is giving you. ⁹
YHWH will establish you as His set apart
people, as He promised you on oath, if you keep
the commands of YHWH your Elohim and
walk in His ways. ¹⁰ Then all the peoples on
earth will see that you are called by the Name
of YHWH, and they will fear you. ¹¹ YHWH
will grant you abundant prosperity - in the
fruit of your womb, the young of your livestock
and the crops of your ground - in the Land He
swore to your forefathers to give you. ¹²
YHWH will open the heavens, the storehouse
of His bounty, to send rain on your Land in
season and to bless all the work of your hands.
You will lend to many nations but will borrow
from none. ¹³ YHWH will make you the head,
not the tail. If you pay attention to the

commands of YHWH your Elohim that I give you this day and carefully follow them, you will always be at the top, never at the bottom. ¹⁴ Do not turn aside from any of the commands I give you today, to the right or to the left, following other gods and serving them. ¹⁵ However, <u>if you do not obey YHWH your Elohim and do not carefully follow all His commands and decrees I am giving you today, all these curses will come upon you and overtake you:</u> ¹⁶ You will be cursed in the city and cursed in the country. ¹⁷ Your basket and your kneading trough will be cursed. ¹⁸ The fruit of your womb will be cursed, and the crops of your land, and the calves of your herds and the lambs of your flocks. ¹⁹ You will be cursed when you come in and cursed when you go out. ²⁰ YHWH will send on you curses, confusion and rebuke in everything you put your hand to, until you are destroyed and come to sudden ruin because of the evil you have done in forsaking him. ²¹ YHWH will plague you with diseases until He has destroyed you from the Land you are entering to possess. ²² YHWH will strike you with wasting disease, with fever and inflammation, with scorching heat and drought, with blight and mildew, which will plague you until you perish. ²³ The sky over your head will be bronze, the ground beneath you iron. ²⁴ YHWH will turn the rain of your country into dust and powder; it will come down from the skies until you are destroyed. ²⁵ YHWH will cause you to be

defeated before your enemies. You will come at them from one direction but flee from them in seven, and you will become a thing of horror to all the kingdoms on earth. [26] Your carcasses will be food for all the birds of the air and the beasts of the earth, and there will be no one to frighten them away. [27] YHWH will afflict you with the boils of Egypt and with tumors, festering sores and the itch, from which you cannot be cured. [28] YHWH will afflict you with madness, blindness and confusion of mind. [29] At midday you will grope about like a blind man in the dark. You will be unsuccessful in everything you do; day after day you will be oppressed and robbed, with no one to rescue you. [30] You will be pledged to be married to a woman, but another will take her and ravish her. You will build a house, but you will not live in it. You will plant a vineyard, but you will not even begin to enjoy its fruit. [31] Your ox will be slaughtered before your eyes, but you will eat none of it. Your donkey will be forcibly taken from you and will not be returned. Your sheep will be given to your enemies, and no one will rescue them. [32] Your sons and daughters will be given to another nation, and you will wear out your eyes watching for them day after day, powerless to lift a hand. [33] A people that you do not know will eat what your land and labor produce, and you will have nothing but cruel oppression all your days. [34] The sights you see will drive you mad. [35] YHWH will afflict your knees and legs with painful boils that

cannot be cured, spreading from the soles of your feet to the top of your head. ³⁶ YHWH will drive you and the king you set over you to a nation unknown to you or your fathers. There you will worship other gods, gods of wood and stone. ³⁷ You will become a thing of horror and an object of scorn and ridicule to all the nations where YHWH will drive you. ³⁸ You will sow much seed in the field but you will harvest little, because locusts will devour it. ³⁹ You will plant vineyards and cultivate them but you will not drink the wine or gather the grapes, because worms will eat them. ⁴⁰ You will have olive trees throughout your country but you will not use the oil, because the olives will drop off. ⁴¹ You will have sons and daughters but you will not keep them, because they will go into captivity. ⁴² Swarms of locusts will take over all your trees and the crops of your land. ⁴³ The sojourner (ger) who lives among you will rise above you higher and higher, but you will sink lower and lower. ⁴⁴ He will lend to you, but you will not lend to him. He will be the head, but you will be the tail. ⁴⁵ All these curses will come upon you. They will pursue you and overtake you until you are destroyed, because you did not obey YHWH your Elohim and observe the commands and decrees He gave you. ⁴⁶ They will be a sign and a wonder to you and your descendants forever. ⁴⁷ Because you did not serve YHWH your Elohim joyfully and gladly in the time of prosperity, ⁴⁸ therefore in hunger and thirst, in nakedness and dire

*poverty, you will serve the enemies YHWH
sends against you. He will put an iron yoke on
your neck until He has destroyed you.* ⁴⁹
*YHWH will bring a nation against you from
far away, from the ends of the earth, like an
eagle swooping down, a nation whose language
you will not understand,* ⁵⁰ *a fierce-looking
nation without respect for the old or pity for
the young.* ⁵¹ *They will devour the young of
your livestock and the crops of your land until
you are destroyed. They will leave you no
grain, new wine or oil, nor any calves of your
herds or lambs of your flocks until you are
ruined.* ⁵² *They will lay siege to all the cities
throughout your Land until the high fortified
walls in which you trust fall down. They will
besiege all the cities throughout the Land
YHWH your Elohim is giving you.* ⁵³ *Because
of the suffering that your enemy will inflict on
you during the siege, you will eat the fruit of
the womb, the flesh of the sons and daughters
YHWH your Elohim has given you.* ⁵⁴ *Even
the most gentle and sensitive man among you
will have no compassion on his own brother or
the wife he loves or his surviving children,* ⁵⁵
*and he will not give to one of them any of the
flesh of his children that he is eating. It will be
all he has left because of the suffering your
enemy will inflict on you during the siege of all
your cities.* ⁵⁶ *The most gentle and sensitive
woman among you - so sensitive and gentle that
she would not venture to touch the ground with
the sole of her foot - will begrudge the husband*

she loves and her own son or daughter [57] the afterbirth from her womb and the children she bears. For she intends to eat them secretly during the siege and in the distress that your enemy will inflict on you in your cities. [58] If you do not carefully follow all the words of this Torah, which are written in this Scroll, and do not revere this glorious and awesome Name – YHWH your Elohim [59] YHWH will send fearful plagues on you and your descendants, harsh and prolonged disasters, and severe and lingering illnesses. [60] He will bring upon you all the diseases of Egypt that you dreaded, and they will cling to you. [61] YHWH will also bring on you every kind of sickness and disaster not recorded in this Scroll of the Torah, until you are destroyed. [62] You who were as numerous as the stars in the sky will be left but few in number, because you did not obey YHWH your Elohim. [63] Just as it pleased YHWH to make you prosper and increase in number, so it will please Him to ruin and destroy you. You will be uprooted from the Land you are entering to possess. [64] Then YHWH will scatter you among all nations, from one end of the earth to the other. There you will worship other gods - gods of wood and stone, which neither you nor your fathers have known. [65] Among those nations you will find no repose, no resting place for the sole of your foot. There YHWH will give you an anxious mind, eyes weary with longing, and a despairing heart. [66] You will live in constant suspense,

filled with dread both night and day, never sure of your life. [67] In the morning you will say, 'If only it were evening!' and in the evening, 'If only it were morning!' because of the terror that will fill your hearts and the sights that your eyes will see. [68] YHWH will send you back in ships to Egypt on a journey I said you should never make again. There you will offer yourselves for sale to your enemies as male and female slaves, but no one will buy you." Debarim 27:12-28:68.

It was made abundantly clear that when they entered the Land there were responsibilities and there were consequences for neglecting those responsibilities. The consequences for disobedience were presented in nightmarish terms. It likely sent shivers down the spines of those who considered the possibility of experiencing such things. It was meant to have a deterent effect so that the people would obey and be blessed. YHWH desired so greatly for the people to obey and be blessed that He made disobedience unthinkable due to the horrendous consequences.

To avoid all of this, the people simply needed to diligently and joyfully obey YHWH, which was an expression of their love and appreciation. If they did this, they would be blessed and remain in the Land. Now that they were in the Land, they were responsible for keeping their end of the Covenant – obedience. This was nothing new. We see this as a key characteristic of those who enter into Covenant with YHWH.

This was certainly not the first time that they heard these warnings. Mosheh previously gave them similar warnings of blessings and curses when they were back at Sinai. "³ *If you walk in My decrees and keep My commands and do them,* ⁴ *I will send you rain in its season, and the ground will yield its crops and the trees of the field their fruit.* ⁵ *Your threshing will continue until grape harvest and the grape harvest will continue until planting, and you will eat all the food you want and live in safety in your Land.* ⁶ *I will grant peace in the Land, and you will lie down and no one will make you afraid. I will remove savage beasts from the Land, and the sword will not pass through your country.* ⁷ *You will pursue your enemies, and they will fall by the sword before you.* ⁸ *five of you will chase a hundred, and a hundred of you will chase ten thousand, and your enemies will fall by the sword before you.* ⁹ *I will look on you with favor and make you fruitful and increase your numbers, and* I will keep My Covenant with you. ¹⁰ *You will still be eating last year's harvest when you will have to move it out to make room for the new.* ¹¹ I will put My dwelling place among you, and I will not abhor you. ¹² I will walk among you and be your Elohim, and you will be My people. ¹³ *I am YHWH your Elohim, who brought you out of Egypt so that you would no longer be slaves to the Egyptians; I broke the bars of your yoke and enabled you to walk with heads held high.* ¹⁴ But if you will not listen to Me and carry out all these commands, ¹⁵ *and if you reject My decrees and abhor My judgments and fail to carry out all My commands and so violate My Covenant,* ¹⁶ *then I will do this to you: I will bring upon you sudden terror, wasting diseases and fever that will destroy your sight and drain away your life. You will plant seed in vain, because your enemies will eat it.* ¹⁷ *I will set My face against you so that you will be defeated by your enemies; those who hate you will rule over you, and you will flee even when no one is pursuing you.* ¹⁸ If after all this you will not listen to Me, I will punish you for your sins seven (7) times over. ¹⁹ *I will break down your stubborn pride and*

make the sky above you like iron and the ground beneath you like bronze. ²⁰ Your strength will be spent in vain, because your soil will not yield its crops, nor will the trees of the Land yield their fruit. ²¹ If you remain hostile toward Me and refuse to listen to Me, I will multiply your afflictions seven (7) times over, as your sins deserve. ²² I will send wild animals against you, and they will rob you of your children, destroy your cattle and make you so few in number that your roads will be deserted. ²³ If in spite of these things you do not accept My correction but continue to be hostile toward Me, ²⁴ I Myself will be hostile toward you and will afflict you for your sins seven (7) times over. ²⁵ And I will bring the sword upon you to avenge the breaking of the Covenant. When you withdraw into your cities, I will send a plague among you, and you will be given into enemy hands. ²⁶ When I cut off your supply of bread, ten women will be able to bake your bread in one oven, and they will dole out the bread by weight. You will eat, but you will not be satisfied. ²⁷ If in spite of this you still do not listen to Me but continue to be hostile toward Me, ²⁸ then in My anger I will be hostile toward you, and I Myself will punish you for your sins seven (7) times over. ²⁹ You will eat the flesh of your sons and the flesh of your daughters. ³⁰ I will destroy your high places, cut down your incense altars and pile your dead bodies on the lifeless forms of your idols, and I will abhor you. ³¹ I will turn your cities into ruins and lay waste your sanctuaries, and I will take no delight in the pleasing aroma of your offerings. ³² I will lay waste the Land, so that your enemies who live there will be appalled. ³³ I will scatter you among the nations and will draw out My sword and pursue you. Your Land will be laid waste, and your cities will lie in ruins. ³⁴ Then the Land will enjoy its sabbath years all the time that it lies desolate and you are in the country of your enemies; then the Land will rest and enjoy its sabbaths. ³⁵ All the time that it lies desolate, the Land will have *the rest it did not have during the sabbaths you lived in it.* [36] *As for those of you who are left, I will make their hearts so fearful in the lands of their enemies that the sound of a windblown leaf will put them to flight. They will run as though fleeing from the sword, and they will fall, even though no one is pursuing them.* [37] *They will stumble over one another as though fleeing from the sword, even though no one is pursuing them. So you will not be able to stand before your enemies.* [38] *You will perish among the nations; the land of your enemies will devour you.* [39] *Those of you who are left will waste away in the lands of their enemies because of their sins; also because of their fathers' sins they will waste away.* [40] *But if they will confess their sins and the sins of their fathers their treachery against Me and their hostility toward Me,* [41] *which made Me hostile toward them so that I sent them into the land of their enemies - then when their uncircumcised hearts are humbled and they pay for their sin,* [42] *I will remember My Covenant with Yaakob and My Covenant with Yitshaq and My Covenant with Abraham, and I will remember the Land.* [43] *For the Land will be deserted by them and will enjoy its sabbaths while it lies desolate without them. They will pay for their sins because they rejected My laws and abhorred My decrees.* [44] *Yet in spite of this, when they are in the land of their enemies, I will not reject them or abhor them so as to destroy them completely, breaking My Covenant with them for I am YHWH their Elohim.* [45] *But for their sake I will remember the Covenant with their ancestors whom I brought out of Egypt in the sight of the nations to be their Elohim. I am YHWH.* [46] *These are the decrees, the judgments and the Torah that YHWH established on Mount Sinai between Himself and the Yisraelites through Mosheh."* Vayiqra 26:3-46.

The blessings listed above are wonderful and the curses are dreadful. Obey YHWH and receive the

blessings or disobey and receive the curses. The choice was supposed to be an easy one. It is critical to point out that YHWH would first use others to mete out the curses until finally, He would personally deliver the punishment. Also, it is repeated on four (4) different occasions that the punishment would be multiplied seven (7) times if they did not repent. This becomes very important when calculating the duration of the predicted exiles.

Never does YHWH say that He will forget the Covenant. In fact, all of His actions resulting from Yisrael breaking the Covenant are meant to bring them back into obedience with the Covenant. For the sake of their ancestors, YHWH will not forget the Covenant. He is, after all, YHWH – He does not break His Covenant. This will be an important point to remember as we continue to examine the history of Yisrael.

When the people are in Covenant with YHWH, when they are not only circumcised in their flesh but also in their hearts, they will be blessed. Being in Covenant with YHWH is ultimately about having a circumcised heart and being blessed. The curses were meant to keep people on the straight path, in the way of blessings. When they strayed, the curses were meant to bring Yisrael to repentance, so that their hearts could be circumcised and they could return to YHWH and the subsequent blessings.

This occasion at Shechem must have been exciting, but also sobering. It was bittersweet. While they were finally entering the Land, it was evident that Yisrael would indeed fall away and be punished. In fact, after the death of Yahushua and the elders who brought Yisrael into the Land, things started to disintegrate.

Despite renewing the Covenant, the tribes were constantly struggling within themselves, between each other, with their leaders, with their neighbors and with YHWH. While Yisrael remained tribal in structure, they were bound by a common system of worship with the High Priest as their spiritual leader. This failed to unify all of the tribes, and they often looked for a leader who would function in a leadership role known as a "Judge."

We read in the Book of Judges (Shoftim) how Yisrael lacked cohesive leadership, which led to serious problems. Yisrael was divided and repeatedly falling away from the ways of YHWH. The Book of Judges (Shoftim) ends with the profound statement that essentially summarizes the entire text: "*In those days there was no King in Yisrael – every man did that which was right in his own eyes.*" Judges 21:25.

After hundreds of years of chaos and disunity it was very apparent that Yisrael required cohesive leadership – they needed a King. From the time that they conquered the Land under the leadership of Yahushua, there was a period of approximately 393 years that elapsed until YHWH would raise up a leader who would unite the tribes as a cohesive nation.

8

David

The people eventually cried out for a king. This was inevitable and even foretold by Mosheh. (Debarim 17:14). At that time Samuel (Shemuel)[87] was the undisputed authority figure in Yisrael. Shemuel was a unique individual from the region of Ephraim.

He was dedicated to YHWH, by his mother Hannah, when he was a small child. While he was from the Tribe of Levi (1 Chronicles 6), it appears that he was essentially adopted by the High Priest, the Cohen Gadol, since he stayed in Shiloh and served full time in the Tabernacle, referred to as the Mishkan.[88] At that time the Mishkan was located in Shiloh, which was in the territory of Ephraim. This is important because it was during the period of the Judges that YHWH essentially resided in the territory of Ephraim. That would eventually change.

Eli was the High Priest when Shemuel began his service in the Mishkan. He was not such a good High Priest, because he could not even control his sons, who had corrupted the priesthood. The House of YHWH was not in order, which was a reflection of the condition opf the Land. As a result of their conduct, Eli and his sons were cut off. It was Shemuel who attended to the spiritual needs of Yisrael after Eli and his two sons

Hophni and Phinehas died.

It was thereafter Shemuel who acted as a Priest, a Prophet and a Judge over Yisrael. He had the authority from YHWH to anoint the first king of the Kingdom of Yisrael. How fascinating that this very unique man originally from the region of Ephraim would stand as a judge of Yisrael at the time that Yisrael transitioned into a kingdom.

Shemuel anointed Shaul, who was from the tribe of Benyamin. Benyamin was the only one of the 12 sons of Yisrael that was born in the Land and the tribe of Benyamin was the smallest amongst the tribes. Benyamin was nearly decimated after the sin of Gibeah.[89] This tribe was located geographically between Joseph, the largest tribe, and Yahudah. Joseph and Benyamin were the two youngest sons of Yisrael and they shared the same mother – Rachel.

The reign of Shaul was ultimately cut off because he did not diligently obey the commandments. Here is what Shemuel told Shaul: "[13] *You have done foolishly. You have not kept the commandment of YHWH your Elohim, which He commanded you. For now YHWH would have established your kingdom over Yisrael forever. [14] But now your kingdom shall not continue. YHWH has sought for Himself a man after His own heart, and YHWH has commanded him to be commander over His people, because you have not kept what YHWH commanded you.*" 1 Shemuel 13:13-14.

If you are going to be the King of a Covenant people, the Covenant must be at the center of your life. Shaul failed, just as Adam had failed. He did not keep, guard, watch over and protect (shamar) the commandments.[90] As we have repeatedly seen, this is the trait that YHWH expects from someone in Covenant

with Him. You cannot simply be circumcised in the flesh, you must have a circumcised heart.

As a result, YHWH found a man like Yahushua and Caleb - a man who would follow Him with his whole heart. David was a giant slayer as were Yahushua and Caleb. David was a shepherd who trusted in his Elohim, and we know from the Psalms (Tehillim)[91] that he loved the Torah. These are the character traits of a man that YHWH will allow to lead His people Yisrael.

David was the youngest child of Jesse (Yeshai)[92] and was born and raised in Bethlehem. The reign of King David is looked upon as the Golden years of Yisrael. Before David, the tribes were generally divided between the North, led by Ephraim (Joseph) and the South, led by Yahudah. David first ruled over the Southern tribes – the House of Yahudah - for seven (7) years. After that time the Northern tribes - the House of Yisrael - submitted to his kingship. He united Yisrael and ruled for a total of forty (40) years. Once again, the number forty (40) demonstrates a link with the Messiah.

He made mistakes, but his heart for YHWH never wavered. As a result, YHWH covenanted with David that the throne would never depart from his offspring. Interestingly, we read about this Covenant when David expressed concern about building a House for YHWH.

"*4 But it happened that night that the Word of YHWH came to Nathan, saying, 5 'Go and tell My servant David, Thus says YHWH: Would you build a house for Me to dwell in? 6 For I have not dwelt in a house since the time that I brought the children of Yisrael up from Egypt, even to this day, but have moved about in a tent and in a tabernacle. 7 Wherever I have moved about with all the children of Yisrael,* *have I ever spoken a word to anyone from the tribes of Yisrael, whom I commanded to shepherd My people Yisrael, saying, 'Why have you not built Me a house of cedar?* ⁸ *Now therefore, thus shall you say to My servant David, 'Thus says YHWH of hosts: I took you from the sheepfold, from following the sheep, to be ruler over My people, over Yisrael.* ⁹ *And I have been with you wherever you have gone, and have cut off all your enemies from before you, and have made you a great name, like the name of the great men who are on the earth.* ¹⁰ *Moreover I will appoint a place for My people Yisrael, and will plant them, that they may dwell in a place of their own and move no more; nor shall the sons of wickedness oppress them anymore, as previously,* ¹¹ *since the time that I commanded judges to be over My people Yisrael, and have caused you to rest from all your enemies.* Also YHWH tells you that He will make you a house.* ¹² *When your days are fulfilled and you rest with your fathers,* I will set up your seed after you, who will come from your body, and I will establish his kingdom.* ¹³ *He shall build a house for My Name, and I will establish the throne of his kingdom forever.*¹⁴ I will be his Father, and he shall be My son. If he commits iniquity, I will chasten him with the rod of men and with the blows of the sons of men.* ¹⁵ *But My mercy shall not depart from him, as I took it from Saul, whom I removed from before you.* ¹⁶ *And your house and your kingdom shall be established forever before you. Your throne shall be established forever.* ¹⁷ *According to all these words and according to all this vision, so Nathan spoke to David."* 2 Shemuel 7:4-17.

So we read from this Covenant that it was still made within the framework of the Covenant made with Abraham. David was one of the seed of Abraham, and he was made King of Yisrael. Abraham was told that kings would come from him, and through David we can see the

fulfillment of that aspect of the Covenant. That portion of the Covenant was now extended through the seed of David. YHWH was now promising that a throne and a kingdom would be established through this particular seed of Abraham.

It is also important to note that although punishment is promised for disobedience. He promised that His mercy would not depart from David's seed, and that his throne would be established forever.

What we also see through this Covenant is an actual adoption. YHWH is continuing to build His House, and He actually adopted this man who had a heart to build Him a house. The heart of David was so aligned with the heart of YHWH that he was adopted by YHWH. Through this adoption process we begin to see the Messianic fulfillment of the Son of Elohim pattern that was previously demonstrated through Abraham and Yitshaq.

In fact, while there was an immediate fulfillment of this Word through David's physical seed, it is very apparent that there is a deeper, future prophetic aspect to this Word that concerns the Messiah. This is evident throughout the Psalms (Tehillim).

"*3 You said, 'I have made a Covenant with My chosen one, I have sworn to David My servant, 4 I will establish your line forever and make your throne firm through all generations. Selah 5 The heavens praise your wonders, O YHWH, your faithfulness too, in the assembly of the holy ones. 6 For who in the skies above can compare with YHWH? Who is like YHWH among the heavenly beings? 7 In the council of the holy ones Elohim is greatly feared; He is more awesome than all who surround Him. 8 O YHWH Elohim Almighty, who is like You? You are mighty, O YHWH, and Your faithfulness* surrounds You. ⁹ You rule over the surging sea; when its waves mount up, You still them. ¹⁰ You crushed Rahab like one of the slain; with Your strong Arm You scattered Your enemies. ¹¹ The heavens are Yours, and Yours also the earth; You founded the world and all that is in it. ¹² You created the north and the south; Tabor and Hermon sing for joy at Your Name. ¹³ Your Arm is endued with power; Your Hand is strong, Your right Hand exalted. ¹⁴ Righteousness and justice are the foundation of Your throne; love and faithfulness go before You. ¹⁵ Blessed are those who have learned to acclaim You, who walk in the light of Your presence, O YHWH. ¹⁶ They rejoice in Your Name all day long; they exult in Your righteousness. ¹⁷ For You are their glory and strength, and by Your favor You exalt our horn. ¹⁸ Indeed, our shield belongs to YHWH, our king to the Holy One of Yisrael. ¹⁹ Once You spoke in a vision, to Your faithful people you said: I have bestowed strength on a warrior; I have exalted a young man from among the people. ²⁰ I have found David My servant; with My sacred oil I have anointed him. ²¹ My Hand will sustain him; surely My Arm will strengthen him. ²² No enemy will subject him to tribute; no wicked man will oppress him. ²³ I will crush his foes before him and strike down his adversaries. ²⁴ My faithful love will be with him, and through My Name his horn will be exalted. ²⁵ I will set his hand over the sea, his right hand over the rivers. ²⁶ He will call out to me, 'You are my Father, my Elohim, the Rock my Savior.' ²⁷ I will also appoint him My firstborn, the most exalted of the kings of the earth. ²⁸ I will maintain My love to him forever, and My Covenant with him will never fail. ²⁹ I will establish his line forever, his throne as long as the heavens endure. ³⁰ If his sons forsake My Torah and do not follow My statutes, ³¹ if they violate My decrees and fail to keep My commands, ³² I will punish their sin with the rod, their iniquity with flogging; ³³ but

I will not take My love from him, nor will I ever betray My faithfulness. [34] *I will not violate My Covenant or alter what My lips have uttered.* [35] *Once for all, I have sworn by My holiness and I will not lie to David* [36] *that his line will continue forever and his throne endure before Me like the sun;* [37] *it will be established forever like the moon, the faithful witness in the sky."* Tehillim 89:3-37.

David was anointed (moshiach) with the set apart oil of YHWH, like Yisrael anointed the Rock. The Rock is a picture for the provision and salvation of YHWH. Therefore, David is likened to that Rock, which ultimately is a picture of the Messiah. His line would continue forever, and his throne would be a visible witness – like the sun and the moon. The Scriptures indicate that the sun and the moon are for signs and Appointed Times, for days and years. (Beresheet 1:14).

Therefore, the throne of David would be woven into the fabric of time and particularly the Appointed Times, which are Covenant events. Something very special was occurring in the Royal Covenant. It was another cycle in the Covenant made with Abraham.

David was responsible for moving the capital of the Kingdom to Jerusalem. It is no coincidence that this was the location from which the Melchizedek reigned. Again, we see the connection with Abraham, and another completion in the cycle of the Covenant. This is a picture of the Righteous King - a priest to El Most High working within and through the Covenant.

Once David established his throne in Jerusalem he desired to build a House for YHWH. Up until then the Tabernacle, made in the wilderness, was still being used and had moved to various locations. David set his heart to build a permanent house.[93]

At the direction of the prophet Gad, David purchased the threshing floor of Araunah, along with oxen to slaughter.[94] There he built an altar to YHWH, and it was chosen as the location of the House of YHWH. There is no coincidence that this particular location was chosen.

A threshing floor is a specially flattened surface made either of rock or beaten earth where the farmer would thresh the grain harvest. The threshing floor was either owned by the entire village or by a single family. It was usually located outside the village in a place exposed to the wind.[95]

Once the grain was threshed, a process of separating it from the stalks, it needed to be separated from the chaff through a process known as winnowing. The fact that the location of the House of YHWH was a threshing floor has profound implications when you consider that the Appointed Times, known as the moadim, were centered around the harvests.[96]

It is even more profound that it was at this very location that the Messenger of YHWH stopped during a plague on Yisrael due to the sin of David. When he was initially chosen as King, in a state of humility he declared that he was chosen to rule over "*a great people, too numerous to count or number.*" (1 Kings 3:8). Later in his reign the Scriptures record: "*Satan rose up against Yisrael and incited David to take a census of Yisrael.*" 1 Chronicles 21:1. Another Scripture states that: "*The anger (literal the nostril) of YHWH was kindled and He moved David against them to say 'Go number Yisrael and Yahudah.*" 2 Shemuel 24:1.

YHWH was greatly displeased by this act, and David was given three choices of punishment. He chose

to fall under the sword of YHWH, and a plague went throughout the Land. Interestingly, the punishment resulting from numbering people occurred at the time when the people were supposed to be numbering time – cycles of time.

This event took place while wheat was being threshed, so it would have been around the time of Shavuot, when cycles of seven are being counted. (Vayiqra 20:15; Debarim 16:9). As a result of the plague, Seventy thousand (70,000) Yisraelites had died, and the plague stopped at the threshing floor around the Feast of Weeks (Sevens).

While David purchased the land, he was not permitted to build the House, because he had blood on his hands. He was responsible for making the plans and preparations for building the House, as well as developing the songs, the instruments and other aspects of the worship service.[97]

After the death of King David, things deteriorated very rapidly. His son, Solomon (Shlomo),[98] built and dedicated the House of YHWH. He also built other great structures and accrued incredible wealth. He was known for his great wisdom, but sadly he fell into serious idolatry at the end of his life.

Read how his heart turned away from YHWH: *"[1] But King Shlomo loved many foreign women, as well as the daughter of Pharaoh: women of the Moabites, Ammonites, Edomites, Sidonians, and Hittites - [2] from the nations of whom YHWH had said to the children of Yisrael, 'You shall not intermarry with them, nor they with you. Surely they will turn away your hearts after their gods.' Shlomo clung to these in love. [3] And he had seven hundred wives, princesses, and three hundred concubines; and his wives turned away his heart. [4] For*

it was so, when Shlomo was old, that his wives turned his heart
after other gods; and his heart was not loyal to YHWH his
Elohim, as was the heart of his father David. ⁵ *For Shlomo*
went after Ashtoreth the goddess of the Sidonians, and after
Milcom the abomination of the Ammonites. ⁶ *Shlomo did evil in*
the sight of YHWH, and did not fully follow YHWH, as did
his father David. ⁷ *Then Shlomo built a high place for*
Chemosh the abomination of Moab, on the hill that is east of
Jerusalem, and for Molech the abomination of the people of
Ammon. ⁸ *And he did likewise for all his foreign wives, who*
burned incense and sacrificed to their gods. ⁹ *So YHWH*
became angry with Shlomo, because his heart had turned from
YHWH Elohim of Yisrael, who had appeared to him twice, ¹⁰
and had commanded him concerning this thing, that he should
not go after other gods; but he did not keep what YHWH had
commanded. ¹¹ *Therefore YHWH said to Shlomo, because you*
have done this, and have not kept My Covenant and My
statutes, which I have commanded you, I will surely tear the
kingdom away from you and give it to your servant. ¹²
Nevertheless I will not do it in your days, for the sake of your
father David; I will tear it out of the hand of your son. ¹³
However I will not tear away the whole kingdom; I will give
one tribe to your son for the sake of My servant David, and for
the sake of Jerusalem which I have chosen." 1 Kings 11:1-13.

This man who began his reign renowned for his
wisdom ended up an idolater. He failed to keep (shamar)
the commandments, which separated him from the One
Who had blessed him so greatly. The Scriptures are very
clear that it was his disobedience that led to his demise.

The Torah specifically forbids kings from
obtaining great wealth or taking many wives. (Debarim
17:16-17) They were supposed to prepare their own Torah
Scroll to remind them to live and rule according to the

instructions of YHWH. (Debarim 17:18). They were, after all, kings of a Covenant people.

Shlomo was provided with everything he needed to be a great king, but he failed miserably. He ended up being involved in abominable conduct, some of the worst pagan rituals that existed, including the sacrifice of children. He blatantly disobeyed the commandments, and the Kingdom would suffer as a result. Before his death, it was prophesied by Ahiyah of Shiloh that the Kingdom would be torn apart.

The prophet confronted the servant of Shlomo, Jereboam, as he was leaving Jerusalem. Ahiyah took a new cloak, and tore it into twelve (12) pieces. He told Jereboam to take 10 pieces and spoke the following to him:

"*[31] See, I am going to tear the kingdom out of Shlomo's hand and give you ten (10) tribes. [32] But for the sake of My servant David and the city of Jerusalem, which I have chosen out of all the tribes of Yisrael, he will have one (1) tribe. [33] I will do this because they have forsaken Me and worshiped Ashtoreth the goddess of the Sidonians, Chemosh the god of the Moabites, and Molech the god of the Ammonites, and have not walked in My ways, nor done what is right in My eyes, nor kept My statutes and laws as David, Shlomo's father, did. [34] But I will not take the whole kingdom out of Shlomo's hand; I have made him ruler all the days of his life for the sake of David My servant, whom I chose and who observed My commands and statutes. [35] I will take the kingdom from his son's hands and give you ten tribes. [36] I will give one tribe to his son so that David My servant may always have a lamp before Me in*

*Jerusalem, the city where I chose to put my Name. [37]
However, as for you, I will take you, and you will
rule over all that your heart desires; you will be king
over Yisrael. [38] If you do whatever I command you
and walk in My ways and do what is right in My eyes
by keeping My statutes and commands, as David my
servant did, I will be with you. I will build you a
dynasty as enduring as the one I built for David and
will give Yisrael to you. [39] I will humble David's
descendants because of this, but not forever."* 1 Kings
(Melakim) 11:31-39.

This was an incredible prophecy given to
Jereboam – an Ephraimite. The Scriptures record that
Jereboam was a mighty man of valour - he was a
powerful man. Shlomo recognized this and placed him in
charge of the whole labor force of the House of Joseph.

Jereboam eventually rebelled against the throne of
Shlomo. His people, the House of Yisrael, were being
oppressed, and YHWH chose Jereboam to punish
Shlomo's house for the idolatry and sin committed by
Shlomo. YHWH also gave Jereboam great promises, if
he would only do what Shlomo failed to do – be like
David. In other words, this Ephraimite would be a great
king over Yisrael if he would simply obey and guard
(shamar) the commands, walk in His ways and do what
was right.[99]

9

Division

After the death of King Shlomo, the prophecy given by Ahiyah came to pass. The House of Yisrael, also known as the Northern Kingdom, petitioned Solomon's son, King Rehoboam, essentially asking for tax relief. In the past, King Shlomo, had put a heavy burden on the people amassing great wealth and building mighty structures.

Instead of taking the advice of the elders, Rehoboam took the advice of his young friends and responded to the apparent reasonable request by stating: *"My father laid on you a heavy yoke - I will make it even heavier. My father scourged you with whips - I will scourge you with scorpions."* 1 Kings (Melakim) 12:11.

His "unwise" response resulted in a split in the Kingdom of Yisrael. Under the rule of Shlomo, Yisrael had broken the Covenant with YHWH, so they suffered the punishment of breaking the Covenant. Yisrael was split in two – as was pictured by the pieces in the Covenant process involving Abram.

The House of Yisrael, which consisted of the ten northern Tribes, aligned with Jeroboam, son of Nebat. The House of Yahudah, which consisted of the southern Tribes, aligned with Rehoboam. While the House of Yahudah maintained the worship of YHWH in

Jerusalem, the northern Tribes set up their own false worship system. This is where things started to go very bad for the House of Yisrael.

Apparently, Jeroboam feared that if the people from his kingdom, the House of Yisrael, continued to go to Jerusalem they would eventually join back with the House of Yahudah and reunite the Kingdom of Yisrael. This notion was unfounded, self-serving and contrary to the promise given to him by YHWH. His fear and concern demonstrated that he did not believe the promise of YHWH, so he took matters into his own hands.

After seeking some bad advice he set up pagan worship in the north.

"^{26} *Jeroboam thought to himself, the kingdom will now likely revert to the house of David.* ^{27} *If these people go up to offer sacrifices at the House of YHWH in Jerusalem, they will again give their allegiance to their master, Rehoboam king of Yahudah. They will kill me and return to King Rehoboam.* ^{28} *After seeking advice, the king made two golden calves. He said to the people, 'It is too much for you to go up to Jerusalem. Here are your gods, O Yisrael, who brought you up out of Egypt.* ^{29} *one he set up in Bethel, and the other in Dan.'* ^{30} *And this thing became a sin; the people went even as far as Dan to worship the one there.* ^{31} *Jeroboam built shrines on high places and appointed priests from all sorts of people, even though they were not Levites.* ^{32} *He instituted a festival on the fifteenth day of the eighth month, like the festival held in Yahudah, and offered sacrifices on the altar. This he did in*

Bethel, sacrificing to the calves he had made. And at Bethel he also installed priests at the high places he had made. ³³ On the fifteenth day of the eighth month, a month of his own choosing, he offered sacrifices on the altar he had built at Bethel. So he instituted the festival for the Yisraelites and went up to the altar to make offerings." 1 Kings (Melakim) 12:26-33.

This is really quite incredible, because Jereboam was already promised a perpetual throne like David's if he would simply obey. Instead of trusting the Word of YHWH, he tried to hold onto power using his own intellect and setting up his own system of worship – in direct contravention to the ways of YHWH!

Jeroboam not only established new places of worship, he also established different Appointed Times and set up a false priesthood. Notice that he chose a familiar place to offer sacrifices. Beth El was, after all, the "House of El." It was the place where Yaakob, and later Yisrael, built altars and offered sacrifices. The problem was that Jereboam actually violated the Torah. He changed the priesthood, the Appointed Times and he set up idols.

The sin of Jeroboam was even worse than the sin of his predecessors at Sinai. Despite warnings, Jeroboam refused to repent. As a result of this great sin, Yisrael was scheduled for punishment. It was not a mystery that they would be punished, Mosheh had told them long ago, but they apparently did not remember or they simply did not care. His new priests likely neglected to teach the curses associated with their actions to the people.

As you might imagine, not everyone in this new breakaway kingdom was pleased with the idolatry that was introduced by Jeroboam. While everyone must have surely appreciated the tax relief, they needed to choose whether the trade was worth it or not – they had a choice to make.

The Scriptures record the following: "*¹³ And from all their territories the priests and the Levites who were in all Yisrael took their stand with him (Rehoboam). ¹⁴ For the Levites left their common-lands and their possessions and came to Yahudah and Jerusalem, for Jeroboam and his sons had rejected them from serving as priests to YHWH. ¹⁵ Then he appointed for himself priests for the high places, for the goat and the calf idols which he had made. ¹⁶ And after them, those from all the tribes of Yisrael, such as set their heart to seek YHWH Elohim of Yisrael, came to Jerusalem to sacrifice to YHWH Elohim of their fathers. ¹⁷ So they strengthened the kingdom of Yahudah, and made Rehoboam the son of Shlomo strong for three years, because they walked in the way of David and Shlomo for three years.*" 2 Chronicles 11:13-17

This tells us that at least the Levites from the Northern Kingdom left and went to dwell with Yahudah. While others from the Northern Kingdom "*came to Jerusalem to sacrifice*" we do not know for certain if they moved there. We can safely assume from the language that the statement: "*they strengthened the kingdom of Yahudah*" means that they were added to the kingdom by moving to Judea. This is important to recognize, because it is highly likely that the Southern Kingdom ended up becoming a mixture of all of the tribes, although primarily Yahudah, Benyamin and Levi.

Sadly, the entire ordeal stemmed from a continuing sibling rivalry between Ephraim and Yahudah. Jeroboam, after all, was from the tribe of Ephraim (Joseph) and Rehoboam was from the tribe of

Yahudah. We see this as a continuing theme throughout the Scriptures. It is a very important concept to understand – the battle between the first born status and the rulership – because it continues to this day.

The matter was aptly summarized in 1 Melakim 12:19: "*So Yisrael has been in rebellion against the house of David to this day.*" The split in the kingdom was no accident, as proclaimed by Shemayah, the man of Elohim, when Rehoboam was about to suppress the rebellion of the House of Yisrael. "*This is what YHWH says: 'Do not go up to fight against your brothers, the Yisraelites. Go home, every one of you, for this is My doing. So they obeyed the Word of YHWH and went home again, as YHWH had ordered.'*" 1 Melakim 12:24. YHWH had a plan for this division which was much greater than people could imagine, and it was all about the Covenant.

As we read from the Scriptures, neither King followed good advice and both Kingdoms ended up getting into trouble. The audacity of the sin of the House of Yisrael resulted in a more immediate and severe judgment. Ultimately, both Kingdoms ended up receiving the promised curses of YHWH that are found within the Torah.

Since they were divided, and acting independently of one another, YHWH treated them differently. They committed different sins, and were given different punishments. The House of Yahudah staved off judgment as they drifted in and out of idolatry throughout the succession of many kings. Both ended up suffering the punishment foretold by Mosheh. They were evicted from the House, which was physical expulsion from the Land.

10

Exile

Before the tribes of Yisrael entered the Land they were given detailed and repeated guidance concerning the blessings of obedience and the curses of disobedience. As with Adam and Hawah they were given instructions, and they were warned of the punishment that awaited them if they disobeyed. Likewise, if they wanted to dwell in the Household of YHWH, they needed to obey the rules of the House. Yisrael could live in the Land as long as they obeyed the Torah.

There are many who proclaim that the Torah, which they call "the Law," was too difficult for Yisrael to obey. This is simply untrue. After detailing the blessings and the curses to Yisrael, Mosheh specifically stated: "*[11] Now what I am commanding you today is not too difficult for you or beyond your reach. [12] It is not up in heaven, so that you have to ask, 'Who will ascend into heaven to get it and proclaim it to us so we may obey it?' [13] Nor is it beyond the sea, so that you have to ask, 'Who will cross the sea to get it and proclaim it to us so we may obey it?' [14] No, the Word is very near you; it is in your mouth and in your heart so you may obey it.*" Debarim 30:11-14 NIV.

The ultimate punishment for the people of Yisrael was exile. It was specifically provided that if Yisrael did not obey the Torah: "*[36] YHWH will drive you*

and the king you set over you to a nation unknown to you or your fathers. There you will worship other gods, gods of wood and stone. *37* You will become a thing of horror and an object of scorn and ridicule to all the nations where YHWH will drive you." Debarim 28:36-37.

Again they were told: *"62* You who were as numerous as the stars in the sky will be left but few in number, because you did not obey YHWH your Elohim. *63* Just as it pleased YHWH to make you prosper and increase in number, so it will please Him to ruin and destroy you. You will be uprooted from the land you are entering to possess. *64* Then YHWH will scatter you among all nations, from one end of the earth to the other. There you will worship other gods - gods of wood and stone, which neither you nor your fathers have known. *65* Among those nations you will find no repose, no resting place for the sole of your foot. There YHWH will give you an anxious mind, eyes weary with longing, and a despairing heart. *66* You will live in constant suspense, filled with dread both night and day, never sure of your life. *67* In the morning you will say, 'If only it were evening!' and in the evening, 'If only it were morning!' - because of the terror that will fill your hearts and the sights that your eyes will see. *68* YHWH will send you back in ships to Egypt on a journey I said you should never make again. There you will offer yourselves for sale to your enemies as male and female slaves, but no one will buy you." Debarim 28:62-68.

Notice that although they had been as numerous as the stars in the sky, their numbers would be greatly reduced. While YHWH had fulfilled that Covenant promise, because of their disobedience, they would be diminished. Notice that there is no mention of the second Covenant count – the sand of the sea. That would be fulfilled at a later time – a future fulfillmemnt of the

Covenant cycle.

Besides these prescribed punishments, there was also provision for multiplying their punishment. In Vayiqra 26 the Yisraelites were told on four separate occasions that their punishment would be multiplied seven (7) times if they continued to disobey. This is extremely important to understand when examining the duration of the exiles for the different kingdoms.

So Mosheh told the children of Yisrael that they would, in fact, be exiled. He also provided them with the hope of an eventual restoration described as follows:

"¹ When all these blessings and curses I have set before you come upon you and you take them to heart wherever YHWH your Elohim disperses you among the nations, ² and when you and your children return to YHWH your Elohim and obey Him with all your heart and with all your soul according to everything I command you today, ³ then YHWH your Elohim will restore your fortunes and have compassion on you and gather you again from all the nations where He scattered you. ⁴ Even if you have been banished to the most distant land under the heavens, from there YHWH your Elohim will gather you and bring you back. ⁵ He will bring you to the Land that belonged to your fathers, and you will take possession of it. He will make you more prosperous and numerous than your fathers. ⁶ YHWH your Elohim will circumcise your hearts and the hearts of your descendants, so that you may love Him with all your heart and with all your soul, and live. ⁷ YHWH your Elohim will put all these curses on your enemies who hate and persecute you. ⁸ You will again obey YHWH and follow all His commands I am giving you today. ⁹ Then YHWH

your Elohim will make you most prosperous in all the work of your hands and in the fruit of your womb, the young of your livestock and the crops of your land. YHWH will again delight in you and make you prosperous, just as He delighted in your fathers, [10] if you obey YHWH your Elohim and keep His commands and decrees that are written in this Scroll of the Torah and turn to YHWH your Elohim with all your heart and with all your soul." Debarim 30:1-10.

So we see a pattern being repeated - just as Adam and Hawah were cut off and expelled from the "household" because of their disobedience – so were the two Houses of Yisrael. This is an interesting parallel because, as we shall see, all of the tribes of Yisrael were not exiled together, rather the Kingdom was divided in two and the House of Yisrael was exiled separate from the House of Yahudah.

Let us first read what happened to the House of Yisrael:

"[1] *In the twelfth year of Ahaz king of Yahudah, Hoshea son of Elah became king of Yisrael in Samaria, and he reigned nine years. [2] He did evil in the eyes of YHWH, but not like the kings of Yisrael who preceded him. [3] Shalmaneser king of Assyria came up to attack Hoshea, who had been Shalmaneser's vassal and had paid him tribute. [4] But the king of Assyria discovered that Hoshea was a traitor, for he had sent envoys to So king of Egypt, and he no longer paid tribute to the king of Assyria, as he had done year by year. Therefore Shalmaneser seized him and put him in prison. [5] The king of Assyria invaded the entire land, marched against Samaria and laid siege to it for three years. [6] In the ninth year of Hoshea, the king of Assyria captured Samaria and deported the Yisraelites to*

Assyria. He settled them in Halah, in Gozan on the Habor River and in the towns of the Medes. [7] All this took place because the Yisraelites had sinned against YHWH their Elohim, who had brought them up out of Egypt from under the power of Pharaoh king of Egypt. They worshiped other gods [8] and followed the practices of the nations YHWH had driven out before them, as well as the practices that the kings of Yisrael had introduced. [9] The Yisraelites secretly did things against YHWH their Elohim that were not right. From watchtower to fortified city they built themselves high places in all their towns. [10] They set up sacred stones and Asherah poles on every high hill and under every spreading tree. [11] At every high place they burned incense, as the nations whom YHWH had driven out before them had done. They did wicked things that provoked YHWH to anger. [12] They worshiped idols, though YHWH had said, 'You shall not do this. [13] YHWH warned Yisrael and Yahudah through all his prophets and seers: Turn from your evil ways. Observe My commands and decrees, in accordance with the entire Torah that I commanded your fathers to obey and that I delivered to you through My servants the prophets.' [14] But they would not listen and were as stiff-necked as their fathers, who did not trust in YHWH their Elohim. They rejected His decrees and the Covenant He had made with their fathers and the warnings He had given them. They followed worthless idols and themselves became worthless. They imitated the nations around them although YHWH had ordered them, 'Do not do as they do,' and they did the things YHWH had forbidden them to do. [16] They forsook all the commands of YHWH their Elohim and made for themselves two idols cast in the shape of calves, and an Asherah pole. They bowed down to all the starry hosts, and

they worshiped Baal. ¹⁷ They sacrificed their sons and daughters in the fire. They practiced divination and sorcery and sold themselves to do evil in the eyes of YHWH, provoking Him to anger. ¹⁸ So YHWH was very angry with Yisrael and removed them from His presence. Only the tribe of Yahudah was left, ¹⁹ and even Yahudah did not keep the commands of YHWH their Elohim. They followed the practices Yisrael had introduced. ²⁰ Therefore YHWH rejected all the people of Yisrael; He afflicted them and gave them into the hands of plunderers, until He thrust them from His presence. ²¹ When He tore Yisrael away from the house of David, they made Jeroboam son of Nebat their king. Jeroboam enticed Yisrael away from following YHWH and caused them to commit a great sin. ²² The Yisraelites persisted in all the sins of Jeroboam and did not turn away from them ²³ until YHWH removed them from His presence, as He had warned through all His servants the prophets. So the people of Yisrael were taken from their homeland into exile in Assyria, and they are still there." 2 Melakim 17:1-24.

The Assyrians actually removed all of the House of Yisrael from the Land. This is a fact debated by some, but the Scriptures clearly state that "YHWH rejected ALL the people of Yisrael" and "ONLY the Tribe of Yahudah was left." Remember that a remnant of the Northern Tribes, along with the Levites, likely "moved in" with the House of Yahudah after Jeroboam set up his idolatrous system of worship. Therefore, while Assyria removed the Northern Tribes from their Land, there was probably a remnant of these Tribes who lived in Judea

and joined the House of Yahudah.

As was their custom, Assyrian Kings did not just defeat their enemies – they transplanted them in order to better gain control of the territories that they conquered. In the case of the House of Yisrael, this appears to have been a process which took place through the reigns of three Assyrian Kings, Tiglath-pileser III, Shalmaneser V and Sargon II – possibly others.

 One can read in the Khorsebad Annals how Sargon II took Samaria and carried away 27,290 of the population of Yisrael. This is often used by those who desire to contradict the Scriptures by claiming that not all of the House of Yisrael was sent into exile. That is a weak argument because this particular incident recorded by Sargon II was only one event of many that occurred in the 700's BCE.

"In the late 1800's some clay Assyrian cuneiform tablets were discovered and they were finally translated in the 1930's. These tablets were Assyrian records of this 700's [Y]israelite deportation. There were records of four deportations, which proved the ten tribes of the northern Nation of [Y]israel were assembled into Assyrian culture and became identifiable as the C[i]merians, the Sythians, and the Goths. Our records of ancient history show that over several hundred years, and through different 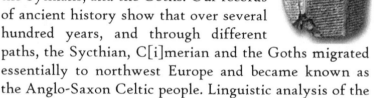 paths, the Sycthian, C[i]merian and the Goths migrated essentially to northwest Europe and became known as the Anglo-Saxon Celtic people. Linguistic analysis of the

word 'Anglo-Saxon' shows the word 'Saxon' means 'sons of Isaac.'"[100]

The exile of the northern tribes was a result of their grievous sins – YHWH had to remove them from His presence. They were participating in the worst forms of idolatry, even offering their children as sacrifices – likely to the god Chemosh. Not only were the Yisraelites removed from their land, they were replaced by foreigners.

"[24] *The king of Assyria brought people from Babylon, Cuthah, Avva, Hamath and Sepharvaim and settled them in the towns of Samaria to replace the Yisraelites.* *They took over Samaria and lived in its towns.* [25] *When they first lived there, they did not worship YHWH; so He sent lions among them and they killed some of the people.* [26] *It was reported to the king of Assyria: The people you deported and resettled in the towns of Samaria do not know what the Elohi of that country requires. He has sent lions among them, which are killing them off, because the people do not know what He requires.* [27] *Then the king of Assyria gave this order: 'Have one of the priests you took captive from Samaria go back to live there and teach the people what the Elohi of the land requires.'* [28] *So one of the priests who had been exiled from Samaria came to live in Bethel and taught them how to worship YHWH.* [29] *Nevertheless, each national group made its own gods in the several towns where they settled, and set them up in the shrines the people of Samaria had made at the high places.* [30] *The men from Babylon made Succoth Benoth, the men from Cuthah made Nergal, and the men from Hamath made Ashima;* [31] *the Avvites made Nibhaz and Tartak, and the Sepharvites burned* their children in the fire as sacrifices to Adrammelech and Anammelech, the gods of Sepharvaim. [32] *They worshiped YHWH, but they also appointed all sorts of their own people to officiate for them as priests in the shrines at the high places.* [33] *They worshiped YHWH, but they also served their own gods in accordance with the customs of the nations from which they had been brought.* [34] To this day they persist in their former practices. They neither worship YHWH nor adhere to the decrees and ordinances, the Torah and commands that YHWH gave the descendants of Yaakob, whom He named Yisrael. [35] When YHWH made a Covenant with the Yisraelites, He commanded them: 'Do not worship any other gods or bow down to them, serve them or sacrifice to them. [36] But YHWH, who brought you up out of Egypt with mighty power and outstretched arm, is the One you must worship. To Him you shall bow down and to Him offer sacrifices. [37] You must always be careful to keep the decrees and ordinances, the Torah and commands He wrote for you. Do not worship other gods. [38] Do not forget the Covenant I have made with you, and do not worship other gods. [39] Rather, worship YHWH your Elohim; it is He who will deliver you from the hand of all your enemies.' [40] They would not listen, however, but persisted in their former practices. [41] Even while these people were worshiping YHWH, they were serving their idols. To this day their children and grandchildren continue to do as their fathers did." 2 Melakim 17:24-41.

Notice that YHWH sent lions to destroy these new settlers because they too were not worshipping Him. As a result, the King of Assyria sent back a priest to instruct the foreigners how to serve YHWH, which they did along with their pagan worship. We can see this very  day the foreigners who still live in Samaria. The Samaritans currently practice a hybrid religion, centered at Mount Gerizim. Their religion is based primarily upon the Torah, which retains the Paleo Hebrew Script, although it includes a certain amount of deviation. This has resulted in ancient and underlying tensions between the Samaritans and those from the House of Yahudah.

How interesting that the Kingdom of Yisrael was chosen to be a kingdom of priests who, through their obedience, were to shine as a light to the nations. They were delivered from Egypt and brought to their own Land so that they could be set apart and obey YHWH. Through their obedience they would be blessed, and all the world would see it. Instead, they disobeyed, but even through their disobedience they would give testimony to the nations. Only now they would be scattered throughout the nations, and the nations were brought into the Land.

The Scriptures indicate that the House of Yahudah also followed the ways of the House of Yisrael, although their punishment was withheld due to their repentance and restoration that occurred under the reign of various kings. The tribes of the House of Yisrael were removed from their Land and scattered by the Assyrians around 721 - 722 BCE. The House of Yahudah was not exiled until around 586 BCE. These specific dates are disputed by some in academia, but they are certainly close.

Ezekiel (Yehezqel)[101] was one of the major prophets who prophesied to the House of Yahudah concerning their sin during their exile. He began his prophetic ministry in the *"fifth year of King Jehochin's captivity."* Yehezqel 1:2. This Jehochin was the king of Yahudah who was taken captive into Babylon about 610 BCE. Accordingly, this would place the beginning of Yehezqel's prophecies at about 606 BCE.

The last dates which Yehezqel mentions in his prophecy are the "twenty-seventh year" and "the twenty fifth year of our captivity" Yehezqel 29:17, 40:1. Therefore, Yehezqel prophesied for at least 20 years among the captives, until 584 BCE.

The Babylonians exiled captives from Jerusalem in three different stages. In an early campaign around 618 BCE, the prophet Daniel was among the Yahudim taken to Babylon. A second attack against the city occurred in 610 BCE, when many more captives were taken. Yehezqel was likely taken captive at this time. Then in the extensive campaign of 601 BCE - 599 BCE, Nebuchadnezzar destroyed Jerusalem and took most of the remaining inhabitants into exile.[102]

Thus we have the House of Yisrael, often referred to as Ephraim, separated from the House of Yahudah and completely removed from the Land by the Assyrians. We later see the House of Yahudah removed by the Babylonians. Both Kingdoms strayed from YHWH. As we previously saw Ephraim (represented by Yahushua) and Yahudah (represented by Caleb) enter in

to the Land because they followed YHWH wholeheartedly (Debarim 1:36) – now both Houses were expelled because of their disobedience.

Over the decades that followed, many prophets were sent to try to restore them to a right relationship with YHWH by pointing the way back to the Torah. This, after all, is the primary function of a prophet - restoration. There were different prophets sent to the different Kingdoms to warn them, and they would often stand in the gap and encourage Yisrael (Ephraim) and Yahudah to get cleaned up and get right with their Creator. It was all about the Covenant and these prophets acted like marriage counselors.

Sadly, both Kingdoms failed to heed their warnings. They refused to give up their whoring and thus they remained separated from their Husband - YHWH.

Read what YHWH spoke through the Prophet Hoshea: "*⁴ What can I do with you, Ephraim? What can I do with you, Yahudah? Your love is like the morning mist, like the early dew that disappears. ⁵ Therefore I cut you in pieces with My prophets, I killed you with the words of My mouth; My judgments flashed like lightning upon you. ⁶ For I desire mercy, not sacrifice, and acknowledgment of Elohim rather than burnt offerings. ⁷ Like Adam, they have broken the Covenant - they were unfaithful to Me there.*" Hoshea 6:4-7.

Notice how YHWH speaks to Ephraim and Yahudah separately, and notice the connection with Adam. Adam was supposed to commune with YHWH. Adam was literally and metaphorically split in two when Hawah was taken from his side - and both Adam and Hawah individually broke the Covenant. This was similar to what happened with Yisrael. The Kingdom

was divided into Ephraim and Yahudah and both of them broke the Covenant.

It might have seemed like all was lost as YHWH sent His prophets to proclaim the punishment that would befall both Houses. Thankfully, these prophets did not only proclaim judgment, they also give hope to both the House of Yisrael and the House of Yahudah. They provided the promise that someday, these people would be restored back into the fullness of the Covenant.

II

The Prophets

Both Houses of Yisrael broke the Covenant allowing YHWH to declare it null and void. YHWH actually predicted that this would happen. He told Mosheh and Yahushua ahead of time.[103]

We know that YHWH divorced the House of Yisrael, although there is nothing to indicate that He divorced the House of Yahudah. That does not mean that Yahudah's conduct was any better than Yisrael's. In fact, she was actually described as being treacherous, and Yisrael was described as being more righteous in her backsliding than Yahudah.

"*⁶ YHWH said also to me in the days of Josiah the king: Have you seen what backsliding Yisrael has done? She has gone up on every high mountain and under every green tree, and there played the harlot. ⁷ And I said, after she had done all these things, 'Return to Me.' But she did not return. And her treacherous sister Yahudah saw it. ⁸ Then I saw that for all the causes for which backsliding Yisrael had committed adultery, I had put her away and given her a certificate of divorce; yet her treacherous sister Yahudah did not fear, but went and played the harlot also. ⁹ So it came to pass, through her casual harlotry, that she defiled the Land and committed adultery with stones and trees. ¹⁰ And yet for all this her treacherous sister Yahudah has not turned to Me with her whole heart, but in pretense, says* YHWH. [11] *Then* YHWH *said to me, backsliding Yisrael has shown herself more righteous than treacherous Yahudah.* [12] *Go and proclaim these words toward the north, and say:* '*Return, backsliding Yisrael,*' *says* YHWH; '*I will not cause My anger to fall on you. For I am merciful,*' *says* YHWH; '*I will not remain angry forever.* [13] *Only acknowledge your iniquity, that you have transgressed against* YHWH *your Elohim, and have scattered your charms to alien deities under every green tree, and you have not obeyed My voice,*' *says* YHWH. [14] '*Return, O backsliding children,*' *says* YHWH '*for I am married to you. I will take you, one from a city and two from a family, and I will bring you to Zion* . . . [20] *Surely, as a wife treacherously departs from her husband, so have you dealt treacherously with Me, O House of Yisrael,*' *says* YHWH." Jeremiah 3:6-14, 20.

So we see that the House of Yisrael dealt treacherously with YHWH, and He issued her a certificate of divorce. The House of Yahudah observed this entire event, and still continued to backslide. This was what made her treacherous. It was likely only because of the Covenant made with David that YHWH spared her from complete separation, although she too was exiled for her deeds.

The amazing part of the Word given by Jeremiah was the hope given to Yisrael. Despite the divorce YHWH indicated that He would not forget Yisrael forever. This same hope was given through the prophet Hoshea. According to Hoshea, YHWH would forget Yisrael, but he also provided the hope of restoration.

When the Scriptures first introduce Hoshea, they provide us with a general time frame. "*The word of* YHWH *that came to Hoshea son of Beeri during the reigns of Uzziah, Jotham, Ahaz and Hezekiah, kings of Yahudah, and*

during the reign of Jeroboam son of Yahoash king of Yisrael."
Hoshea 1:1. This is important because we know that
Hoshea was a prophet while both Kingdoms were still in
the Land – prior to the exile of the House of Yisrael.

YHWH used the life of Hoshea to demonstrate
what He was going to do to the House of Yisrael. He
instructed Hoshea as follows: "*'2 Go, take to yourself an
adulterous wife and children of unfaithfulness, because the
Land is guilty of the vilest adultery in departing from
YHWH.' 3 So he married Gomer daughter of Diblaim, and she
conceived and bore him a son. 4 Then YHWH said to Hoshea,
'Call him Yezreel, because I will soon punish the house of Yahu
for the massacre at Yezreel, and I will put an end to the
kingdom of Yisrael. 5 In that day I will break Yisrael's bow in
the Valley of Yezreel.'" Hoshea 1:2-5.

Yezreel means both "Elohim scatters" and
"Elohim sows." As He "scattered" them under Yahu, and
finally by the Assyrian deportation, so He will "sow"
them again.[104] So, through Hoshea's first child, we know
that the Kingdom of Yisrael would come to an end and
would be scattered.

"*6 Gomer conceived again and gave birth to a daughter.
Then YHWH said to Hoshea, 'Call her Lo-Ruhamah, for I
will no longer show love to the House of Yisrael, that I should
at all forgive them. 7 Yet I will show love to the House of
Yahudah; and I will save them - not by bow, sword or battle,
or by horses and horsemen, but by YHWH their Elohim."
Hoshea 1:6-7.

The definition for the name Lo-Ruhamah is given
in the passage. In essence it means "no pity, no mercy,
no compassion." In other words, YHWH was going to
show restraint while the House of Yisrael was scattered
and suffering – He would stop showing love to them. At

the same time, He would continue to show love to the House of Yahudah, and would save them in a way which they could not take credit.

After Gomer had weaned Lo-Ruhamah, she gave birth to another son. *"Then YHWH said, 'Call him Lo-Ammi, for you are not My people, and I am not your Elohim.'"* Hoshea 1:9. It could not get much worse than this. Not only would the Kingdom of Yisrael come to an end and be scattered - they would no longer be loved by YHWH, and they would no longer be considered to be His people. In other words, they would be divorced from YHWH because they were adulterous.

Despite this devastating prophecy Hoshea continued with a message of hope. *"¹⁰ Yet the Yisraelites will be like the sand on the seashore, which cannot be measured or counted. In the place where it was said to them, 'You are not My people,' they will be called 'sons of the living Elohim.' ¹¹ The people of Yahudah and the people of Yisrael will be reunited, and they will appoint one leader and will come up out of the Land, for great will be the day of Yezreel."* Hosea 1:10-11.

Not only will the House of Yisrael be restored to the status of "sons of Elohim" they will also be reunited with Yahudah, and they will be too numerous to count – like the sand on the seashore. This is the promise of the Covenant. They will appoint one leader, which is a clear reference to the reign of the Messiah. So we see this prophesied event as another cycle of the Covenant with Abraham.

Before this great promise would occur, the House of Yisrael would literally lose their identity. YHWH describes this progression from rejection to restoration through the family of Hoshea. Gomer represented the

present day House of Yisrael, and her children represented the future House of Yisrael.

"*¹ Say of your brothers, 'My people,' and of your sisters, 'My loved one.' ² Rebuke your mother, rebuke her, for she is not My wife, and I am not her Husband. Let her remove the adulterous look from her face and the unfaithfulness from between her breasts. ³ Otherwise I will strip her naked and make her as bare as on the day she was born; I will make her like a desert, turn her into a parched land, and slay her with thirst. ⁴ I will not show My love to her children, because they are the children of adultery. ⁵ Their mother has been unfaithful and has conceived them in disgrace. She said, 'I will go after my lovers, who give me my food and my water, my wool and my linen, my oil and my drink.' ⁶ Therefore I will block her path with thorn bushes; I will wall her in so that she cannot find her way. ⁷ She will chase after her lovers but not catch them; she will look for them but not find them. Then she will say, 'I will go back to my Husband as at first, for then I was better off than now.' ⁸ She has not acknowledged that I was the one who gave her the grain, the new wine and oil, who lavished on her the silver and gold-which they used for Baal. ⁹ Therefore I will take away My grain when it ripens, and My new wine when it is ready. I will take back My wool and My linen, intended to cover her nakedness. ¹⁰ So now I will expose her lewdness before the eyes of her lovers; no one will take her out of My Hands. ¹¹ I will stop all her celebrations: her yearly festivals, her New Moons, her Sabbath days - all her Appointed Times. ¹² I will ruin her vines and her fig trees, which she said were her pay from her lovers; I will make them a thicket, and wild animals will devour them. ¹³ I will punish her for the days she burned incense to the Baals; she decked herself with rings and jewelry, and went after her lovers, but Me she forgot, declares YHWH."* Hoshea 2:1-13.

YHWH vividly illustrates the adulterous conduct of the House of Yisrael through her idolatry – chasing after other gods. When things start to go bad, Yisrael thinks that she can simply return to YHWH, but it was too late. All of the curses start to come upon her, and she even loses the Appointed Times when the people of YHWH meet with their Elohim. This is a vivid demonstration of the separation that she would experience.

Jeremiah (Yirmeyahu)¹⁰⁵ was called a prophet to the nations, although he primarily prophesied to the House of Yahudah concerning their impending exile. There was a time when he prophesied to both the Northern Kingdom and the Southern Kingdom. Just as Mosheh had told all of the tribes of Yisrael that they would be scattered because they did not obey the Torah, so too did Yirmeyahu.

We already read the prophecy of Yirmeyahu declaring that YHWH *"gave faithless Yisrael her certificate of divorce and sent her away because of all her adulteries."* Yirmeyahu 3:8. Yirmeyahu also prophesied specifically to the House of Yahudah of their impending exile.

"¹⁰ When you tell these people all this and they ask you, Why has YHWH decreed such a great disaster against us? What wrong have we done? What sin have we committed against YHWH our Elohim? ¹¹ then say to them, 'It is because your fathers forsook Me,' declares YHWH, 'and followed

other gods and served and worshiped them. *They forsook Me and did not keep My Torah. ¹² But you have behaved more wickedly than your fathers. See how each of you is following the stubbornness of his evil heart instead of obeying Me. ¹³ So I will throw you out of this Land into a land neither you nor your fathers have known, and there you will serve other gods day and night, for I will show you no favor.*'" Yirmeyahu 16:10-13.

He went on to proclaim: "*¹ Yahudah's sin is engraved with an iron tool, inscribed with a flint point, on the tablets of their hearts and on the horns of their altars. ² Even their children remember their altars and Asherah poles beside the spreading trees and on the high hills. ³ My mountain in the land and your wealth and all your treasures I will give away as plunder, together with your high places, because of sin throughout your country. ⁴ Through your own fault you will lose the inheritance I gave you. I will enslave you to your enemies in a land you do not know, for you have kindled My anger, and it will burn forever.*" Yirmeyahu 17:1-4.

Yahudah's hearts had become like stone. Instead of the Torah being inscribed upon their hearts, as it was inscribed upon the tablets of stone, their sins were inscribed upon their hearts. Just as Mosheh smashed the tablets, and later renewed the Covenant at Sinai, Yahudah needed to have the Covenant renewed because they had broken the Covenant. This time, the Torah would be written on their hearts instead of on tablets of stone.

So we see that despite the fact that both Yahudah and Yisrael sinned and received punishment, it did not mean that the Covenant was abolished. It needed to progress to the next level of fulfillment, and the participants now needed their hearts to be circumcised, not just their flesh.

Remember that the Covenant with Abram was unconditional, while the Covenant with Abraham was conditional. Abraham needed to walk perfect, just as Yisrael was to walk perfect, according to the ways of YHWH. The perfect way was found within the instructions – the Torah. Their deliverance from slavery was a free gift, provided by the blood of the lamb. Dwelling in the House of YHWH, represented by the Land, was another matter – that was conditioned upon their obedience.

The important point is that YHWH would not give up on His people, even when they broke the Covenant. He made provision for renewal of the Covenant, and Mosheh provided the pattern for renewal when he carved out the second set of Tablets and brought them up the mountain.

The question that one might logically ask at this point is: What happened to the House of Yisrael? We see the House of Yahudah living throughout the world collectively labeled as "Jews" practicing their unique religion called Judaism. Judaism is far removed from the Way of YHWH due to the predominance of tradition, as well as the unscriptural Rabbinic oversight and control derived from the Pharisaic sect.

The House of Yisrael has remained in exile, apparently lost. There are many who speculate concerning the "Lost Ten Tribes." We can trace the House of Yahudah from their seventy (70) year exile into Babylon and back to the Land. In fact, not all of them were exiled and some remained in the Land during the exile. We can continue to follow them when they were later banished from Jerusalem in 70 CE by the Romans. Throughout history, the House of Yahudah

never lost her identity, because of the Covenant with David.

The House of Yisrael, on the other hand, completely lost her identity. The words spoken, and the life lived out by Hoshea, came to pass. YHWH would no longer be her Elohim, and she would no longer be His people. Remember that Joseph was a prince among his brothers. Joseph's children, Ephraim and Manashah, were later adopted by Yisrael and shared in their father's status.

They were both given promises of multitudes of people. These were definitely tribes that carried the Covenant promises, and they were the chief Tribes, particularly Ephraim, of the House of Yisrael. YHWH has not forgotten this treasured firstborn, and the House of Yisrael does not consist of some small scattered groups of people hidden in little pockets throughout the world.

The House of Yisrael truly was scattered and lost, but only for a time. Just as Yisrael became a great multitude while in Egypt, the House of Yisrael has become an exceedingly great multitude while scattered throughout the world. This is so the prophecies concering Ephraim and Manassah involving great numbers could be fulfilled. It is actually through the House of Yisrael that the promises of Kings and Nations would come to pass. Presently, the House of Yisrael is woven into the fabric and power structures of the nations of the world.

The House of Yisrael is hidden from most people's view, because they are not readily identified with the Covenant. In fact, most of the House of Yisrael currently look and act like pagans, because they do not understand their identity. That is all about to change. Joseph provides us with the patters. While he was exalted in Egypt, he was hidden from his brother's eyes because of his pagan exterior. Joseph stood above his brothers and judged them. They did not even know him, until the appointed time.[106]

Through the prophets we are able to discern when the House of Yisrael's punishment will end, which will lead to the "unveiling" of Joseph. The Prophet Yehezqel actually provided a vivid description of the duration of punishment in arguably the most unique and extraordinary prophecy provided in the Scriptures.

"*[1] You also, son of man, take a clay tablet and lay it before you, and portray on it a city, Jerusalem. [2] Lay siege against it, build a siege wall against it, and heap up a mound against it; set camps against it also, and place battering rams against it all around. [3] Moreover take for yourself an iron plate, and set it as an iron wall between you and the city. Set your face against it, and it shall be besieged, and you shall lay siege against it. This will be a sign to the House of Yisrael. [4] Lie also on your left side, and lay the iniquity of the House of Yisrael upon it. According to the number of the days that you lie on it, you shall bear their iniquity. [5] For I have laid on you the years of their iniquity, according to the number of the days, three hundred and ninety (390) days; so you shall bear the iniquity of the House of Yisrael. [6] And when you have completed them, lie again on your right side; then you shall bear the iniquity of the House of Yahudah forty (40) days. I have laid on you a day for each year. [7] Therefore you shall set your face toward the siege of Jerusalem; your arm shall be uncovered, and you shall prophesy against it. [8] And surely I will restrain you so that you cannot turn from one side to another till you have ended the days of your siege. [9] Also take*

for yourself wheat, barley, beans, lentils, millet, and spelt; put them into one vessel, and make bread of them for yourself. During the number of days that you lie on your side, three hundred and ninety days, you shall eat it. ¹⁰ And your food which you eat shall be by weight, twenty shekels a day; from time to time you shall eat it. ¹¹ You shall also drink water by measure, one-sixth of a hin; from time to time you shall drink. ¹² And you shall eat it as barley cakes; and bake it using fuel of human waste in their sight. ¹³ Then YHWH said, So shall the children of Yisrael eat their defiled bread among the Nations, where I will drive them." Yehezqel 4:1-13.

This was extremely unusual behavior. Yehezqel actually had to lie on his two sides four hundred and thirty (430) days to demonstrate the different punishments for the two kingdoms. His prophecy was so unusual in order to grab people's attention and make them focus on what was happening. These were not just words spoken and lost in time or written on scrolls that were stored away somewhere or destroyed. This was a mental image and a vivid picture that was etched in the minds of those who saw it, and it is critical to understand what was happening.

Yehezqel was a prophet who was with the captives of the House of Yahudah in Babylon. This prophecy was given in Babylon, and it provided specific periods of punishment for both the House of Yahudah and the House of Yisrael. The House of Yisrael had already been taken captive by the Assyrians. They experienced 5 different exiles between the years 723 BCE and 714 BCE.

Their punishment, according to Yehezqel would be three hundred and ninety (390) years. Under normal circumstances that would have ended around 333 BCE to

324 BCE, although that is not what happened. Remember, Mosheh provided that the people's punishment would be multiplied seven (7) times if they did not turn from their wicked ways.

As it turns out, the House of Yisrael would be punished for a period of three hundred and ninety (390) years multiplied by seven (7), which makes their full punishment period two thousand seven hindred and thirty (2,730) years. As a result, their period of punishment would end between 2006 CE and 2015 CE. This is not something taught in any mainstream religion, and very few are actually even looking for the return of the outcasts of Yisrael.

Does this mean that all the House of Yisrael would return to their Land by 2015 CE? Maybe, but not necessarily. If we use the pattern of Yahudah returning from their Babylonian exile, it might take some time. When the House of Yahudah returned from their seventy (70) year exile prophesied by Yirmeyahu, it was not immediate, nor was their return complete. They would also experience the punishment of forty (40) years prophesied by Yehezqel, multiplied by seven (7), prior to the turn of the millennium.[107] The House of Yahudah is not presently restored to the Land according to the Covenant.

So it is possible that the return of the House of Yahudah is not the pattern for the return of the House of Yisrael. In fact, there are further prophecies that actually provide some clues as to how the final restoration and return will occur. The House of Yisrael and the House of Yahudah must both return to the Covenant. The House of Yahudah as an identifiable people having gone astray, and the House of Yisrael is a lost people who

must be regathered. These sheep, from two different folds, will eventually be brought together by One Shepherd.

On numerous occasions Elohim promised "*Return to Me and I will return to you.*" (Zechariah 1:3; Malachi 3:7). This was certainly good news and this reconciliation could only occur through a renewal of the Covenant.

12

Renewal

We read throughout the Scriptures how the Covenant was broken and punishment was rendered upon the appropriate parties. While many believe that was the end of the story for Yisrael and Yahudah. In fact, many Christians believe that YHWH is finished with Yisrael, and now works through a new Covenant made with an entirely new entity called "The Church."

The problem with this notion is that it is simply not true. It is a fabricated doctrine, completely unsupported by the Scriptures – fostered and perpetuated by poor translations and even worse teaching. There is no basis in the Scriptures for a Covenant being made with any other people than Yisrael.

In fact, there is no such thing as a "new" Covenant that replaces an "old" Covenant. Rather, the Scriptures detail a perpetual Covenant that flows through the cycles of time and gets renewed this process. Each renewal sheds new light upon the Covenant path.

The Scriptures repeatedly provide patterns and promises that speak, not only to a restoration of the divided Kingdom of Yisrael, but also a renewal of the Covenant with Yisrael. At Sinai we were provided with a pattern for renewal, and the prophets describe how the renewal will take place with the House of Yisrael and the

House of Yahudah.

First we will look at what Yirmeyahu prophesied concerning a renewal of the Covenant that was broken.

"*[31] 'The time is coming,' declares YHWH, 'when I will make a renewed (חדשה) Covenant with the House of Yisrael and with the House of Yahudah.' [32] 'It will not be like the Covenant I made with their forefathers when I took them by the hand to lead them out of Egypt, because they broke My Covenant, though I was a Husband to them,' declares YHWH. [33] 'This is the Covenant I will make with the House of Yisrael after that time,' declares YHWH. 'I will put My Torah in their minds and write it on their hearts. I will be their Elohim, and they will be My people. [34] No longer will a man teach his neighbor, or a man his brother, saying, Know YHWH, because they will all know Me, from the least of them to the greatest, declares YHWH. For I will forgive their wickedness and will remember their sins no more.' [35] This is what YHWH says, He Who appoints the sun to shine by day, Who decrees the moon and stars to shine by night, Who stirs up the sea so that its waves roar - YHWH Almighty is His Name: [36] 'Only if these decrees vanish from My sight, declares YHWH, will the descendants of Yisrael ever cease to be a nation before Me.' [37] This is what YHWH says: 'Only if the heavens above can be measured and the foundations of the earth below be searched out will I reject all the descendants of Yisrael because of all they have done,' declares YHWH. [38] 'The days are coming,' declares YHWH, 'when this city will be rebuilt for Me from the Tower of Hananel to the Corner Gate. [39] The measuring line will stretch from there straight to the hill of Gareb and then turn to*

Goah. *⁴⁰ The whole valley where dead bodies and ashes are thrown, and all the terraces out to the Kidron Valley on the east as far as the corner of the Horse Gate, will be holy to YHWH. The city will never again be uprooted or demolished.'"* Yirmeyahu 31:31-40.

You see, YHWH will never forget Yisrael, and He promises to rebuild Jerusalem as part of the renewed Covenant. The renewed Covenant is with the House of Yisrael and the House of Yahudah, and it still involves the Torah. Only now it will be written in their minds and on their hearts. There is no "new" covenant made with anyone else, simply a "renewed" Covenant with Yisrael.

The confusion regarding this issue derives from the Hebrew word "hadashah" (𐤀𐤅𐤔𐤃𐤇), which is often translated as "new." The word "hadashah" (𐤀𐤅𐤔𐤃𐤇) actually means: "to renew, rebuild or refresh." It can also be translated as new or fresh, but we are not talking about something brand new.

The best example of this word can be seen in the moon. The Hebrew for "new moon" is "chodesh" (𐤔𐤃𐤇), which shares the same root as "hadashah" (𐤀𐤅𐤔𐤃𐤇) so essentially they share the same meaning. Everyone knows that the so-called "new moon" is not actually a brand new moon, but rather the reappearance or renewal of the moon after it has gone through its monthly cycle.

This monthly picture is provided so that we can understand the renewal cycle of the Covenant. The renewed Covenant is not a brand new Covenant. Like the moon, it is the same Covenant going through the completion of a cycle, and it too will be renewed.

The correlation with the cycle of the moon cannot be ignored, because this cycle also parallels a woman's monthly menstrual cycle. That cycle essentially involves the same length of time and involves blood. It involves a period of "uncleanness" which then leads to washing and a renewed relationship between a husband and wife.

These cycles are all blended into creation so that we can understand the Covenant cycles and the relationship between YHWH and His people Yisrael.

Notice how Yirmeyahu indicated that there will be a time when the Covenant would be renewed with both Houses, but then goes on to describe the Covenant with the House of Yisrael. The reason for the unique treatment with the House of Yisrael is the same as what occurred at Sinai – adultery.

Yehezqel further elaborates on this renewed Covenant with the House of Yisrael.

"*[14] The Word of YHWH came to me: [15] Son of man, your brothers - your brothers who are your blood relatives and the whole House of Yisrael - are those of whom the people of Jerusalem have said, 'They are far away from YHWH; this Land was given to us as our possession.' [16] Therefore say: This is what the Sovereign YHWH says: 'Although I sent them far away among the nations and scattered them among the countries, yet for a little while I have been a sanctuary for them in the countries where they have gone.' [17] Therefore say: This is what the Sovereign YHWH says: 'I will gather you from the nations and bring you back from the countries where you have been scattered, and I will give you back the Land of Yisrael again. [18] They will return to it and remove all its vile images and detestable idols. [19] I will give them an undivided*

heart and put a renewed (חדשה) spirit in them; I will
remove from them their heart of stone and give them a
heart of flesh. [20] Then they will follow My decrees and
be careful to keep My ordinances. They will be My
people, and I will be their Elohim. [21] But as for those
whose hearts are devoted to their vile images and
detestable idols, I will bring down on their own heads
what they have done,' declares the Sovereign
YHWH." Yehezqel 11:14-21.

So we can see how the renewed Covenant still
involves the Torah, but it is now focused inward. This
prophecy describes the circumcision of the heart. The
pattern of circumcising the flesh will be repeated, but
through this renewal process hearts of stone will be
replaced with hearts of flesh. This restoration and
renewal is a fulfillment of the Covenant of circumcision
and is reiterated later by the prophet as follows:

"[16] Again the Word of YHWH came to me: [17] 'Son
of man, when the people of Yisrael were living in their
own Land, they defiled it by their conduct and their
actions. Their conduct was like a woman's monthly
uncleanness in My sight. [18] So I poured out My wrath
on them because they had shed blood in the Land and
because they had defiled it with their idols. [19] I
dispersed them among the nations, and they were
scattered through the countries; I judged them
according to their conduct and their actions. [20] And
wherever they went among the nations they profaned
My holy Name, for it was said of them, These are
YHWH's people, and yet they had to leave His Land.
[21] I had concern for My holy Name, which the House of
Yisrael profaned among the nations where they had
gone.' [22] Therefore say to the House of Yisrael, This is

what the Sovereign YHWH says: 'It is not for your sake, O House of Yisrael, that I am going to do these things, but for the sake of My holy Name, which you have profaned among the nations where you have gone. [23] I will show the holiness of My great Name, which has been profaned among the nations, the Name you have profaned among them. Then the nations will know that I am YHWH,' declares the Sovereign YHWH, 'when I show Myself holy through you before their eyes. [24] <u>For I will take you out of the nations; I will gather you from all the countries and bring you back into your own Land.</u> [25] I will sprinkle clean water on you, and you will be clean; I will cleanse you from all your impurities and from all your idols. [26] <u>I will give you a renewed (hadash) heart and put a renewed (hadashah) spirit in you; I will remove from you your heart of stone and give you a heart of flesh.</u> [27] <u>And I will put My Spirit in you and move you to follow My decrees and be careful to keep My judgments.</u> [28] <u>You will live in the Land I gave your forefathers; you will be My people, and I will be your Elohim.</u> [29] I will save you from all your uncleanness. I will call for the grain and make it plentiful and will not bring famine upon you. [30] I will increase the fruit of the trees and the crops of the field, so that you will no longer suffer disgrace among the nations because of famine. [31] Then you will remember your evil ways and wicked deeds, and you will loathe yourselves for your sins and detestable practices. [32] I want you to know that I am not doing this for your sake, declares the Sovereign YHWH. Be ashamed and disgraced for your conduct, O House of Yisrael!" Yehezqel 36:16-32.

Notice that it was The Word of YHWH Who

came and appeared to Yehezqel, just as He appeared to Abram. The Hebrew word used in the text is "hayah" (ﬡﬡﬡ), which actually can mean: "to exist." It actually forms part of the Name of YHWH (ﬡﬡﬡﬡ). So this was not simply an audible voice. The Word of YHWH was YHWH manifesting Himself to these individuals. Yehezqel is told that YHWH desired to reveal Himself through Yisrael. To do this He would circumcise their hearts and He would place His Spirit within them.

Essentially, Yisrael was in her period of uncleanness. She needed to get cleansed before she could, once again, join with YHWH in Covenant relationship. This is the pattern of renewal between a husband and a wife that occurs every month as they are separated by her period of uncleanness, known as the "nidah" (ﬡﬡﬡ) (Vayiqra 15:19-24, 18:19, 20:18).

This is not a subject taught in most mainline religions that base their faith upon the Scriptures. Sadly, if you fail to recognize this information you will not correctly comprehend the plan of YHWH. There is no new and different Covenant, simply the same Covenant promise renewed, expanded and fulfilled. Now, instead of words chiseled in stone, placed in the Ark, set apart from the people – the Covenant words would be inscribed upon their hearts. They would all receive the Spirit of YHWH within them so that they could obey and dwell in the Covenant Land.

Both the House of Yisrael and the House of Yahudah were given different durations for their exiles. Their status under the Covenant had changed and each needed to follow their own unique path back to being restored into a Covenant relationship with YHWH.

As we briefly touched upon in the previous

chapter, the House of Yahudah returned to the Land precisely according to schedule while the House of Yisrael remained in exile.

Since the House of Yisrael was apparently divorced, they required remarriage in order to reestablish their Covenant relationship with YHWH. For this to occur, YHWH must regather those who were scattered. They must then be prepared to join the Covenant by undergoing circumcision - only this time it involves circumcision of the heart. The renewal of the Covenant involves hearts being circumcised, just as Mosheh had explained. This was not a new concept or a new Covenant, it was simply how the Covenant would be renewed. Only when their hearts are circumcised can they remain faithful to YHWH.

The purpose of the Renewed Covenant is clear: *"that they may walk"* in the ways of YHWH and *"do them."* YHWH continues to expect obedience to the same instructions - the same Torah - that has existed from the beginning. It is to prepare the people so that they can live in the Land.

This is the same Covenant, only this time it will be written on hearts of flesh instead of tablets of stone. It is the fulfillment of the Covenant of Circumcision when the hearts of those in the Covenant are circumcised. This is an internal spiritual event, rather than an external cutting of the flesh. It will be done by YHWH as He places His Spirit within them.

It is the picture provided by Mosheh as he first went up the mountain and received tablets of stone, which were broken. He thereafter cut another set and brought them up the mountain and presented them to YHWH so that YHWH could write His Torah upon

these new tablets, which represented the hearts and the minds of men. (Shemot 34:1).

Now that the renewal process is properly understood, we will continue to examine what happened to the divided Kingdom of Yisrael after the exiles of the House of Yisrael and the House of Yahudah.

13

The Return of Judah

The exile of the House of Yahudah was much different than that of the House of Yisrael. Not only was the duration of each exile different, but they also adapted to their exiles in different ways. The House of Yisrael was completely displaced from their Land by the Assyrians. They were relocated throughout that empire, which was later conquered by the Babylonians and the Medes. The House of Yisrael was gradually scattered to the "four corners" of the earth, and assimilated into those various cultures. As a result, they eventually completely lost their identity and became, in essence, Gentiles as they were mixed into the nations.

The House of Yahudah, on the other hand, was conquered and exiled by the Babylonians who were later conquered by the Medes. In their exile they largely maintained their identity, and it is important to understand that not all of the Yahudim were exiled from the Land. Some remained, although it does not appear that they maintained any cohesive governmental structure. Also, they were greatly encroached upon by their surrounding neighbors.

Historical and archaeological evidence shows that the Yahudim who were exiled to Babylonia. They assimilated into that culture, but maintained their distinctive tribal identity. Many retained Hebrew names, they signed and witnessed contracts, they gave and received inheritances and some even operated in governmental positions. It appears that they lived and functioned as Yahudim, and even had their own city called "Al Yahudah" – this was a far different exile than that of the House of Yisrael.

So while the House of Yisrael was completely removed from the Land and seemingly "lost" in history, the House of Yahudah was exiled until the time of their prophesied return. When it was time for their return, they knew who they were and they knew where their people could be found.

The Scriptures record the following: "²⁰ *He carried into exile to Babylon the remnant, who escaped from the sword, and they became servants to him and his sons until the kingdom of Persia came to power.* ²¹ *The land enjoyed its Sabbath rests; all the time of its desolation it rested, until the seventy (70) years were completed in fulfillment of the word of YHWH spoken by Yirmeyahu.* ²² *In the first year of Cyrus king of Persia, in order to fulfill the Word of YHWH spoken by Yirmeyahu, YHWH moved the heart of Cyrus king of Persia to make a proclamation throughout his realm and to put it in writing:* ²³ *This is what Cyrus king of Persia says: 'YHWH, the Elohim of heaven, has given me all the kingdoms of the earth and He has appointed me to build a Temple for Him at Jerusalem in Yahudah. Anyone of His people among you - may YHWH his Elohim be with him, and let him go up.'"* 2 Chronicles 36:20 – 23.

This portion of 2 Chronicles is referring specifically to the prophecy of Yirmeyahu wherein he stated to the House of Yahudah: "*This whole country will*

become a desolate wasteland, and these nations will serve the king of Babylon seventy (70) years." Yirmeyahu 25:11. The House of Yahudah was indeed exiled by the King of Babylon and their exile lasted for seventy (70) years.

Again in Yirmeyahu 29 we read the warning of judgment along with the promise of a return for the House of Yahudah: "*¹⁰ This is what YHWH says: 'When seventy (70) years are completed for Babylon, I will come to you and fulfill my gracious promise to bring you back to this place. ¹¹ For I know the plans I have for you,' declares YHWH, 'plans to prosper you and not to harm you, plans to give you hope and a future. ¹² Then you will call upon Me and come and pray to Me, and I will listen to you. ¹³ You will seek Me and find Me when you seek Me with all your heart. ¹⁴ I will be found by you, declares YHWH, and will bring you back from captivity. I will gather you from all the nations and places where I have banished you,' declares YHWH, 'and will bring you back to the place from which I carried you into exile.'"* Yirmeyah 29:10-14.

"And YHWH will take possession of Yahudah as His inheritance in the Holy Land, and will again choose Jerusalem." Zechariah 2:12. The promise of return from the Babylonian exile was fulfilled, as prophesied, and some of the descendants of those who were exiled returned to the Land. We read about this return primarily in the accounts of Haggai, Zechariah, Nehemiah and Ezra.

It is important to recognize that only the House of Yahudah was given the promise of return within seventy (70) years, and only a remnant of the House of Yahudah was returned from exile. Many attempt to imply that the House of Yisrael somehow snuck back in along the way and resettled into their tribal territories,

but that is simply not the case.

The House of Yisrael and the House of Yahudah both engaged in idolatry against YHWH, and both were dealt punishments. Because the House of Yisrael committed different sins than the House of Yahudah they were both punished separately and their exiles had different durations.

These were described previously and Yehezqel aptly demonstrated the different periods as he was commanded to lie on his left side for three hundred and ninety (390) days and his right side for forty (40) days. The time that he laid on his left side represented a day for every year of sin committed by the House of Yisrael and the time that he laid on his right side represented a day for every year of sin committed by the House of Yahudah. (see Yehezqel 4).

The restoration of the divided Kingdom of Yisrael could not occur until the sins of both Houses were dealt with according to the Torah. Only then can there be a renewal and restoration. That restoration will involve another wedding.

"[1] For Zion's sake I will not keep silent, for Jerusalem's sake I will not remain quiet, till her righteousness shines out like the dawn, her salvation like a blazing torch. [2] The nations will see your righteousness, and all kings your glory; you will be called by a new name that the mouth of YHWH will bestow. [3] You will be a crown of splendor in YHWH's hand, a royal diadem in the hand of your Elohim. [4] No longer will they call you Forsaken, or call your Land Desolate. But you will be called Hephzibah (My delight is in her), and your land Beulah (Married); for YHWH will take delight in you, and your Land married. [5] As a young man marries a maiden, so will your sons marry you; as a bridegroom rejoices over his bride, so will

your Elohim rejoice over you." Yeshayahu 62:1-5.

While some of the exiles of the House of Yahudah were restored to the Land under the successive returns of Zerubbabel, Ezra and Nehemiah, among others - the House of Yisrael has yet to be restored to the Land. They fell under a different punishment and their return was prophesied to be at a different time and in a different fashion than their brethren, the House of Yahudah.

Since the exile of the House of Yisrael by the Assyrians, the tribes that constituted the House of Yahudah have generally been the only identifiable and recognizable remnant of the Commonwealth of Yisrael within and without the Land. While it is highly probable that there was a mixing of the Tribes after the division of the Kingdoms, those that came from the north joined with Yahudah and became part of Yahudah. Therefore, after the return from Babylon, the vast majority, if not all, of the recognizable Tribes that constituted the Commonwealth of Yisrael were from the Tribes of Yahudah, Benyamin and Levi – those that had been taken captive by the Babylonians.

It is also important to understand the apparent friction that existed between those who were exiled from Judea and those who remained in Judea during the exile. Remember that not everyone from Judea was taken captive by the Babylonians. The royalty, nobility and priests of the House of Yahudah had been taken into captivity, but others remained. As a result, there were many of the descendents of the former ruling class who were returning with a mandate to reestablish the Kingdom of Yahudah.

Those who were punished by being taken into

exile believed that through their exile they had been "cleansed" or "purified" from the former sins of Yahudah and therefore in a position to reestablish the Kingdom. In contrast, the ones that stayed apparently felt that they were the righteous ones because they were not punished by being taken into exile. As a result, they put up some opposition to these returning exiles.

Because of their differences and varying attitudes, the two groups of Yahudim often clashed and experienced conflict within their ranks. Nevertheless, the Scriptures record that under the authority of Cyrus, King of Persia, Zerubabbel, a prince of Yahudah, returned to the Land and he was encouraged by YHWH to complete the work of rebuilding the Altar and the Temple. (Zechariah 4:9).

Zerubbabel was joined by Yahushua, the High Priest, along with prophets and many Levites. They completed the House of YHWH and reestablished the Temple service. They were later joined by Ezra and Nehemiah. We read about their efforts in books named after these two individuals, which are one book in the Hebrew Scriptures.

While Ezra and Nehemiah detail the ones who returned from captivity (Ezra 2 and Nehemiah 7), it is important to note that many of the Yahudim remained in Babylonia. They had built homes, married wives, had children, jobs and generally life was going on for them. They apparently were content with their lives and saw no need to return – not unlike what we see today with the Modern State of Israel. While many Yahudim have returned to the Land to restore the Kingdom of Yahudah, many more continue to reside outside the Land.

As such we know that some of the exiled

Yahudim returned to the Land while many continued to be dispersed through out the Babylonian and Mede territories. The Yahudim also migrated south into Egypt, Ethiopia, Libya and throughout Africa and the mediteranean region.

Therefore, the return from exile was not a complete return and the House of Yahudah was never restored as a fully autonomous Kingdom, except for brief periods of rebellion from the ruling empires to which they had been subjected. These Yahudim continued to be ruled and influenced by the Greeks, Selucids and Romans while the Parthians eventually ruled over the former Mede Empire to the east.

The House of Yahudah experienced a second exile according to the punishment described by Yehezqel, which was multiplied seven (7) times, like the punishment described for the House of Yisrael. The Scriptures do not specifically describe a subsequent return for either House and we are left with a sense that the promise of the Renewed Covenant provided by the prophets has yet to occur.

When we look at organized religion, it seems that noone is really examining this outstanding issue. Judaism has essentially moved on, and while some in Judaism anticipate a messiah, there is little agreement as to the purpose and identity of their messiah. Since Judaism generally considers itself the sole progeny of Yisrael, few in that religion are concerned with the renewed Covenant and the regathering of the lost House of Yisrael.

Christianity, which claims to believe in the Messiah of Yisrael, rarely spends any time on this vital subject because they generally feel that Yisrael had its

opportunity and failed. According to popular Christian doctrine the reins have now been passed to "The Church," which they believe is "Spiritual Yisrael." Since the Christian Church believes that there is a "new" Covenant that replaced the "old" Covenant, they are certainly not interested in a renewal of the Covenant with the House of Yisrael and the House of Yahudah.

As a result, no one is really looking for the House of Yisrael or expecting their return from exile. Consequently, very few are expecting that the House of Yahudah and the House of Yisrael will be reunited, as in the days of King David. In short, few are expecting the Kingdom of Yisrael to be restored to the Covenant as provided by the prophets.

This is a pity because the ministry of the Messiah largely involves the restoration of the House of Yisrael and reuniting the divided Kingdom. If Christianity believes in the Messiah of Yisrael, then it must recognize that the Messiah is interested in the renewal of the Covenant that involved the restoration of the Kingdom of Yisrael.

The Christian religion has failed to understand that the House of Yisrael was divorced from YHWH because she committed adultery, she whored after different pagan gods. (Yirmeyahu 3:8). This sin was very grievous in the eyes of YHWH and as a result, the Northern Tribes were scattered throughout the nations. YHWH also declared that He would be a Husband to the House of Yisrael if she would return to Him. (Yirmeyahu 3:14).

Therefore, in order to unite and restore the Kingdom to YHWH, the House of Yahudah and the House of Yisrael need to be cleansed from their

defilements. They need to be restored to Elohim and restored to the Land.

So, for there to be a restoration there was needed a Shepherd who could gather the sheep, a Prophet who could direct His people, a High Priest who could atone for their transgressions, and a King who could rule over the restored Kingdom – what was needed was the Messiah of the Covenant.

14

Messiah and the Covenant

So far, we seen a sampling of the Messianic hints woven throughout the Scriptures, and surrounding the Covenant. From the Garden, after the fall of man, we saw that Adam and Hawah were permitted to live, but there were punishments issued. The primary focus of the Scriptures, from that point onward, was how the Creator would fix this problem and restore His creation. That is where we see a very strong message concerning the Messiah.

The Scriptures record that the seed of the woman would be harmed, but ultimately would crush the nachash. This was the hope given after the Garden event. Despite this promise, blood was shed as an atonement. The blood of animals was only a temporary solution, and it did not resolve the underlying problem that now faced mankind – death.

How could a living Elohim restore lie to His dying creation. Clearly, the message was that the shedding of blood would be involved in the solution. The Scriptures tell us that the life is in the blood. The mystery is how the shedding of blood, which is linked with death, would ultimately lead to life. This mystery would be revealed through the Covenant. In the meantime, the effects of this sin were allowed to spread

throughout the earth until Noah.

Once again man had disobeyed and rebelled against the ways of YHWH. Only Noah walked perfectly before YHWH in his generation. Noah listened and obeyed the instructions of YHWH. He heard the instructions and he believed the Word. His actions of building the Ark and storing the food demonstrated that belief.

He did not just hear and expect YHWH to provide the Ark. YHWH and this man were collaborating to save Creation. The judgment would come from YHWH, although He would provide a way of deliverance, through the work of a man. This is a powerful Messianic pattern.

Because of Noah's obedience and his efforts, his family and the select animals were protected from a worldwide judgment of water that took place over a period of forty (40) days and forty (40) nights. The number forty (40) will repeatedly be associated with the Messiah.

As long as Noah continued to walk perfect by obeying YHWH he would be saved, along with his family and future mankind for that matter. They were not removed from the planet, they endured the judgment in the protection of the Covenant House that they dwelled within.

YHWH provided the instruction, the path to life – the Torah. Noah then followed the instruction. This obedience led to his deliverance. This was the pattern established in the Garden. When man obeys the instructions he is provided life within the Covenant House. Those within the house are protected from judgment and death outside the House.

Noah was a "second Adam" in a sense. He was given dominion over the entire earth – a planetary land grant, if you will. Contrary to Adam, Noah diligently obeyed and was spared from judgment. As a result, he was the father of all people who would thereafter populate the earth, although he was ultimately still under the curse of death inherited from Adam. While his obedience kept him safe from judgment, there was nothing he could do to save himself from old age and death.

When the waters receded he built an altar and slaughtered clean animals to YHWH. This man in the Ark, which represented the Covenant House, then entered into Covenant with YHWH after the judgment was over. This Covenant impacted all of mankind from that point on. It was an unconditional Covenant. It revealed that YHWH did not want to destroy His creation again, but He did want obedience. He set up the rainbow as a sign of the Covenant.

From that point on people should remember the flood, and they should also remember the reason for the flood. While YHWH indicated that He would not judge the entire planet again by a flood, He did not say that the planet would not be judged by disease, pestilence, hail, blood or fire!

Noah went on to populate the planet, and the Scriptures trace a righteous line that flowed through his son named Shem. We then follow this seed ten (10) generations to another man living in a pagan culture. We are first introduced to Abram, an uncircumcised man, who is called out of a pagan culture to a new Land. After this man obeyed and journeyed to the Land he is given a great promise of Land and descendants.

He entered into a Covenant with YHWH while he was in a "deep sleep," which should direct us to the event where Hawah was birthed from Adam. That was the marriage Covenant that originally occurred in the Garden. So it appears that YHWH was going to birth something from this man.

During the blood Covenant ceremony, Abram did not walk through the blood of the Covenant. Only the flame and the cloud of smoke passed through the cuttings of the Covenant. This was understood to represent the Messiah. Therefore, we see the Messiah being subject to the penalty for the Covenant being broken. The Messiah alone would be responsible for paying the price for the sin of Adam and Hawah in the Garden. That penalty and that price was death.

This provides us with a better understandingof the mystery of the blood atonement revealed at the Garden. Since life only comes from YHWH, it makes sense that only YHWH Himself, through the Messiah, could provide healing for the infection of sin that was killing mankind.

Many years later, YHWH appeared to Abram and told him to "walk perfect" before Him. He was given a new name and told to circumcise himself and his household. His wife was also given a new name and it is from the union of these two "renewed" individuals came the seed through which the Covenant will flow. This was another revelation of the mystery of the seed of the woman provided in the Garden.

The new names, Abraham and Sarah, were all about the Covenant. They represented the fact that these people were now new beings, filled with the Spirit or breath of YHWH, represented by the hey (ℷ) added to each of their names. These two heys (ᐅ) represented the two heys found in the Name of YHWH (ᐅYᐅႱ).

Notice that between the two heys (ᐅ) is the vav (Y), which represents a "nail" or a "stake." This symbolized the two heys (ᐅ) being joined together in a marriage – The Marriage Covenant. The two heys (ᐅ) became joined together as one (echad), and this marital relationship leads to the final character in the Name of YHWH to be revealed in the Covenant plan, which is actually the first.

The first character in the Name is yud (Ⴑ), which represents an arm. This can clearly be seen in more ancient renderings of the yud (ᴗ). So the yud (Ⴑ) in the Name of YHWH represents the Arm of YHWH. Therefore, further in this Covenant cycle, we should be looking for another name change involving a yud (Ⴑ). This would show us the Covenant Son, the offspring of the Marriage Covenant.

Land and seed were already promised to Abram, although a larger portion than was described to the seed of Abraham. The seed of Abraham was promised the Land of Canaan. This particular seed would pass through the sign of the Covenant, etched in the flesh of Abraham. That seed would pass into a womb, specifically prepared for the seed. This seed would also have to bear the mark of the Covenant on the eighth day, a very significant picture of the future impact of this Covenant.

Just as the seven days of creation represented the duration of this present physical world (7,000 years), so the selection of the eighth day as the marking day for the Covenant of Circumcision signifies when the fulfillment of this Covenant would occur – the beginning of the eighth day. This is a mystery shown through the

Appointed Time of Shemini Atzeret. (see Vayiqra 23:36).

The most significant part of this Covenant of Circumcision was when Abraham was later instructed to offer up the promised son of the Covenant as a sacrifice. He was told to take his son to a very specific location within the Land of Canaan, known as Moriah. Only when Abraham obeyed, and was prepared to offer up "his only son," was the fulfillment of the Covenant revealed. It turns out that YHWH would provide the Lamb. Further revelation of this "promised son" sacrifice was provided through the Passover.

This promised son named Yitshaq was later married and he had two sons. His younger son Yaakob was given the firstborn blessing, and he had twelve sons. Like Abraham, his name was changed. He essentially became a new man before he returned to the Promised Land – his new name was Yisrael. It is through "am Yisrael" that a Covenant people would arise.

His youngest son, when he returned to the Land, was Joseph. Joseph was treated as a prince and given the firstborn status symbolized by a royal robe. As with his father, Joseph was not the oldest son but he received the blessing of the first born. Joseph was given visions of greatness that made his brothers jealous. They wanted to kill him and actually feigned his death. They killed a goat and tore his garment. They placed the blood upon the garment and asked the father to inspect it. The implication was that Joseph had been killed, and he was essentially "dead" to his father Yisrael.

Joseph was sold into slavery, but was exhalted in the Kingdom of Egypt. He was given favor and power so that he could save his brethren, all of Egypt and the surrounding peoples from starvation. He was later

"resurrected" to his father Yisrael, but it was during his period of death that he worked out the salvation of the people.[108]

Joseph had two sons, Ephraim and Manasah. Once again, the younger son, Ephraim, was elevated to first born, and both of the sons of Joseph were actually adopted by Yisrael. So these two sons of Joseph, born and raised in Egypt, were adopted into this Covenant community. Another pattern that would reveal how the House of Yisrael would come back into the Covenant through adoption. The life of Joseph provided a very important Messianic pattern, as do all of the patterns associated with the firstborn sons.

After the revelation of Joseph to his family, the household of Yisrael actually moved into Egypt. They were a group of seventy (70), which represents the nations. Interestingly, they were inside the boundaries of the land promised to Abram, but outside of the Covenant Land promised to the seed of Abraham. So they were taking the promise of the Covenant outside of the Land to the nations before it was time to enter into the next cycle of the Covenant of Circumcision.

For the time being, they were mixed with the nations. It was while they were in Egypt that they actually became a great assembly of people. They were brought there by Joseph, and this is a pattern that would later be repeated by the House of Yisrael (Joseph), when they were exiled by the Assyrians.

When their time in Egypt was over we saw YHWH raise up another man in an ark named Mosheh. This man was like a god to the people, and he would mediate the Covenant between YHWH and His Bride – Yisrael. The path of Yisrael is the path of the Covenant.

It is the path back to the garden, which represents the House.

Yisrael was delivered from Egypt through the Passover, when their households were covered by the blood of the lamb. It was through this event that we saw the significance of the promised Lamb of Elohim. The Passover Lamb provided a covering from death.

The Yisraelites were led by Mosheh out of Egypt along with a mixed multitude of people. This is how YHWH would draw the nations to Him. He used Yisrael as a net, and gathered the nations back to Him through His Covenant.

This great assembly of people, "gathered in the net," collectively passed through the waters of the Red Sea and received the Words of the Covenant at Sinai. This was a marriage ceremony and they agreed to the terms of the marriage. Through this process at Sinai we saw Mosheh repeatedly ascending and descending the mountain and remaining forty (40) days and forty (40) nights – pointing to the Messianic fulfillment of this marriage Covenant process.

The Children of Yisrael rebelled and refused to enter into the Land and they were forced to wander in the wilderness for forty (40) years. During this forty (40) year period a new generation was raised up to enter in. This new generation confirmed the Covenant at Moab. They were led across the waters of the Jordan and into the Land under the leadership of Yahushua, an individual whose name was changed from Hoshea.

This name change is significant because a yud (𐤉) was added to his name. This is the yud (𐤉) from the Name of YHWH (𐤄𐤅𐤄𐤉). That yud (𐤉) represented the son who would come from the Marriage Covenant –

symbolized by the union between Abraham and Sarah.

Therefore, when we look at Yahushua, we are looking directly at the pattern of the promised son of Elohim – the Messiah. His name is actually a direct clue to the identity of the Messiah. Yahushua was first a servant of Mosheh, and then he took over where Mosheh left off. He actually led Yisrael into the fulfillment of the Covenant of Circumcision. He led the Yisraelites through an "immersion" in the Jordan, and into the Land where they were circumcised and they ate the Passover. He led them as they conquered and settled into the Land – the Marital Home.

After entering the Land they, once again, confirmed the Covenant at Shechem. They proclaimed the blessings and the curses from Mt. Ebal and Mt. Gerezim. The Covenant cycle that began with Abram was completed, or fulfilled, by Yahushua. This completion did not do away with the Covenant, or end the Covenant. Rather, the Covenant was filled full of meaning, and begin another cycle toward a further fulfillment.

After the passage of hundreds of years of disunity and repeated backsliding, the Yisraelites cried out for a King. Initially, Saul (Shaul) was chosen from the tribe of Benjamin, the youngest son of Yisrael. Saul was a tall handsome man, seemingly appropriate characteristics for a king. The problem was his heart.

As a result, YHWH replaced Saul with David, a shepherd, the youngest of eight (8) sons of Jesse. Through the selection process YHWH confirmed that: "*Man looks at the outward appearance but YHWH looks at the heart.*" 1 Shemuel 16:7. The number eight (8) as we saw with Abram, is closely linked with the Covenant

and new beginnings.

David was a son of the Covenant. He had a heart for YHWH, and he is a powerful pattern for the Messiah. It is particularly significant to note that he first ruled over the House of Yahudah for seven (7) years, and then the House of Yisrael joined under his rulership. He united the Kingdom and ruled a total of forty (40) years. He brought the Tabernacle to Jerusalem and made plans to build YHWH a permanent House.

Because of his heart, YHWH made a special Covenant with David that his throne would remain forever. David was adopted by YHWH, and this draws many to understand that the Messiah would reign on David's throne. The prophets repeatedly refer to David in the future sense, which is understood to be a Messianic reference.

The Covenant cycles were not yet fulfilled, and the patterns were not complete. We had been given many patterns provided by men that would ultimately be fulfilled by the Messiah. Men could not completely fulfill these Covenant cycles, it had to be through the very Arm of YHWH, represented by the yud (ז).

As a result, Yisrael's time in the Land was full of problems. While the reign of David is looked upon as a great period, it was clearly not perfect, and things began to deteriorate after his death. Shlomo fell away from YHWH, and as a result, YHWH tore much of the Kingdom away from the throne of David.

The Kingdom was divided between the House of Yisrael in the north, and the House of Yahudah in the south. Both Houses fell away from YHWH. As a result, they were punished and exiled. The Covenant was broken, as had happened at Sinai, and needed to be

renewed.

Remember that when Mosheh broke the tablets he ordered the punishment of 3,000 people. Just because there was punishment did not mean that the Covenant would automatically be renewed. Mosheh had to cut the new tablets and present them before YHWH. YHWH said that there would be another like Mosheh.

"[18] *I will raise up for them a Prophet like you from among their brothers; I will put My words in His mouth, and He will tell them everything I command Him.* [19] *If anyone does not listen to My Words that the Prophet speaks in My Name, I Myself will call him to account.*" Debarim 18:18-19.

So when we think of the Messiah we should be looking for a Prophet like Mosheh – One Who speaks the Words of YHWH with authority and One Who renews the Covenant with Yisrael.

There were prophets who specifically spoke of the renewal of the Covenant, and the restoration of the Kingdom of Yisrael. For there to be renewal, there must first be atonement – a cleansing from the sin that brought about the punishment. As we already saw, the Covenant of Circumcision would now include the Circumcision of the heart.

Yehezqel prophesied that YHWH would provide atonement for Yisrael by renewal of the Covenant that had been broken. "[59] *This is what the Sovereign YHWH says: I will deal with you as you deserve, because you have despised my oath by breaking the Covenant.* [60] *Yet I will remember the Covenant I made with you in the days of your youth, and I will establish an everlasting Covenant with you.* [61] *Then you will remember your ways and be ashamed when you receive your sisters, both those who are older than you and those who are younger. I will give them to you as daughters,*

but not on the basis of My Covenant with you. [62] *So I will establish My Covenant with you, and you will know that I Am YHWH.* [63] *Then, when I make atonement for you for all you have done, you will remember and be ashamed and never again open your mouth because of your humiliation, declares the Sovereign YHWH.*" Yehezqel 16:59-63.

It is this understanding for the need for atonement that has led to confusion regarding the Messiah. A mere man could not atone for the sins of Yisrael. Through the Akeda we saw the promised son, the only son, of Abraham being offered up. That is a picture of the Father YHWH offering up His Son, the Lamb of Elohim. Just as the blood of the Passover Lamb was shed and covered the occupants of the House – the Covenant House.

That begs the question of whether YHWH can have a Son. The answer is unequivocally yes. If YHWH can create, He can surely procreate, if that is His desire. The pattern of the seed is probably the most powerful and compelling pattern provided in the Scriptures. It would defy all logic or reason to attempt to claim that the source of all life would not desire to procreate. That, as it turns out, is the ultimate purpose of our existence and all of creation.

That leads to other questions: How can the Messiah, being the Son of Elohim, pays the price for sin by dying? Further, how can He die and then unify and rule over the restored Kingdom of Yisrael?

The Scriptures clearly reveal two roles for the Messiah, 1) Joseph - the One Who atones for the sin of Yisrael; and 2) David – the One who will reunite Yisrael, and bring them back into Covenant with YHWH. These two roles seem to contradict each other, which has resulted in some believing that there will be two different Messiahs. This is because, they saw the Messiah function through the Scriptures in two roles, as two sons: 1) the son of Joseph and 2) the son of David.

The Messiah, son of Joseph would suffer, as Joseph suffered. Remember that Joseph essentially died and was "resurrected" in the eyes of his father Yisrael. He was reported to be dead, and was removed from his father's house. This is the same pattern of death and resurrection presented through the Abrahamic Covenant with Abraham the Father and his "only son" Yitshaq.

Both of these "blood shedding" events are pictures of the ultimate atonement that YHWH would provide through His "only son" - The Messiah. Atonement was necessary in order to renew the Covenant and restore mankind. This Messiah "Son of Joseph" would die as the Lamb of Elohim – the atonement for the people of the Covenant – the fulfillment of the Passover lamb.

The reason for these two Messianic roles should be evident as we just examined the division of the Kingdom of Yisrael into two houses. It is important to recognize that Joseph represented the leadership of the Northern Kingdom through the Tribe of Ephraim, and David represented the leadership of the Southern Kingdom through the Tribe of Yahudah.

These two kingdoms were punished differently and they needed One Who could resolve both of their unique circumstances. They both had sinned and needed to be restored into right relationship with YHWH. This was not a new problem – it goes back to the Garden.

Therefore, according to the patterns provided through the Scriptures, Yisrael and all of mankind needed a Mediator who could resolve this problem. One

who could restore all of Creation to the Creator and atone for the sin that separated mankind from YHWH – the Son of Joseph.

They also needed a Shepherd Who could gather the lost shee that had been scattered throughout the nations and a King Who could restore the divided Kingdom of Yisrael. They needed a Shepherd King – the Son of David.

No passage of Scripture better exemplifies this seeming contradiction between the roles of the Messiah than Yeshayahu 52 and 53, which provide the following description of the Arm of YHWH, also identified as the Servant.

"*52:10 YHWH will lay bare His Set Apart Arm in the sight of all the nations, and all the ends of the earth will see the salvation of our Elohim.* 11 *Depart, depart, go out from there! Touch no unclean thing! Come out from it and be pure, you who carry the vessels of YHWH.* 12 *But you will not leave in haste or go in flight; for YHWH will go before you, the Elohim of Yisrael will be your rear guard.* 13 *See, My Servant will act wisely; He will be raised and lifted up and highly exalted.* 14 *Just as there were many who were appalled at Him - His appearance was so disfigured beyond that of any man and His form more than the sons of men-* 15 *so will He sprinkle many nations, and kings will shut their mouths because of Him. For what they were not told, they will see, and what they have not heard, they will understand.* 53:1 *Who has believed our message and to whom has the Arm of YHWH been revealed?* 2 *He grew up before Him like a tender shoot (twig), and like a root out of dry ground. He had no beauty or majesty to attract us to Him, nothing in*

His appearance that we should desire Him. ³ He was despised and rejected by men, a Man of sorrows, and familiar with suffering. Like One from whom men hide their faces He was despised, and we esteemed Him not. ⁴ Surely He took up our infirmities and carried our sorrows, yet we considered Him stricken by Elohim, smitten by Him, and afflicted. ⁵ But He was pierced for our transgressions, He was crushed for our iniquities; the punishment that brought us peace was upon Him, and by His wounds we are healed. ⁶ We all, like sheep, have gone astray, each of us has turned to his own way, and YHWH has laid on Him the iniquity of us all. ⁷ He was oppressed and afflicted, yet He did not open His mouth. He was led like a lamb to the slaughter, and as a sheep before her shearers is silent, so He did not open His mouth. ⁸ By oppression and judgment He was taken away. And who can speak of His descendants? For He was cut off from the land of the living; for the transgression of My people He was stricken. ⁹ He was assigned a grave with the wicked, and with the rich in His death, though He had done no violence, nor was any deceit in His mouth. ¹⁰ Yet it was YHWH's will to crush Him and cause Him to suffer, and though YHWH makes His life a guilt offering. He will see His offspring and prolong His days, and the will of YHWH will prosper in His Hand. ¹¹ After the suffering of His soul, He will see the labor of His soul and be satisfied; by His knowledge My righteous Servant will justify many, and he will bear their iniquities. ¹² Therefore I will give Him a portion among the great, and He will divide the spoils with the strong, because He poured out His life unto death, and was numbered with the transgressors. For He bore the sin

of many, and made intercession for the transgressors."
Yeshayahu 52:10-53:12.

This clear Messianic prophecy describes the Servant, the Arm of YHWH. This is the Messiah Son of Joseph, described as One who was not handsome and One who was afflicted. Yeshayahu describes this Servant as One who would be despised and rejected by men, although He would carry the punishment of Yisrael.

He would be led to the slaughter like a lamb – the Lamb of YHWH. He would be killed and actually bear the sins of many. His life would be a guilt offering, yet He would later be satisfied by the labor of His soul. He would be "cut off" from the land of the living, and have no physical descendants, yet He will see His offspring and prolong His days.

The mouth of kings will be shut because of this Servant, who will divide the spoils with the strong and be given a portion with the great. The life of this Servant will actually atone for the sins of many, and by His wounds Yisrael would be healed.

This is an incredible prophecy and very difficult for some to understand. It was hard to comprehend how this Servant could die, yet live. This was the solution that Yisrael needed, One who could atone for their sins and restore their relationship with their Husband, YHWH.

It is important to remember that the blood of animals could never accomplish such a feat. Blood was shed after the sin of Adam and Hawah, but they were still not permitted back into the Garden.

The sacrificial system was instituted by YHWH as a practical way of instructing mankind in matters of sin and atonement. YHWH wanted man to understand that if sin was committed, it would take the blood of an innocent to cover the sin. Since all life derives from YHWH, atonement that leads to restoration and life must ultimately come directly from Him.

Interestingly, the Servant will perform a work that will affect the Nations and the entire earth – not just Yisrael. *"¹ Behold! My Servant whom I uphold, My Elect one in whom My soul delights! I have put My Spirit upon Him; He will bring forth justice to the Gentiles (Nations). ² He will not cry out, nor raise His voice, nor cause His voice to be heard in the street. ³ A bruised reed He will not break, and smoking flax He will not quench; He will bring forth justice for truth. ⁴ He will not fail nor be discouraged, till He has established justice in the earth; and the coastlands shall wait for His Torah. ⁵ Thus says Elohim YHWH, Who created the heavens and stretched them out, Who spread forth the earth and that which comes from it, Who gives breath to the people on it."* Yeshayahu 42:1-5.

In order for the nations to be justified, a sacrifice would have to be made that cleansed them from the effects of sin. This sacrifice would be accomplished by the Servant in Whom Elohim delighted. This Servant would bring justice, or rather judgment, to the Nations. He would accomplish this through the Covenant.

"¹ Listen, O coastlands, to Me, and take heed, you peoples from afar! YHWH has called Me from the womb; from the matrix of My mother He has made mention of My Name. ² And He has made My mouth like a sharp sword; in the shadow of His Hand He has hidden Me, and made Me a polished shaft; in His quiver He has hidden Me. ³ And He said to Me, You are My servant, O Yisrael, in whom I will be glorified. ⁴ Then I said, I have labored in vain, I have spent my strength for nothing and in vain; yet surely my just reward is

with YHWH, and my work with my Elohim. [5] *And now YHWH says, Who formed Me from the womb to be His Servant, to bring Yaakob back to Him, so that Yisrael is gathered to Him (For I shall be glorious in the eyes of YHWH, and My Elohim shall be My strength),* [6] *Indeed He says, It is too small a thing that You should be My Servant to raise up the Tribes of Yaakob, and to restore the preserved ones of Yisrael; I will also give You as a light to the Gentiles (Nations), that You should be My salvation to the ends of the earth.* [7] *Thus says YHWH, The Redeemer of Yisrael, their Holy One, to Him whom man despises, to Him whom the nation abhors, to the Servant of rulers: Kings shall see and arise, Princes also shall worship, because of YHWH who is faithful, The Holy One of Yisrael; and He has chosen You.* [8] *Thus says YHWH: In an acceptable time I have heard You, and in the day of salvation I have helped You; I will preserve You and give You as a Covenant to the people, to restore the earth, to cause them to inherit the desolate heritages;* [9] *That You may say to the prisoners, Go forth, to those who are in darkness, show yourselves. They shall feed along the roads, and their pastures shall be on all desolate heights.* [10] *They shall neither hunger nor thirst, neither heat nor sun shall strike them; for He who has mercy on them will lead them, even by the springs of water He will guide them.* [11] *I will make each of My mountains a road, and My highways shall be elevated.* [12] *Surely these shall come from afar; Look! Those from the north and the west, and these from the land of Sinim.* [13] *Sing, O heavens! Be joyful, O earth! And break out in singing, O mountains! For YHWH has comforted His people, and will have mercy on His afflicted."* Yeshayahu 49:1-13.

There are some who argue the Servant is actually Yisrael, but when read in context that is clearly not the case. Yisrael was intended to be a light to the nations but she failed. It is the Messiah Who will now be that Light and it will be Messiah Who will "*raise up the Tribes of Yaakob, and . . . restore the preserved ones of Yisrael.*"

The prophecy clearly speaks of One Who will do the necessary work of YHWH. The Servant was hidden in the Hand of YHWH and would be formed in the womb, have a mother and obviously be born and live as a son of Adam. He would raise up and restore Yisrael. His life would be marked with suffering, and He would actually become the Covenant with Yisrael that was broken. He would be the Renewed Covenant.

"*[1] Eli, Eli, why have you spared Me? Why are you so far from saving Me, so far from the words of My groaning? [2] O My Elohim, I cry out by day, but You do not answer, and by night, but I find no rest. [3] Yet you are set apart, enthroned on the praises of Yisrael. [4] In You our fathers put their trust; they trusted and You delivered them. [5] They cried to You and were saved; in You they trusted and were not disappointed. [6] But I am a worm and not a man, scorned by men and despised by the people. [7] All who see Me mock Me; they hurl insults, shaking their heads: [8] He trusts in YHWH; let YHWH rescue Him. Let Him deliver Him, since He delights in Him. [9] Yet You brought Me out of the womb. You made Me trust in You even at My mother's breast. [10] From birth I was cast upon You. From My mother's womb you have been My Elohim. [11] Do not be far from Me, for trouble is near and there is no one to help. [12] Many bulls surround Me; strong bulls of Bashan encircle Me. [13] Roaring lions tearing their prey open their mouths wide against Me. [14] I am poured out like water, and all My bones are out of joint. My heart has turned to wax; it has melted away within Me. [15] My*

strength is dried up like a potsherd, and My tongue
sticks to the roof of My mouth; you lay Me in the dust
of death. *16* Dogs have surrounded Me; a band of evil
men has encircled Me, they have pierced My hands and
My feet. *17* I can count all My bones; people stare and
gloat over Me. *18* They divide My garments among
them and cast lots for My clothing. *19* But You, O
YHWH, be not far off; O My Strength, come quickly
to help Me. *20* Deliver My life from the sword, My
precious life from the power of the dogs. *21* Rescue Me
from the mouth of the lions; save Me from the horns of
the wild oxen. *22* I will declare Your Name to My
brothers; in the congregation I will praise You. *23* You
who fear YHWH, praise Him! All you descendants of
Yaakob, honor Him! Revere Him, all you descendants
of Yisrael! *24* For He has not despised or disdained the
suffering of the afflicted one; He has not hidden His
face from Him but has listened to His cry for help. *25*
From you comes the theme of My praise in the great
assembly; before those who fear You will I fulfill My
vows. *26* The poor will eat and be satisfied; they who
seek YHWH will praise Him - may your hearts live
forever! *27* All the ends of the earth will remember and
turn to YHWH, and all the families of the nations will
bow down before Him, *28* for dominion belongs to
YHWH and He rules over the nations. *29* All the rich
of the earth will feast and worship; all who go down to
the dust will kneel before Him - those who cannot keep
themselves alive. *30* Posterity will serve Him; future
generations will be told about YHWH. *31* They will
proclaim His righteousness to a people yet unborn - for
He has done it." Tehillim 22:1-31.

This passage describes One who was born from a

womb, and was with YHWH from birth, although at some point He becomes separated from YHWH. He is despised and undergoes horrific physical pain and suffering. He finds Himself in a position where people can look at Him, shake their heads at Him, mock Him and hurl insults at Him. They will actually look at Him and say: *"He trusts in YHWH; let YHWH rescue Him. Let Him deliver Him, since He delights in Him."* Tehillim 22:8.

He will be encircled by evil men - his hands and his feet will be pierced. People will stare and gloat over him. They will take away His garments and cast lots for His clothes. Most recognize this as a description of a person who is being crucified, only at the time that this Psalm (Mizmor) was written, crucifixion had allegedly not even been invented as a form of punishment. So this Messiah ben Joseph was prophesied to be tortured by a method of execution not yet invented, and would be placed in a position where He actually looked like He needed saving Himself.

With these two different Messiah's, or at least Messianic roles, the next issue to determine is when these Messianic appearances would occur. Since Joseph appeared prior to David, one could reasonably assume that Messiah ben Joseph would appear before Messiah ben David. Further, since the role of Messiah ben Joseph was suffering and atonement, one could reasonably assume that this was a necessary prerequsite to the appearance of Messiah ben David, the conquering King Who reunites and restores the divided Kingdom of Yisrael.

So then the question should be asked: "Did the Messiah ben Joseph ever come and perform the work prophesied. Was there atonement made by the Lamb of

Elohim?"

The prophet Daniel was provided with a very specific timeframe and description of this Messiah by the Messenger Gabriel.

"*²⁴ Seventy weeks are determined for your people and for your holy city, to finish the transgression, to make an end of sins, to make reconciliation for iniquity, to bring in everlasting righteousness, to seal up vision and prophecy, and to anoint the Most Holy. ²⁵ Know therefore and understand, that from the going forth of the command to restore and build Jerusalem until Messiah the Prince, there shall be seven weeks and sixty-two weeks; The street shall be built again, and the wall, even in troublesome times. ²⁶ And after the sixty-two weeks Messiah shall be cut off, but not for Himself; and the people of the prince who is to come shall destroy the city and the sanctuary. The end of it shall be with a flood, and till the end of the war desolations are determined. ²⁷ Then he shall confirm a covenant with many for one week; But in the middle of the week he shall bring an end to sacrifice and offering. And on the wing of abominations shall be one who makes desolate, even until the consummation, which is determined, is poured out on the desolate.*" Daniel 9:24-27.

This text describes the work of Messiah ben Joseph, and a specific number of "weeks" were provided. This seventy week prophecy has been the subject of much debate, but it can only be determined by a proper understanding of the Shemittah Cycles and the Jubilee Cycles. When properly calculated, the times given to Daniel, through Gabriel, point to Messiah ben Joseph right around the turn of the Millenium.[109]

History reveals that there was indeed significant Messianic expectation during this period of time.[110] The Christian religion claims that the Messiah did, indeed appear and die during this period of time, although Christianity has seriously misrepresented the name, the teachings and the purpose of the one that they call Jesus.[111]

In fact, His real name was Yahushua, the same name as the servant of Mosheh. Remember that Yahushua was a unique individual who experienced the Passover in Egypt, as well as the first Passover in the Promised Land. His life spanned the Covenant cycle from Egypt to Sinai and through the renewal at Sinai. He spent forty (40) days on the mountain, forty (40) days in the Land, and then forty (40) years in the wilderness. He led Yisrael, with Mosheh, through the renewal in Moab, and finally into the Land where he built an altar and renewed the Covenant in Shechem. Yahushua was a living example of the Covenant Cycle.

How appropriate that the Messiah would come in the Name of Yahushua.[112] That is a discussion for another text, but the point is simple. There was a specific time for Messiah to come in the past, and there is expectation that the Messiah will once again come, in the end – the end of another cycle.[113]

There will come a time in the future when Jerusalem is under siege, and those who "pierced" the Messiah will see Him – their "eyes will be opened."

"[10] And I will pour out on the house of David and the inhabitants of Jerusalem a spirit of grace and supplication. They will look upon 𐤉𐤄 who they have pierced, and they will mourn for him as one mourns for an only child, and grieve bitterly for him as one grieves for a firstborn son. [11] On that day the weeping in Jerusalem will be great, like the weeping of

Hadad Rimmon in the plain of Megiddo. *¹²* The land will mourn, each clan by itself, with their wives by themselves: the clan of the house of David and their wives, the clan of the house of Nathan and their wives, *¹³* the clan of the house of Levi and their wives, the clan of Shimei and their wives, *¹⁴* and all the rest of the clans and their wives. *¹³:¹* On that day a fountain will be opened to the house of David and the inhabitants of Jerusalem, to cleanse them from sin and impurity. *²* On that day, I will banish the names of the idols from the land, and they will be remembered no more, declares YHWH Almighty. I will remove both the prophets and the spirit of impurity from the land. *³* And if anyone still prophesies, his father and mother, to whom he was born, will say to him, You must die, because you have told lies in YHWH's Name. When he prophesies, his own parents will stab him. *⁴* On that day every prophet will be ashamed of his prophetic vision. He will not put on a prophet's garment of hair in order to deceive. *⁵* He will say, I am not a prophet. I am a tiller of the ground; the land has been My livelihood since My youth. *⁶* If someone asks Him, What are these wounds on your body? He will answer, The wounds I was given at the house of My friends. *⁷* Awake, O sword, against My shepherd, against the Man who is close to Me! declares YHWH Almighty. Strike the shepherd, and the sheep will be scattered, and I will turn My hand against the little ones. *⁸* In the whole land, declares YHWH, two-thirds will be struck down and perish; yet one-third will be left in it. ⁹ This third I will bring into the fire; I will refine them like silver and test them like gold. They will call on My Name and I will answer them; I will say, They are My people, and they will say, YHWH is our Elohim. ¹⁴:¹ A day of YHWH is coming when your plunder will be divided among you. ² I will gather all the nations to Jerusalem to fight against it; the city will be captured, the houses ransacked, and the women raped. Half of the city will go into exile, but the rest of the people will not be taken from the city. ³ Then YHWH will go out and fight against those nations, as He fights in the day of battle. ⁴ On that day His feet will stand on the Mount of Olives, east of Jerusalem, and the Mount of Olives will be split in two from east to west, forming a great valley, with half of the mountain moving north and half moving south. ⁵ You will flee by My mountain valley, for it will extend to Azel. You will flee as you fled from the earthquake in the days of Uzziah king of Yahudah. Then YHWH my Elohim will come, and all the set apart ones with Him. ⁶ On that day there will be no light, no cold or frost. ⁷ It will be a unique day, without daytime or nighttime - a day known to YHWH. When evening comes, there will be light. ⁸ On that day living water will flow out from Jerusalem, half to the eastern sea and half to the western sea, in summer and in winter. ⁹ YHWH will be King over the whole earth. On that day

there will be one YHWH, and His Name the only Name. [10] The whole land, from Geba to Rimmon, south of Jerusalem, will become like the Arabah. But Jerusalem will be raised up and remain in its place, from the Benjamin Gate to the site of the First Gate, to the Corner Gate, and from the Tower of Hananel to the royal winepresses. [11] It will be inhabited; never again will it be destroyed. Jerusalem will be secure. [12] This is the plague with which YHWH will strike all the nations that fought against Jerusalem: Their flesh will rot while they are still standing on their feet, their eyes will rot in their sockets, and their tongues will rot in their mouths. [13] On that day men will be stricken by YHWH with great panic. Each man will seize the hand of another, and they will attack each other. [14] Yahudah too will fight at Jerusalem. The wealth of all the surrounding nations will be collected - great quantities of gold and silver and clothing. [15] A similar plague will strike the horses and mules, the camels and donkeys, and all the animals in those camps. [16] Then the survivors from all the nations that have attacked Jerusalem will go up year after year to worship the King, YHWH Almighty, and to celebrate the Feast of Tabernacles. [17] If any of the peoples of the earth do not go up to Jerusalem to worship the King, YHWH Almighty, they will have no rain. [18] If the Egyptian people do not go up and take part, they will have no rain. YHWH will bring on them the plague he inflicts on the nations that *do not go up to celebrate the Feast of Tabernacles. ¹⁹ This will be the punishment of Egypt and the punishment of all the nations that do not go up to celebrate the Feast of Tabernacles. ²⁰ On that day 'Set Apart to YHWH' will be inscribed on the bells of the horses, and the cooking pots in YHWH's House will be like the sacred bowls in front of the altar. ²¹ Every pot in Jerusalem and Yahudah will be holy to YHWH Almighty, and all who come to sacrifice will take some of the pots and cook in them. And on that day there will no longer be a Canaanite in the house of YHWH Almighty."* Zechariah 12:10-14:21.

This text essentially connects the two Messiahs with the Aleph Taw (✗✗). The Messiah ben Joseph (✗✗) Who was pierced will be alive and He will rule as David. This is the fulfillment of the Shema, when YHWH will be Echad (One) and His Name will be Echad (One).[114]

The House of David and those in Jerusalem will look upon the Aleph Taw (✗✗), whom they pierced. They will grieve over Him as a Firstborn Son. They will understand that, according to the pattern of Abraham and Yitshaq, this was the Firstborn Son of YHWH – the Lamb of Elohim slain for the atonement of mankind. Just as Joseph was hidden from his brothers, so Messiah ben Joseph has been hidden. He will ultimately be revealed at the "appointed time" and they will then recognize the work that Messiah ben Joseph performed through His death and resurrection. They will do this in a time of great distress.

Then, on a unique day, the King – Messiah ben

David, will save His people. He will renew the Covenant with Yisrael. He will establish the Torah throughout the world and will reign from Jerusalem.

The Renewed Covenant could be referred to as The Messianic Covenant since the Messiah is at the very heart the final cycle of fulfillment. Just like Mosheh, the man was like a god and accomplished the deliverance from Egypt, it was a pattern for a future event. The Messiah will gather the Lost Sheep of Yisrael back to the Land just as the prophets foretold.

Remember Hoshea who prophesied to the House of Yisrael. He made it clear that in the end, after they were punished, they would return and they would be restored. "¹⁰ *Yet the sons of Yisrael will be like* <u>*the sand on the*</u> <u>*seashore,*</u> *which cannot be measured or counted. In the place where it was said to them, 'You are not My people,' they will be called 'sons of the living Elohim.* ¹¹ *The sons of Yahudah and the sons of Yisrael will be reunited, and* <u>*they will appoint one*</u> <u>*leader and will come up out of the land,*</u> *for great will be the day of Jezreel.*" Hoshea 1:10-11.

Notice the allusion to the Covenant language spoken to both Abraham and Yaakob relative to their descendants being as numerous as "*the sand on the seashore which cannot be measured or counted.*" (Beresheet 22:17, 32:12). The return of the House of Yisrael and the reuniting of the Kingdom under One Leader or Head speaks directly of David – Messiah ben David.

The prophet Yehezqel makes it very clear: "¹⁹ *This is what the Sovereign YHWH says:* <u>*I am going to take the*</u> <u>*stick of Joseph, which is in Ephraim's hand, and of the*</u> <u>*Yisraelite tribes associated with him, and join it to Yahudah's*</u> <u>*stick, making them a single stick of wood, and they will become*</u> <u>*one in my hand.*</u> ²⁰ *Hold before their eyes the sticks you have* written on [21] and say to them, This is what the Sovereign YHWH says: *I will take the Yisraelites out of the nations where they have gone. I will gather them from all around and bring them back into their own Land.* [22] *I will make them one nation in the Land, on the mountains of Yisrael. There will be one King over all of them and they will never again be two nations or be divided into two kingdoms.* [23] They will no longer defile themselves with their idols and vile images or with any of their offenses, for *I will save them from all their sinful backsliding, and I will cleanse them. They will be My people, and I will be their Elohim.* [24] *My servant David will be King over them, and they will all have one Shepherd. They will follow My laws and be careful to keep My decrees.* [25] They will live in the Land I gave to My servant Yaakob, the Land where your fathers lived. They and their children and their children's children will live there forever, and David My servant will be their Prince forever. [26] *I will make a Covenant of Peace with them; it will be an everlasting Covenant. I will establish them and increase their numbers, and I will put my sanctuary among them forever.* [27] *My dwelling place will be with them; I will be their Elohim, and they will be My people.* [28] Then the nations will know that I YHWH make Yisrael holy, when My sanctuary is among them forever." Yehezqel 37:19-28.

So here we see a completion of the Covenant cycle through what the prophet calls the Covenant of Peace. This Covenant of Peace will be accomplished through the Messiah.

15

In the End

We have seen how YHWH has operated His Covenant through time. Just as the planets rotate and revolve through the process of time, so too does the Covenant of YHWH. This Covenant is actually cycling toward an ultimate fulfillment in synchronicity with all of Creation.

YHWH does not operate in a linear fashion, in a straight line, changing or replacing His Covenant as time passes. Rather, He has operated a continual Covenant plan that flows in and through time, and culminates back to the Garden. This entire process will be fulfilled by and through the Messiah.

The Covenant people, Yisrael, have been under punishment and in exile according to the Torah and the Prophets. This was foretold and it was also promised, as part of the Covenant, that they would once again be restored. "*⁴ For the Yisraelites will live many days without king or prince, without sacrifice or sacred stones, without ephod or idol. ⁵ Afterward the Yisraelites will return and seek YHWH their Elohim and David their king. They will come trembling to YHWH and to His blessings in the last days.*" Hoshea 3:4-5. It is clear that the Messiah, son of David, will bring about a restoration of the Covenant in the end.

"*¹¹ For this is what the Sovereign YHWH says: I*

Myself will search for My sheep and look after them. ¹² *As a shepherd looks after his scattered flock when he is with them, so will I look after My sheep. I will rescue them from all the places where they were scattered on a day of clouds and darkness.* ¹³ *I will bring them out from the nations and gather them from the countries, and I will bring them into their own Land. I will pasture them on the mountains of Yisrael, in the ravines and in all the settlements in the Land.* ¹⁴ *I will tend them in a good pasture, and the mountain heights of Yisrael will be their grazing land. There they will lie down in good grazing land, and there they will feed in a rich pasture on the mountains of Yisrael.* ¹⁵ *I Myself will tend My sheep and have them lie down, declares the Sovereign YHWH.* ¹⁶ *I will search for the lost and bring back the strays. I will bind up the injured and strengthen the weak, but the sleek and the strong I will destroy. I will shepherd the flock with justice.* ¹⁷ *As for you, My flock, this is what the Sovereign YHWH says: I will judge between one sheep and another, and between rams and goats.* ¹⁸ *Is it not enough for you to feed on the good pasture? Must you also trample the rest of your pasture with your feet? Is it not enough for you to drink clear water? Must you also muddy the rest with your feet?* ¹⁹ *Must My flock feed on what you have trampled and drink what you have muddied with your feet?* ²⁰ *Therefore this is what the Sovereign YHWH says to them: See, I Myself will judge between the fat sheep and the lean sheep.* ²¹ *Because you shove with flank and shoulder, butting all the weak sheep with your horns until you have driven them away,* ²² *I will save My flock, and they will no longer be plundered. I will judge between one sheep and another.* ²³ *I will place over them One Shepherd, My Servant David, and He will tend them; He will tend them and be their Shepherd.* ²⁴ *I YHWH will be their Elohim, and My servant David will be prince among them. I YHWH*

have spoken. ²⁵ *I will make a Covenant of Peace with them and rid the land of wild beasts so that they may live in the desert and sleep in the forests in safety.* ²⁶ *I will bless them and the places surrounding My hill. I will send down showers in season; there will be showers of blessing.* ²⁷ *The trees of the field will yield their fruit and the ground will yield its crops; the people will be secure in their land. They will know that I am YHWH, when I break the bars of their yoke and rescue them from the hands of those who enslaved them.* ²⁸ *They will no longer be plundered by the nations, nor will wild animals devour them. They will live in safety, and no one will make them afraid.* ²⁹ *I will provide for them a Land renowned for its crops, and they will no longer be victims of famine in the land or bear the scorn of the nations.* ³⁰ *Then they will know that I, YHWH their Elohim, am with them and that they, the House of Yisrael, are My people, declares the Sovereign YHWH.* ³¹ *You My sheep, the sheep of My pasture, are people, and I am your Elohim, declares the Sovereign YHWH.*" Yehezqel 34:11-31.

This promised Covenant of Peace is not a new Covenant, but rather a renewal of the Covenant with Abraham. It is the final fulfillment of the Abrahamic Covenant. The picture provided is sheep dwelling safely under the protection of their Shepherd in their own land – the Promised Land.

The Promised Land represented the Garden. Abraham was still outside the Garden, just as all men had been since Adam and Hawah were expelled.

Abram was uncircumcised and he had to become a new man and be circumcised before he could emit the promised seed into the woman that he loved, who also was a new person with a new name. From the union of these renewed beings could flow a Covenant people.

The Covenant with Abraham was the path back into the Garden, but only after all of the cycles of this Covenant had been completed. This Covenant process puts us into relationship with the Creator expressed by the word "ahab" ($\mathcal{Y}\mathcal{A}\mathcal{K}$). Abraham was called the "ahab" of Elohim and this word is often translated as "friend." (Yeshayahu 41:8). At the very root of the word is "love."[115]

This is the natural progression in the relationship between a husband and wife when they freely and voluntarily become friends, fall in love and then grow together in that loving union. This is the essence of the Covenant relationship.

In order to complete this Covenant cycle, YHWH needed to provide a new Adam. He needed a second Adam untainted by the sin of the first. This new Adam could then, as an expression of the love of YHWH, atone for the sin that originated in the Garden and "birth" a bride from Himself. That bride would come from the very blood that atoned for her sins. The blood contains the DNA and this bride would become a renewed creation through the renewed Covenant. This second Adam is, of course, the Messiah – the Son of Elohim and the Bride consists of those who are in Covenant with YHWH.

The Covenant is couched within the context of a marriage Covenant, and the pattern of marriage was clear from the beginning. The initial reason why a man and a woman marry is typically for love. Sometimes this is not the case and people are married simply because of cultural or utilitarian motivations. Whatever the reason, procreation is the typical result of the union between a man and a woman.

This was a pattern established from the beginning so that mankind could dwell with YHWH in the end. After the transgression in the Garden, the Covenant cycles continued through time so that YHWH could prepare a Bride for Himself.

That pattern was, once again, revealed and expanded through the Covenant with Abraham. The result of the union between a husband and a wife is a child, and YHWH was using the union between Himself and Yisrael to reveal His "only son" to the world. This was so that He could offer up His Lamb, as Yitshaq and the Passover Lamb to redeem the Covenant people – His family.

Yisrael followed the same pattern as Abraham. When they were in Egypt they were uncircumcised. The offer of deliverance was conditioned only upon their obedience. It was a promise made to Abram, and they had only to circumcise themselves and rely upon the blood of the Passover lamb to protect them from death.

When it came time to enter the Land they were, once again, circumcised. Only then could they partake of the Passover Covenant meal upon entry. This entrance into the Land was symbolic of a return to the Garden, although the original problem of the sin of Adam and Hawah had yet to be dealt with.

Yisrael's entrance into the Land of Canaan was part of the Covenant of Circumcision. In order to remain in the Land they needed to obey the Torah, which included the instructions of the Covenant. This was a condition of the Covenant. Obey and be blessed - disobey and be cursed.

There was a dual nature to this Covenant. There were individuals, and there was the Community - am

Yisrael. Individuals were circumcised and entered into the community. Those individuals were then in the Covenant made with the community of Yisrael. This is an important distinction to remember when on considers being in the family of YHWH versus the Bride of YHWH.

As a result, there was responsibility on the part of each individual within the community to obey, and there was a corporate responsibility for the community as a whole to obey. Yisrael failed to obey and was divided and exiled throughout the world. This was not a mistake or a surprise, it was the way that YHWH could spread His Covenant to the nations.

He would accomplish this goal through either the blessings or the curses promised within the Torah. If Yisrael obeyed, they would be blessed so profoundly that it would attract the nations to them. If they disobeyed, they would be cursed and sent out to all of the nations. Either way, the nations were a major part of the Covenant from the beginning. After all, Nations would come from Abraham, not just Yisrael. The Covenant was not just about Yisrael, it was about the Nations joining with Yisrael in Covenant with YHWH.

It was during this time of exile among the nations that the House of Yisrael would become as numerous as the sands of the sea. While we have seen a remnant of Yahudah returning to the Land, the House of Yisrael has been growing and fulfilling the Covenant promise. (Yeshayahu 10:20-23).

In the future, YHWH will call for His people, and they will be gathered from around the world. Some texts refer to the fact that He will "whistle" for them. (Zechariah 10:8). When His people hear the call they will

get ready to return. Particularly, the House of Yisrael will be returned to the Land as the punishment has been concluded. The Covenant can now be renewed, as was prophesied. It is the same Covenant, only now, through the mediation of Messiah, it will lead to the Covenant of Peace.

Therefore, the ultimate cycle of this Covenant with Abraham will bring about the Covenant of Peace. Again, this is not a new Covenant, simply the renewal of the Covenant through the final work of the Messiah – the Arm of YHWH.

Read how the Prophet Yeshayahu further describes this final fulfillment of the Covenant which leads to restoration. *"¹ Sing, O barren woman, you who have not borne! Break forth into singing, and cry aloud, you who have not labored with child! For more are the children of the desolate than the children of the married woman, says YHWH. ² Enlarge the place of your tent, and let them stretch out the curtains of your dwellings; Do not spare; Lengthen your cords, and strengthen your stakes. ³ For you shall expand to the right and to the left, and your descendants will inherit the nations and make the desolate cities inhabited. ⁴ Do not fear, for you will not be ashamed; Neither be disgraced, for you will not be put to shame; For you will forget the shame of your youth, And will not remember the reproach of your widowhood anymore. ⁵ For your Maker is your Husband, YHWH of hosts is His Name; and your Redeemer is the Holy One of Yisrael; He is called the Elohim of the whole earth. ⁶ For YHWH has called you like a woman forsaken and grieved in spirit, like a youthful wife when you were refused, Says your Elohim. ⁷ For a mere moment I have forsaken you, but with great mercies I will gather you. ⁸ With a little wrath I hid My face from you for a moment; But with everlasting kindness I will have mercy* on you, Says YHWH, your Redeemer. ⁹ *For this is like the waters of Noah to Me; For as I have sworn that the waters of Noah would no longer cover the earth, so have I sworn that I would not be angry with you, nor rebuke you.* ¹⁰ *For the mountains shall depart and the hills be removed, but My kindness shall not depart from you, nor shall My Covenant of Peace be removed, Says YHWH, who has mercy on you.* ¹¹ O you afflicted one, tossed with tempest, and not comforted, behold, I will lay your stones with colorful gems, and lay your foundations with sapphires. ¹² I will make your pinnacles of rubies, your gates of crystal, and all your walls of precious stones.¹³ All your children shall be taught by YHWH, and great shall be the peace of your children. ¹⁴ In righteousness you shall be established; You shall be far from oppression, for you shall not fear; and from terror, for it shall not come near you. ¹⁵ Indeed they shall surely assemble, but not because of Me. Whoever assembles against you shall fall for your sake. ¹⁶ Behold, I have created the blacksmith who blows the coals in the fire, who brings forth an instrument for his work; and I have created the spoiler to destroy. ¹⁷ *No weapon formed against you shall prosper, and every tongue which rises against you in judgment you shall condemn.* This is the heritage of the servants of YHWH, and their righteousness is from Me, Says YHWH." Yeshayahu 54:1-17.

Notice the mention of the Covenant with Noah and the implication is that the Covenant of Peace will encompass the entire planet, and all of mankind. Again we see this Covenant of Peace as a time in the future when the wrath of YHWH is over and His people are, once again, called back to Him.

Just as the Covenant people, the eight (8) residents of the ark, inhabited the planet after exiting the "Covenant House" – so too will a Covenant people

repopulate the Promised Land. There are some who oppose such a notion, arguing that the modern land of Israel is too small to accommodate the multitudes of the returning Lost Sheep of the House of Yisrael.

They forget the prophecies and the Covenant inheritance. Yeshayahu exorts the barren woman Yisrael – *"enlarge the place of your tent . . . for you shall expand to the right and to the left."* It is important to remember that when Abram was uncircumcised, representing the Nations, he was promised land from the Nile to the Euphrates and to the north and to the south. The boundaries of the modern State of Yisrael contain only a portion of the Land of Canaan, but any way you look at it, there is plenty of room "to the right and to the left" to expand and accommodate those returning from the Nations.

The prophet provides a vivid picture of this Covenant of Peace. It should be plain to see that the Covenant of YHWH is in operation through the cycles of time and nothing has been done away with. What, at first glance, appear to be different Covenants described in the Scriptures are essentially the same.

They are all moving in a cyclical fashion through time toward the same destination, back to the beginning, to the Garden. The Covenant is intended to direct and lead us into His Kingdom and into His House. It is there that we have relationship with YHWH. His servants will learn His ways and walk in those ways.

"[2] In the last days the mountain of YHWH's House will be established as chief among the mountains; it will be raised above the hills, and all nations will stream to it. [3] Many peoples will come and say, Come, let us go up to the mountain of YHWH to the House of the Elohim of Yaakob. He will

teach us His ways, so that we may walk in His paths. The Torah will go out from Zion, the Word of YHWH from Jerusalem. [4] *He will judge between the nations and will settle disputes for many peoples. They will beat their swords into plowshares and their spears into pruning hooks. Nation will not take up sword against nation, nor will they train for war anymore.*" Yeshayahu 2:2-4.

The Covenant defines the way back to the House of YHWH. The Covenant defines the relationship between YHWH and His Bride. You must be in Covenant with Him to be in relationship with Him. Failure to understand the Covenant will lead to false doctrines and deception concerning the plan and purpose of YHWH.

The Scriptures, often referred to as the Tanak or the Old Testament, are essentially a description of this Covenant in operation, and the entire Covenant is found therein. If you subscribe to the belief that the Covenant described in the "Old Testament" has been abolished then the same could be said about the so-called "New Covenant" claimed by the Christian religion. Interestingly, the so-called "New Covenant" is actually found within the Tanak.

In fact, the religion of Islam makes a similar argument to that found in Christianity. Islam claims that the Quran is essentially the "newer testament" and final revelation that supersedes the previous Scriptures. Christianity has opened the door for Islam to make this argument by erroneously claiming that YHWH has changed or replaced His Covenant promises.

If Covenant promises established by YHWH, and claimed to be eternal, have been abolished or replaced by YHWH, then how could one be certain that

the "New Covenant" has not or will not be replaced. This belief is false and deceptive, because it is based upon a premise that YHWH changes His mind and does not keep His Word. He always keeps His Word, and the Covenant, which He says is eternal, is still in existence today, and will remain until the end of time as we know it.

YHWH promised that He would not break His Covenant with Yisrael. "*40 But if they confess their iniquity and the iniquity of their fathers, with their unfaithfulness in which they were unfaithful to Me, and that they also have walked contrary to Me, 41 and that I also have walked contrary to them and have brought them into the land of their enemies; if their uncircumcised hearts are humbled, and they accept their guilt - 42 then I will remember My Covenant with Yaakob, and My Covenant with Yitshaq and My Covenant with Abraham I will remember; I will remember the Land.43 The Land also shall be left empty by them, and will enjoy its Sabbaths while it lies desolate without them; they will accept their guilt, because they despised My judgments and because their soul abhorred My statutes. 44 Yet for all that, when they are in the land of their enemies, I will not cast them away, nor shall I abhor them, to utterly destroy them and break My Covenant with them; for I am YHWH their Elohim. 45 But for their sake I will remember the Covenant of their ancestors, whom I brought out of the land of Egypt in the sight of the nations, that I might be their Elohim: I am YHWH.*" Vayiqra 26:40-45.*

King David confirms that the Covenant made and confirmed with the patriarchs will not be superseded. "*14 He is our Elohim; His judgments are in all the earth. 15 He remembers His Covenant forever, the Word He commanded, for a thousand generations, 16 the Covenant He made with Abraham, the oath He swore to Yitshaq. 17 He* confirmed it to Yaakob as a decree, to Yisrael as an everlasting Covenant, [18] Saying, 'To you I give the land of Canaan, the portion of your inheritance,'" 1 Chronicles 16:14-17.

While there are severe penalties for violating the Covenant, there is also a great promise given that YHWH will not forget the Covenant. Despite the fact that Yisrael would break the Covenant with YHWH, He still promised to remember the Covenant. He never gives up on His Children and He has never given up on Yisrael. He knew that they would break the Covenant and they did. He also promised to restore them, and He will.

It was, in fact, His plan and purpose to draw the nations to Him, through either their obedience or their disobedience. It cannot be stressed enough that the Covenant with Yisrael was not just about Yisrael. Rather, it was about drawing the nations to YHWH through Yisrael. The Covenant is for anyone who desires to be restored with YHWH, and if you join the Covenant, you join Yisrael. There is no other path or restoration except through the Covenant.

This was made evident by the prophet Yeshayahu. "[1] This is what YHWH says: 'Maintain justice and do what is right, for My salvation is close at hand and My righteousness will soon be revealed. [2] Blessed is the man who does this, the man who holds it fast, who keeps the Sabbath without desecrating it, and keeps his hand from doing any evil. [3] Let no foreigner who has bound himself to YHWH say, 'YHWH will surely exclude me from His people.' And let not any eunuch complain, 'I am only a dry tree.' [4] For this is what YHWH says: 'To the eunuchs who keep My Sabbaths, who choose what pleases Me and hold fast to My Covenant [5] to them I will give within My House and its walls a memorial

and a name better than sons and daughters; I will give them an everlasting name that will not be cut off. ⁶ *And foreigners who bind themselves to YHWH to serve Him, to love the Name of YHWH, and to worship Him, all who keep the Sabbath without desecrating it and who hold fast to My Covenant* ⁷ *these I will bring to My set apart mountain and give them joy in My House of prayer. Their burnt offerings and sacrifices will be accepted on My altar; for My House will be called a House of prayer for all nations.'* ⁸ *The Sovereign YHWH declares - He who gathers the exiles of Yisrael: 'I will gather still others to them besides those already gathered." Yeshayahu 56:1-8.*

It should now be clear that the plan of YHWH is presented through His progressive Covenant cycles with man. YHWH made a Covenant with creation, individual men, tribes and a kingdom in order to reveal His plan and bring about His will which, simply stated, is to restore His Creation that the world might serve Him as was originally intended. Only now, Creation will be filled with those who were once separated from Him, yet made the choice to follow Him.

If Adam and Hawah had not sinned, there would have been no need for this Covenant. Therefore, the institution of the Covenant cycles was intended to restore. It is vital to understand this Covenant process in order to recognize and participate in this restorative work.

Those who enter into this Covenant relationship join the Assembly of Yisrael, not to be confused with the modern State of Israel, which is established as an exclusively "Jewish State." This nation, comprised of many of the Yahudim, claims the name of Yisrael. Interestingly, those from the House of Yisrael are not welcome to join this state unless they submit to the religion of Judaism. So despite the fact that the modern State of Yisrael consists of many genetic descendants of Yahudah, that does not mean that they are the Covenant Assembly of Yisrael.

As has already been seen through Yishmael, it is not necessarily the physical descendants of Abraham who enter into Covenant with the Living Elohim, but those who are obedient to the Covenant. For many people have claimed to be Abraham's children, but only those who have the faith and obedience that Abraham had, enter the Covenant. This point was made abundantly clear by John the Immerser almost 2,000 years ago.

> "*1* *In those days John the Immerser came preaching in the wilderness of Yudea, *2* and saying, 'Repent, for the kingdom of heaven is at hand!' *3* For this is he who was spoken of by the prophet Yeshayahu, saying: 'The voice of one crying in the wilderness: Prepare the way of YHWH; make His paths straight.' *4* Now John himself was clothed in camel's hair, with a leather belt around his waist; and his food was locusts and wild honey. *5* Then Jerusalem, all Yudea, and all the region around the Jordan went out to him *6* and were immersed by him in the Jordan, confessing their sins. *7* But when he saw many of the Pharisees and Sadducees coming to hisimmersion, he said to them, Brood of vipers! Who warned you to flee from the wrath to come? *8* Therefore bear fruits worthy of repentance, *9* and do not think to say to yourselves, 'We have Abraham as our father.'*

For I say to you that Elohim is able to raise up children to Abraham from these stones. [10] And even now the ax is laid to the root of the trees. Therefore, every tree which does not bear good fruit is cut down and thrown into the fire. [11] I indeed immerse you with water unto repentance, but He who is coming after me is mightier than I, whose sandals I am not worthy to carry. He will immerse you with the Set Apart Spirit and fire. [12] His winnowing fan is in His hand, and He will thoroughly clean out His threshing floor, and gather His wheat into the barn; but He will burn up the chaff with unquenchable fire." Matthew 3:1-12.

By no coincidence, John was Immersing at the same location where Yisrael crossed the Jordan and entered into the Promised Land. Those stones that he was referring to were possibly the 12 Stones set up as a memorial. (Yahushua 4:3). It was a reminder that there were 12 Tribes, not just those in the House of Yahudah. It was a prophetic statement and a reminder that those in the House of Yisrael were also Children of Abraham. They must be raised up as told by Ezekiel. (Ezekiel 37), and they too must enter in to the Land through the Covenant.

Yahushua the Messiah also encountered many who claimed to be descendants of Abraham. They made this claim as they perceived that they were in covenant with YHWH. However, as their works did not align with the works of Abraham, they were not deemed to be in covenant with YHWH. In fact, the Messiah flatly told them to their faces that their father was the devil – not Abraham.

"*39 They answered and said to Him, 'Abraham is our father.' Yahushua said to them, 'If you were Abraham's children, you would do the works of Abraham. 40 But now you seek to kill Me, a Man who has told you the truth which I heard from Elohim. Abraham did not do this. 41 You do the deeds of your father.' Then they said to Him, 'We were not born of fornication, we have one Father - Elohim.' 42 Yahushua said to them, 'If Elohim were your Father, you would love Me, for I proceeded forth and came from Elohim; nor have I come of Myself, but He sent Me. 43 Why do you not understand My speech? Because you are not able to listen to My word. 44 You are of your father the devil, and the desires of your father you want to do. He was a murderer from the beginning, and does not stand in the truth, because there is no truth in him. When he speaks a lie, he speaks from his own resources, for he is a liar and the father of it. 45 But because I tell the truth, you do not believe Me. 46 Which of you convicts Me of sin? And if I tell the truth, why do you not believe Me? 47 He who is of Elohim hears Elohim's words; therefore you do not hear, because you are not of Elohim.'" John 8:39-47.*

This account speaks volumes about who is in the Covenant, and who is not in the Covenant. Claiming to be a descendant of Abraham in no way means one is in Covenant with YHWH Elohim. It is having faith in YHWH Elohim, which amounts to faith in His Word the Messiah, and doing righteous acts commensurate

with that faith. That is outward evidence of someone who is in Covenant with YHWH Elohim.

The Messiah noted that the greatest faith he had observed in Yisrael was through the actions of a Roman centurion. (Matthew 8:5-13). Yahushua also made a point to show that so-called "sinners" would also be considered "sons of Abraham," because He came to seek and save that which was lost. (Luke 19:9-10).

Many people have identified with Abraham including the Muslim religion, the Christian religion and the Jewish religion. However, according to the Messiah, belief supported by actions is evidence of someone in Covenant with YHWH Elohim.

Those within the Covenant Assembly must follow the path demonstrated by Abraham, as individuals and as a people. At present, the Community is fractured and scattered as foretold by the prophets and recorded by history. Soon, the Messiah will gather the flock of YHWH – those who remain in Covenant.

In order to be in this flock you must be covered by the blood of the Lamb of Elohim, and you must keep the Words of the Covenant - the Torah. If you are following some other writing, instructions or oral torah then you are not in Covenant with YHWH, and you are not part of Yisrael. While some might think they are in Covenant and part of Yisrael, they may not be if they are not walking in the Way of the Covenant.

Currently, there is much talk about the end times, and most fail to understand that the future hinges upon the past. We have examined Scriptural Covenants in this text, and it should be abundantly clear by now that they are all essentially one Covenant building through the cycles of time. What appear to be different Covenants

are steps in the progression, revolutions within an orbit, cycles of the one Covenant that will restore mankind back to the Creator. This Covenant defines mankind's relationship with YHWH and reveals the path back to Him.

Ultimately, each person must know YHWH and enter into this Covenant if they desire to be restored to Him. This is not a passive intellectual exercise, as it is treated by some. For one to be in Covenant with YHWH, they must be an active participant in the Covenant process.[116]

The Covenant involves much more than a making a "decision" or saying a prayer. It is a walk – a way of life. YHWH paid the price through His Lamb, Messiah ben Joseph. The blood of the Lamb set people free from bondage, and opened the door back into His House. It is therefore incumbent upon each of us to walk perfect before Him on the path that He established. This is the path that leads to and through the door into His House.

The Covenant that we saw with Abraham continues to this day. It is through this Covenant that we have relationship with YHWH, and that is why it is imperative that we properly understand this Covenant. Someday soon Messiah ben David will restore the Kingdom, and fill the House of Elohim with those who are in the Brit (ברית) – the Covenant.

Endnotes

¹ The term "god" is a generic term which can be attached to any number of powerful beings described in mythology and worshipped in pagan religions. Some use a capital "G" to refer to "the God of the Bible" but I find it a disservice to apply this label to the Creator of the Universe when the Hebrew Scriptures clearly refer to Him as Elohim. The pagan origins of the word "god" are discussed in the Walk in the Light series book entitled *Names*. Elohim (אלהים) is technically plural, but that does not designate more than one Creator. The singular form is El (אל) and could refer to any "mighty one," but because the plural is used to describe the Creator, it means that Elohim is qualitatively stronger or more powerful than any singular El (אל). In Hebrew, the plural form can mean that something or someone is qualitatively greater not just quantitatively greater. We see in the first sentence of the Scriptures that "In the Beginning Elohim created" the Hebrew for "created" is bara (ברא) which literally is "He created." It is masculine singular showing that while Elohim is plural He is masculine singular. For an excellent discussion of the Hebrew Etymology of the Name of Elohim I recommend *His Name is One* written by Jeff A. Benner, Virtualbookworm.com Publishing 2002.

² Many are familiar with modern Hebrew which is commonly used today, but very few recognize that this is not the original language character set of the Scriptures. The Hebrew language has much older characters known as Ancient Hebrew and Paleo Hebrew. As a result, throughout this book we will often use the modern Hebrew character set because of its familiarity, but at times, we will attempt to use the Ancient and Paleo Hebrew Scripts to elucidate certain words, concepts and passages. The Ancient Hebrew font was developed by the author in an attempt to reflect certain scripts found through archaeology.

³ Adam (אדם) is actually a Hebrew name and needs no transliteration. It means "man" and also means "red" as in

"to show blood."

4   Hawah (חוה) means "giver of life" or "mother of all living."
     It is interesting to note that Adam did not name his wife
     until after their transgression.

5   The word et (את), otherwise known as the Aleph Taw,
     consists of two Hebrew characters - the aleph (א) which is
     the first character in the Hebrew alphabet, and the taw (ת)
     which is the last letter in the Hebrew alphabet. "This word
     את is used over 11,000 times (and never translated into
     English as there is no equivalent) to point to the direct
     object of the verb." (from Benner, Jeff A., *Learn to Read
     Biblical Hebrew*, Virtualbookworm.com 2004 Page 41.). It is
     embedded throughout the Hebrew Scriptures and while it
     has a known grammatical function, the Sages have long
     understood that it has a much deeper and mysterious
     function – many believe that it is a direct reference to the
     Messiah. As such, it plays an important part in
     understanding the Scriptural Covenants so we will, at
     times, examine its existence and relevance throughout this
     text.

6   Book nine in the Walk in the Light Series is titled *Kosher*. It
     gives an in depth discussion concerning the Scriptural
     dietary commands and their application to all mankind.
     Because mankind was created by Elohim, Who better to
     provide instruction for proper nutrition than the One Who
     created you. There have been serious misconceptions
     regarding the very important subject and the false teaching
     has been propagated that the dietary instructions only apply
     to "Jews" as if those of Hebrew descent have a different
     physiology or metabolism than the rest of mankind. This is
     nonsense – the dietary instructions were given to those who
     would walk with Elohim and abide in His presence. They
     were given so that those who were obedient would be
     blessed in their bodies. They are instructions from the
     Creator to His Creation to live healthy and disease free
     lives.

7   YHWH (יהוה) is the four letter Name of the Elohim
     described in the Scriptures. This four letter Name has
     commonly been called the "Tetragrammaton" and

traditionally has been considered to be ineffable or unpronounceable. As a result, despite the fact that it is found nearly 7,000 times in the Hebrew Scriptures, it has been replaced with such titles as "The Lord," "Adonai" and "HaShem." I believe that this practice is in direct violation of the First and Third Commandments. Some commonly accepted pronunciations are: Yahweh, Yahuwah and Yahowah. Since there is debate over which pronunciation is correct, I simply use the Name as it is found in the Scriptures, although I spell it in English from left to right, rather than in Hebrew from right to left. For the person who truly desires to know the nature of the Elohim described in the Scriptures, a good place to start is the Name by which He revealed Himself to all mankind.

[8] Some believe that the four letter Name YHWH is ineffable or unspeakable so pronouncing the Name is not an issue. I do not believe that this opinion is compatible with the Scriptures that consistently describe the use of the Name and encourage all to know and use the Name. There is a difference of opinion concerning the pronunciation of the Name. Some pronounce the Name as "Jehovah" which is clearly not correct since there is no "J" in the Hebrew language. A very popular pronunciation is Yahweh. Some say Yahuwah or Yahowah while some simply use the short form of the Name - Yah. Because of this difference in opinion, some simply pronounce the letters "Yud - Hey - Vav - Hey" when referring to the Name. This subject is discussed in detail in the Walk in the Light book entitled *Names*.

[9] Wikipedia citing Cyrus H. Gordon and Gary A. Rendsburg, *The Bible and the Ancient Near East* fourth edition, 1997, Norton & Co.

[10] It is a popular tradition that the fruit of the Tree of Knowledge of Good and Evil was an apple, but this could simply be tradition associated with pagan traditions involving Athena, the goddess of wisdom, with an apple. There is no mention of an apple in the Scriptures, nor is any particular fruit mentioned. According to some tradition, the forbidden fruit was the fig, and this would make sense since the man and the woman sewed fig leaves to cover

themselves. It could be that they reached for the closest thing that they could find. (see Rabbi Nehemia Berachos 40a; Sanhedrin 70a. See also *The Rod of An Almond Tree in God's Master Plan*, Peter A. Michas Wine Press WP Publishing 1997).

[11] This can lead to Dispensationalism that is an incorrect doctrine. Dispensationalism is a system of biblical interpretation formalized in the nineteenth century by John Nelson Darby and later popularized by the publishing of the study Bible of C. I. Scofield and the establishment of Dallas Theological Seminary by Lewis Sperry Chafer. It is the foundation of what is known in eschatological studies as "pre-tribulational premillenialism" and involves the division of history into (usually) seven distinct periods of time known as "dispensations". Twentieth century writers such as John Walvoord, Dwight Pentecost, and Charles Ryrie brought the doctrines of Dispensationalism into mainstream scholarship, which are often summarized by Ryrie's famous "sine qua non", i.e., his statement of the three primary tenets of the system. These are: 1) a clear distinction between Israel and the Church, 2) literal interpretation of Scripture, and 3) the glory of God as the primary goal of history. We find only the third of these principles to be valid. As stated above, God's glory is clearly the driving force behind all things .... We believe there is one people of God, rooted in the Abrahamic Covenant, united in Christ, and consisting of both Jew and Gentile alike. - Christonomy.com

[12] The shedding of blood was traditionally a very important part of the marriage covenant. In fact, the breaking of the virgin bride's hymen and the subsequent blood on the bed was often the final act in consummating the marital relationship. The blood soaked bed cloth was often kept as proof of that covenant. Without the shedding of blood, the marriage could be called off and declared null and void.

[13] The so-called "modern Hebrew" is really not so modern. It developed in the Babylonian exile of the House of Yahudah and is sometimes referred to as Chaldean Flame Letters. This is strictly a Jewish language and belongs to the House of Judah. It is not the original Hebrew language, it was not

used by Abraham, Mosheh, Yisrael, King David or any people described in the Scriptures prior to the exile into Babylon.

14   Some might argue that the word "bar" is actually an Aramaic derivative, but if you look at Psalms 1 and the literal interpretation from the Paleo Hebrew symbols it is certainly acceptable to interpret "bar" as a Hebrew word for "son."

15   Describe the importance of looking at the elements of a word – the different roots to get a full meaning – This is the difference between eastern and western thought. Western thought wants to find the spelling and "definition" of a word whereas eastern looks at the components of a word to discern the "meaning."

16   Fausset's Bible Dictionary, Electronic Database Copyright (c)1998 by Biblesoft.

17   *Hillers, Delbert R.*, Covenant: The History of a Biblical Idea, The Johns Hopkins University Press, 1969.

18   The Salt Covenant is an often overlooked covenant mentioned in the Scriptures. The Salt Covenant is referred to as the brit melah. YHWH commanded that salt be added to all of His offerings. "Season all your grain offerings with salt. Do not leave the salt of the Covenant of your Elohim out of your grain offerings; add salt to all your offerings." Leviticus 2:13. "Traditionally, salt was shared to seal a truce between former enemies or as a symbol of alliance between close friends. Treaties or friendships were often formalized by the partaking of a lick of salt to seal the deal or heal the difference between them. Entering into a Covenant of Salt means binding oneself to another in utmost loyalty and truthfulness, even suffering death, rather than breaking the covenant. For this very reason a Covenant of Salt was never done lightly or haphazardly – it deserves serious respect. To the ancient Hebrews, salt represented purification, and was also symbolic of enduring friendship, honesty, and loyalty (2Kings 2:19-21; 2 Chronicles 13:5). Today some Eastern people still use the phrase: '*There is salt between us.*' Having no salt, meant disloyalty and barrenness." homeworship101.com/fyi_salt_covenant. The Covenant of salt was made with the Levites, representing

the adopted firstborn sons of YHWH and the ones who served Yisrael. It is actually a Covenant with them. The prophet Malachi refers to the Covenant. "*³ Because of you I will rebuke your descendants; I will spread on your faces the offal from your festival sacrifices, and you will be carried off with it. ⁴ And you will know that I have sent you this admonition so that My Covenant with Levi may continue, says YHWH Almighty. ⁵ My Covenant was with him, a Covenant of life and peace, and I gave them to him; this called for reverence and he revered me and stood in awe of My Name. ⁶ True instruction was in his mouth and nothing false was found on his lips. He walked with me in peace and uprightness, and turned many from sin.*" Malachi 2:3-6. See also Ezekiel 43:23-24

19   Qayin (קָיִן) means: "acquired" and is an accurate transliteration of the name commonly referred to as Cain.

20   Hebel (הבל) means: "breath" and is an accurate transliteration of the name commonly referred to as Abel. This name also can mean "vanity," and the Book of Yasher actually states that this was the intended meaning of the name as Hawah declared: "In vanity we came into the earth, and in vanity we shall be taken from it." Book of Yasher 1:13.

21   It is very interesting to view the sacrifices that were rendered by these two, because it reveals a pattern that is repeated in Scriptures. It shows us behavior that is pleasing, and that which is displeasing to YHWH. We read in Beresheet that "in the process of time" they both provided an offering to YHWH. In the Hebrew we read "miqetz yamiym" (מקץ ימים), which literally means "in the end of days." It seems clear that this was an Appointed Time when both knew that an offering was expected of them. The Scriptures reveal that Qayin brought an offering of the fruit of the ground to YHWH, and Hebel ALSO brought the firstborn of his flock and their fat. In other words, Hebel brought an offering of the fruit of the ground to YHWH but he also brought the firstborn of his flock. The Hebrew word used for flock is tsone (צאון), which implies a goat or a lamb. I believe that this was likely the Appointed Time of Yom Kippur, when atonement is made by shedding the

blood of a goat. Now many believe that the Appointed Times first began at Sinai when the Torah was given to Yisrael through Mosheh, but this notion is not supported by the Scriptures. I believe that the Torah and the patterns found within the Appointed Times go back to the beginning. (see also Endnotes 63, 66, 74 and 116 for a discussion of The Appointed Times as well as the Walk in the Light series book entitled The Appointed Times). YHWH repeatedly tells us that He has declared the end from the beginning. (Yeshayahu 41:26, 46:10, 48). His patterns and His ways go all the way back to the beginning and are demonstrated through cycles – one of those cycles being harvests. Throughout the Scriptures we see the terms "in the beginning" (beresheet) referring to the beginning of a harvest or the firstfruits of a harvest, and the term "in the end of days" (miqetz yamiym) referring to the end of that harvest. Many interpret this passage with Qayin and Hebel as if to show that raising animals was better than tilling the ground, but this is not the relevant point. We see that Hebel offered his firstfruits, while there was no mention of this for Qayin. Also note that the offering of Hebel involved blood, while the offering of Qayin did not. Thus the offering of Qayin was not acceptable – it did not include blood and he did not receive atonement. As a result, he was overtaken by sin and he ultimately did shed blood – the blood of his brother. This provides us with the patterns of Messiah's fulfillment of the Passover. The Scriptures provided Appointed Times that are described by YHWH as "My Appointed Times." (Vayiqra 23:2). In other words, they belong to Him. The Appointed Times described in Vayiqra 23, as well as other portions of the Torah, are often erroneously referred to as the Jewish Holidays. This is a grave mistake because YHWH specifically says that these are "My Appointed Times." They belong to no ethnic or religious group. This topic is discussed in greater detail in the Walk in the Light series book entitled Appointed Times.

22 Michael Wise, Martin Abegg Jr., and Edward Cook, The Dead Sea Scrolls - A New Translation, Harper Collins, 2005, p. 94.

23 For further discussions concerning this issue, reference is

made the Walk in the Light series books entitled *The Messiah, Appointed Times,* and *The Final Shofar.*

[24] The instructions of YHWH are known as the Torah. In a very general sense, the word Torah is used to refer to the first five books of the Scriptures which some call the Pentateuch, or the five books of Moses. Torah may sound like a strange word to anyone who reads an English translation of the Scriptures, but it is found throughout the Hebrew text. The reason is because it is a Hebrew word which translators have chosen to replace with "the Law." Whenever the word "Torah" is found in the Hebrew, it has been translated as "the Law" in English Bibles. Therefore, if you grew up reading an English Bible then you would never have come across this word. On the other hand, if you read the Hebrew Scriptures the word Torah is found throughout the text. The word Torah (תורה) in Hebrew means: *"utterance, teaching, instruction or revelation from Elohim."* It comes from horah (הורה) which means *to direct, to teach* and derives from the stem yara (ירה) which means to **shoot** or **throw.** Therefore there are two aspects to the word Torah: 1) aiming or pointing in the right direction, and 2) movement in that direction. The Torah (תורה) is the first five books of the Hebrew and Christian Scriptures. The Torah is more accurately defined as the "instruction" of YHWH for His set apart people. The Torah contains instruction for those who desire to live righteous, set apart lives in accordance with the will of YHWH. Contrary to popular belief, people can obey the Torah. (Debarim 30:11-14). It is the myriads of regulations, customs and traditions men attach to the Torah that make it impossible and burdensome for people to obey. The Torah has been in existence as long as Creation and arguably forever because the instructions of YHWH are the ways of YHWH. The names of the five different "books" are transliterated from their proper Hebrew names as follows: Genesis – Beresheet, Exodus – Shemot, Leviticus – Vayiqra, Numbers – Bemidbar, Deuteronomy – Debarim. While it is generally considered that the Torah is contained exclusively within the 5 Books of Moses, in a broader sense one might

292

argue that they are included in the entire Tanak – The Torah, The Nebiim (The Prophets) and the Ketubim (The Writings).

[25] It is important to recognize that there is no such thing as a Hebrew numeral set, separate and apart from the Hebrew letters. As a result, each Hebrew character has a corresponding numeric value. This adds an interesting dimension to the study of Scriptures. Commonly called gematria, the study of the numeric values of characters and words can be quite revealing.

[26] Yeshayahu (יְשַׁעְיָהוּ) is the proper transliteration for the Prophet commonly called Isaiah. His name in Hebrew means "YHWH saves."

[27] The description of the rainbow in the Throne Room in Heaven is actually found in the Book of Revelation at 4:3.

[28] Nechama Leibowitz, *New Studies in Bereshit*, p. 86.

[29] As we continue to examine the Covenant process between YHWH and man it becomes increasingly clear that the Messiah, represented by the Aleph Taw (✕𐤊), is at the center of it all. The Aleph Taw (✕𐤊) and the Messiah are discussed in greater detail in the Walk in the Light series book entitled *The Messiah*.

[30] Throughout this text you may find that the words "Jewish," "Jews" and "Jew" are in italics because they are ambiguous and sometimes derogatory terms. At times these expressions are used to describe all of the genetic descendants of the man named Yaakob (Jacob), later named Yisrael (Israel). At other times the words are used to describe those who adhere to the religion of Judaism. The terms are commonly applied to ancient Israelites as well as modern day descendents of those tribes, whether they are atheists or Believers in YHWH. The word "Jew" originally referred to a member of the tribe of Judah (Yahudah) or a person that lived in the region of Judea. After the different exiles of the House of Yisrael and the House of Yahudah, it was the Yahudim that returned to the Land while the Northern Tribes, known as the House of Yisrael, were scattered to the ends of the earth (Yirmeyahu 9:16). The Yahudim retained their identity to their culture

and the Land and thus came to represent all of Yisrael, despite the fact that the majority of Yisrael, the 10 tribes of the Northern Kingdom, remained "lost." As a result, the word "Jew" is erroneously used to describe a Yisraelite. While this label became common and customary, it is not accurate and is the cause of tremendous confusion. This subject is described in greater detail in The Walk in the Light Series book entitled *The Redeemed*.

[31] Interestingly, the Aleph Taw (✗✗) is located next to the individuals who left with Abram and then it is located next to "the Land" so we see an intimate connection between the people who follow YHWH and the Land with the Aleph Taw (✗✗) as the One binding them together.

[32] Shechem means "between the shoulders" and is aptly named as it sits between two mountains - Mt. Gerizim and Mt. Ebal. This is a place rich in history as it was where Abram built an altar to YHWH when he entered the Land. It is also one of the few places where we read about a land transaction in the Scriptures. This is also the resting place for the bones of Joseph. To this day, in the heart of the newly named city of Nablus there is a tomb where Joseph's bones are kept. The Yisraelites brought them out of Egypt and this is also the place where the blessings and the curses were proclaimed. Shechem is located within the tribal Land of Manasseh.

[33] The Melchizedek priesthood is one of the most mysterious aspects of the Torah. Very little information is provided except when Abraham actually paid tithes to Melchizedek – The Righteous King of Jerusalem. Abraham, a man who met and Covenanted with YHWH paid an honor to this King/Priest that should give us pause for reflection. This Priest was not a Levite because there were no Levites at that time. The Levitic Priesthood would later come from Abraham's descendants. As a result it is vital that we understand that YHWH has another priesthood that operated before Abraham and one that is in operation even now, which is separate and apart from the line of Aharon and the Levitic Priesthood established in the Torah. The Levitic Priesthood requires an earthly sacrificial system,

and operated almost exclusively during the Age of Instruction. The Melchizedek line, on the other hand, transcends both time and space. This has great Messianic significance and it should help us understand the dual nature of the Messiah as both King and High Priest.

34 The reference to the "fourth generation" is interesting and reinforces the fact that we need to look at the Scriptures and the Covenants described therein in a cyclical fashion. In the Hebrew we read dowr rebiyiy (דור רביעי) which literally means "fourth revolution of time." It refers to a "foursquare" "period" or "age." This could be referring to the completion of the building of the house that, as we saw, is always present in the Covenants.

35 There is something very special going on here that is not always apparent from the English translations that simply refer to "The Word." The Aramaic Targums emphasize "the Word" by referring to it as "The Memra." There is considerable commentary of this "Word" and how the Sages of old grappled to explain this aspect of the Creator. Ultimately, the Memra is tied with the Messiah and as a result we should expect the Messiah to be intimately involved with the Covenant with Abram.

36 The Scriptures clearly provide – from the beginning – that a day begins in darkness (the evening) and then proceeds to light (the morning). From the Creation account we see how the days are repeatedly reckoned beginning in the evening, then proceeding to the morning – a day. This is a very important "cycle" and as you study the Scriptures it will become evident that the time of day when things occur is very significant.

37 A *Comprehensive Etymological Dictionary of the Hebrew Language for Readers of English*, Ernest Klein, Carta Jerusalem 1987 p. 107.

38 This is an important distinction. A Covenant had previously been made with the uncircumcised man Abram. Now there was another Covenant made with this circumcised man Abraham. It was not a new Covenant, but rather a Covenant within a Covenant. This is an important pattern to understand as we examine the process of entering into Covenant with YHWH.

Ancient Hebrew was a visual language wherein every letter
has a visual meaning and told a story. When those letters
were put together, their meanings combined to form
concepts. I have made it a part of my studies to look beyond
the Modern Hebrew to the Ancient Hebrew pictographs to
find out the original concepts behind various words. This
adds a whole new dimension to the study of the Scriptures
that is both exciting and authentic. I highly recommend
that you visit www.ancient-hebrew.org, which has a great
deal of useful information. There is so much that we can
glean from this passage. The fact that YHWH put
Abraham to sleep immediately makes us think of Adam. If
YHWH did not want Abraham to see Him, He could have
easily told him not to look, or even covered him like He did
with Mosheh on Mount Sinai. The fact that YHWH put
him to sleep seems to raise a red flag and call special
attention to this incident. I believe that it reflects the fact
that YHWH was in the process of making for Himself a
Bride through the Seed of Abraham, and as He put Adam to
sleep to take something out of him to create his bride - so
He did the same with Abram. Only instead of taking
something out – YHWH added something to Abram which
is symbolized in the hey (ה) that was later added to his
name. Rabbi Yosef Kalatsky in a Beyond Pshat article
provides the following commentary: "Based on a verse in
Tehillim [Psalms] which alludes to the fact that Hashem
[YHWH] formed the worlds with the letters 'yud' and
'hey,' the Gemara in Tractate Menachos states, 'The
physical world was created with the spirituality of the letter
'hey,' and the world to come was created with the
spirituality of the letter 'yud.' Meaning, the spiritual energy
contained within the letter 'hey' brought about all physical
existence. G-d said to Abraham, Just as the spiritual energy
in the letter 'hey' was needed to bring about all physical
existence, that same energy is needed to bring a change
within you to be able to be the father, the Patriarch, of the
Jewish people.' The additional 'hey' is not merely another
letter added to Abraham's name; but rather, it brought about
a profound change within him; his dimension of person
became the equivalent of all existence." www.torah.org. If

YHWH (יהוה) did form the physical world with the (יה) which are the first two characters in His Name then one might reasonably ask – what about the last two letters of His Name. We can see the answer in the name of the first woman who is commonly called Eve, but her Hebrew name is Hawah (חוה). Her name means "life giver" and notice that it includes the last two letters of the Name of YHWH (וה). This life is not the same as the rest of creation, which was already formed. This "life" was the Life of YHWH that was breathed into Adam – it was what "made him in the image of YHWH." Now back to Abraham and Sarah – it is important to emphasize that there was not just one hey (ה) added – there were two. YHWH added one to the male Abraham and one to the female Sara<u>h</u>, and when the two were joined together, it was that Seed and that Womb which would provide the promised line from which Messiah would come forth. Those two heys are the two heys found in the Name of YHWH (יהוה).

[40] The Creator's reckoning of time is discussed at length in the Walk in the Light series book entitled "Appointed Times." It is critical that anyone who claims to follow the Almighty understand His times and seasons in order to synchronize their lives with His plan.

[41] The birth of Yitshaq at Passover is supported by the Targums, which were Aramaic translations of the Torah that often extrapolated facts that were implied or understood to be part of the Torah, likely through tradition.

[42] The Third Day, known as Yom Shliyshiy (יום שלישי) has great significance in the Scriptures and should be the subject of much study for the serious student.

[43] The Book of Yasher is not a "canonized" text, but it is mentioned twice in the Scriptures, which appears to validate its existence and authenticity. See Joshua 10:13 and II Samuel 1:18. The issue of canonization is discussed in the Walk in the Light series book entitled *The Scriptures*.

[44] The Hebrew Scriptures are the original texts and the Hebrew language was uniquely chosen by the Creator to transmit His message. There is critical information below the surface of the text which often gets lost, particularly

when you start translating this ancient eastern language into a modern western language. As a result, I encourage students of the text to learn and study in the original Hebrew whenever possible.

45 Shaul of Tarsus, commonly referred to as the Apostle Paul in Christianity, recognized that the Seed of Abraham was the Messiah. In his Torah teaching to the Galatians he writes: *"Now to Abraham and his Seed were the promises made. He does not say, 'And to seeds,' as of many, but as of one, 'And to your Seed,' who is Messiah."* Galatians 3:16. This man was a well educated man, taught by the renowned Sage Gamaliel. Through his various writings he was attempting to instruct Gentiles in the Hebrew Scriptures. Sadly, many of his writings have been twisted and misconstrued and some actually believe that he was the founder or a co-founder of the Christian religion.

46 The Red Heifer sacrifice is intimately connected with the Lamb of Elohim. It is the one sacrifice that makes a person clean. Every person is tarnished from sin, which is the transgression of the Torah perpetuated from the Garden. All must be made clean before they can be reconciled to YHWH. This process of becoming clean, so that you can enter into the House of YHWH is provided through the picture of the Red Heifer, which is slaughtered "outside the camp," not on the Altar which is within the courts of the House of YHWH. The Red Heifer sacrifice provides cleansing so that one can approach the Altar. We then receive atonement from the Passover Sacrifice on the Altar that allows us to enter the House. The description of the Red Heifer slaughtering can be found in Numbers (Bemidbar) 19.

47 Jewish and Early Christian Methods of Bible Interpretation, Judah Gross, Hashtaumd, Quoting [ix] Levenson 181 [x] Manns 60.

48 The theme of the promised son, born at the Appointed Time, dying and later being resurrected is repeated in the incident involving the Shunammite woman and Elisha. (2 Melakim 4:1-37).

49 Numbers are very significant in the Scriptures, particularly when examining the Hebrew Scriptures where each letter

has a corresponding numerical value. As a result, every letter and word in the Hebrew language has a numerical equivalent. The study of numbers in the Scriptures is referred to as Gematria. Through the study of the numbers in Scriptures we can see patterns and connections that are not readily observable through most translations.

50 For further discussion regarding the dawning of the day and the Messianic significance including specific examples, reference is made to the Walk in the Light series book entitled *The Messiah*.

51 Shemot (שמות) is the transliteration for the Hebrew word that is often written Exodus in English Bibles. Shemot actually means: "names."

52 Egypt is the modern word used to describe the land inhabited by the descendents of Mitsrayim, who was the son of Ham (Beresheet 10:6). Thus, throughout this text the word Mitsrayim may be used in place of the English word Egypt since that is how it is rendered in the Torah.

53 Mosheh (משה) is the proper transliteration for the name of the Patriarch commonly called Moses.

54 Most agree that the name Mosheh is actually an Egyptian name that refers to his miraculous appearance from the waters of the Nile.

55 *Pharaoh's and Kings – A Biblical Quest*, David Rohl, Crown Publishers, New York p. 252-256. See also *Digging up the Past*, David Downs and *Unwrapping the Pharaohs*, John Ashton and David Downs, pp. 92 – 93, Master Books 2006.

56 The Book of Yasher 68:17, 71:1 and 72:25. The Book of Yasher is not a canonized text, but it is referred to twice in the Tanak and recent research has been performed verifying the accuracy of the dates provided therein, making it a valuable resource for "filling in the gaps" that are present throughout the Torah. Research performed by Eliyahu David ben Yissachar.

57 Book of Yasher 72:37.

58 Yasher 76:3-5 and Shemot 2:16-20. There is significant tradition in Judaism and Christianity that Mosheh was 40 years old when he fled Egypt. The tradition in Judaism comes from Rabbi Yohanan ben Zakkai and Rabbi Akiba. Both of these men were significant figures in turning the

covenant people away from the truth conserning the Torah of Mosheh and Yahushua the Messiah. It was they who said in Midrash Rabbah C:10, "Mosheh spent forty years in Pharaoh's palace, forty years in Midian, and served Israel forty years." This tradition eventually seeped into Christianity and the interpretation of Acts 7:23 and Acts 7:30. The 40 years mentioned in Acts 7:23 refers to the period of time between when the king in Acts 7:18 *arose*, and when Mosheh decided to *visit his brethren the children of Israel*. The king who did not know Joseph was Neferhotep I. There were 40 years between when Neferhotep I was born in 1539 BCE until when Mosheh decided to visit the children of Israel in 1499 BCE. Whereas the 40 years mentioned in Acts 7:30 refers to the period when Mosheh was king of Cush between 1490-1451 BCE.

59 Book of Yasher 76:23.

60 Book of Yasher 77:51 and Shemot 2:21.

61 The man Aaron, whose Hebrew name is better transliterated as Aharon, was the brother of Mosheh. They both were born into the Tribe of a Levi, although Mosheh had been adopted into the household of Pharaoh.

62 This is likened to the Commandment concerning the mezzuzah. Undoubtedly, the most significant prayer in the Torah is known as The Shema found at Debarim 6:4. The Shema proclaims: "*4 Hear, O Yisrael: YHWH our Elohim, YHWH is one. 5 Love YHWH your Elohim with all your heart and with all your soul and with all your strength. 6 These commandments that I give you today are to be upon your hearts. 7 Impress them on your children. Talk about them when you sit at home and when you walk along the road, when you lie down and when you get up. 8 Tie them as symbols on your hands and bind them on your foreheads. 9 Write them on the doorframes of your houses and on your gates.*" Debarim 6:4-9. The Command to write the commands on our doorposts and our gates means that YHWH is in control of that space. His Commandments are the rule of that property, which represents His Kingdom on the Earth.

63 The Scriptures speak of a future event when YHWH will gather His sheep from the four corners of the planet. (Amos 9:14; Jeremiah 23:3-8; Isaiah 11:0-16; Isaiah 35:3-10; Zekaryah

10:6-12; Ezekiel 39:28). Passover is not just a Feast, it is a "moadi" which means an Appointed Time which is essentially a "rehearsal." It is not simply a remembrance of something that happened in the past, it is also a rehearsal for a future event. As a result, those who continue to celebrate the Appointed Times of YHWH should do so with joy and anticipation of future fulfillment. This subject is discussed in further detail in the Walk in the Light series books entitled *Appointed Times* and *The Final Shofar*.

[64] The first born is a very important subject, especially in ancient days. The firstborn was typically entitled to a "double portion" of the father's estate and was expected to carry on in the father's stead after death. In the Exodus we see YHWH killing the firstborn of all in Egypt that were not under the "covering" of the blood of the slaughtered lambs and kids of the first year. After this incident, the Tribe of Levi was later set apart to YHWH as firstborn from the nation of Yisrael. *"[11] YHWH also said to Mosheh, [12] 'I have taken the Levites from among the Israelites in place of the first male offspring of every Yisraelite woman. The Levites are mine, [13] for all the firstborn are mine. When I struck down all the firstborn in Egypt, I set apart for Myself every firstborn in Yisrael, whether man or animal. They are to be Mine. I am YHWH."* Bemidbar 3:11-13.

[65] Beresheet 33:17

[66] Succot, also known as the Feast of Booths or the Feast of Tabernacles is specifically mentioned as a celebration, which will occur every year when the Messiah reigns from Zion. All the Nations, not just Jews, will be required to celebrate or they will be punished. This is perfectly consistent with the notion that the Appointed Times belong to YHWH and that it is the time when His Creation will meet with Him. It is commanded in Shemot 23:16; Shemot 34:22; Vayiqra 23:34; Debarim 16:16 and Debarim 31:10. We understand from the Prophet Zechariah (Zekaryah) that all of the nations of the Earth will be required to celebrate this feast when Messiah reigns. *"[16] Then the survivors from all the nations that have attacked Jerusalem will go up year after year to worship the King, YHWH Almighty, and to celebrate the Feast of Tabernacles. [17] If any of the peoples of the earth do not go up to*

Jerusalem to worship the King, YHWH Almighty, they will have no rain. [18] If the Egyptian people do not go up and take part, they will have no rain. YHWH will bring on them the plague He inflicts on the nations that do not go up to celebrate the Feast of Tabernacles. [19] This will be the punishment of Egypt and the punishment of all the nations that do not go up to celebrate the Feast of Tabernacles." Zekaryah 14:16-19.

[67] The mikvah is where the Christian doctrine of baptism derives, although it did not begin with Christianity and was commanded by YHWH long before Messiah came. It was a natural thing for Yisraelites to do. In fact, there were numerous mikvaote (plural form of mikvah) at the Temple and it was required that a person be immersed in a mikvah prior to presenting their sacrifice. The Hebrew word for baptize is tevila (טביל), which is a full body immersion that takes place in a mikvah (מקוה). This comes from the passage in Beresheet 1:10 when YHWH "gathered together" the waters. The mikvah is the gathering together of flowing waters. The "tevila" immersion is symbolic for a person going from a state of uncleanliness to cleanliness. The priests in the temple needed to tevila regularly to insure that they were in a state of cleanliness when they served in the Temple. Anyone going to the Temple to worship or offer sacrifices would tevila at the numerous pools outside the Temple. There are a variety of instances found in the Torah when a person was required to tevila. It is very important because it reminds us of the filth of sin, and the need to be washed clean from our sin in order to stand in the presence of a set apart Elohim. Therefore, it makes perfect sense that we be immersed in a mikvah prior to presenting the sacrifice of the perfect lamb as atonement for our sins. It also cleanses our "temple" which the Spirit of Elohim will enter in, to tabernacle with us. The tevila is symbolic of becoming born again, and is an act of going from one life to another. Being born again is not something that became popular in the seventies within the Christian religion. It is a remarkably Yisraelite concept that was understood to occur when one arose from the mikvah. In fact, people witnessing an immersion would often cry out "Born Again!" when a person came up from an immersion. It was also an integral

part of the Rabbinic conversion process, which, in many ways is not Scriptural, but in this sense is correct. For a Gentile to complete their conversion, they were required to be immersed, or baptized, which meant that they were born again - born into a new life. Many people believe that immersion is a newly instituted Christian concept because of the exchange between Messiah and Nicodemus. Let us take a look at that conversation in the Gospel according to Yahanan: *"¹ Now there was a man of the Pharisees named Nicodemus, a ruler of the Yahudim. ² He came to Yahushua at night and said, 'Rabbi, we know you are a teacher who has come from Elohim. For no one could perform the miraculous signs You are doing if Elohim were not with him.' ³ In reply Yahushua declared, 'I tell you the truth, no one can see the kingdom of Elohim unless he is born again.' ⁴ 'How can a man be born when he is old?' Nicodemus asked. 'Surely he cannot enter a second time into his mother's womb to be born!' ⁵ Yahushua answered, 'I tell you the truth, no one can enter the kingdom of Elohim unless he is born of water and the Spirit. ⁶ Flesh gives birth to flesh, but the Spirit gives birth to spirit. ⁷ You should not be surprised at My saying, You must be born again. ⁸ The wind blows wherever it pleases. You hear its sound, but you cannot tell where it comes from or where it is going. So it is with everyone born of the Spirit.' ⁹ 'How can this be?' Nicodemus asked. ¹⁰ 'You are Yisrael's teacher,' said Yahushua, 'and do you not understand these things? ¹¹ I tell you the truth, we speak of what we know, and we testify to what we have seen, but still you people do not accept our testimony. ¹² I have spoken to you of earthly things and you do not believe; how then will you believe if I speak of heavenly things? ¹³ No one has ever gone into heaven except the One who came from heaven - the Son of Man. ¹⁴ Just as Mosheh lifted up the snake in the desert, so the Son of Man must be lifted up, ¹⁵ that everyone who believes in Him may have eternal life.'"* Yahanan 3:1-15. From this exchange it seems that Nicodemus is unfamiliar with immersion, but he was not surprised by the fact that a person needed to be "born again." His first question: *"How can a man be born when he is old?"* demonstrated he did not see how it applied to him, because he was already a Yahudim. His second question *"How can this be,"* only affirmed that fact. And this is why Yahushua asked: *"You are Yisrael's teacher and do you not understand these things?"* In other words, "You're supposed to be the one teaching Yisrael about these spiritual matters and you're not. You think only the Gentiles need to be immersed and born again, but all Yahudim need to be immersed and born again because everyone has sinned, and this needs to be taught to everyone - not just the Gentiles." So you see, being born again through immersion was not new to Yisrael. This is why many readily were immersed by Yahanan the Immerser - they understood their need. It was often the leaders who failed to see their need for cleansing because they were blinded by the notion that their Torah observance justified them. It is important to note that the tevila must occur in "living waters" - in other words, water that is moving and ideally which contains life. These living waters are symbolic of the Messiah. In a Scriptural marriage, a bride would enter the waters of purification prior to her wedding. These are the same waters that we are to enter when we make a confession of faith and become part of the Body of Messiah - His Bride.

⁶⁸ Elim was a very special place and one cannot ignore the numerical significance of twelve (12) and seventy (70). Some interpret Elim to mean: "Palm trees" or better yet "strong trees." Twelve is a number typically associated with Yisrael – the Community of YHWH. Seventy (70) is an number typically associated with "the Nations." Here at this place we see a picture of the Nations being nourished by Yisrael. This was an oasis in the desert, and a picture of a future event when the Nations leave their bondage of the Egyptian system of sorcery that now envelopes the world. They will come together to the waters that flow to Yisrael. This is not only a place, but a time which is rehearsed yearly called Succot, when Palm Branches are waved. This subject is discussed further in the Walk in the Light series books entitled *Appointed Times* and *The Final Shofar*.

⁶⁹ A Ketubah (כתובה) is simply a marriage contract. It was quite common in ancient cultures, and continues to be common primarily in eastern cultures. It established the rights and responsibilities of the parties and often included the damages for a parties' breach of the contract. In western

culture, similar contracts are used and called pre-nuptial agreements.

[70] See Beresheet 15:13. We have already mentioned the concept of Gematria and the study of numbers in the Scriptures. Along that line the numbers 4, 40, 400 are repeatedly linked with Messiah. This subject is discussed further tin the Walk in the Light book entitled *The Messiah*.

[71] Yisrael was to be a set apart people, a kingdom of priests so that they could be an example to the rest of the nations. YHWH spoke the following to Mosheh at Sinai: "*⁵ Now if you obey Me fully and keep My Covenant, then out of all nations you will be My treasured possession. Although the whole earth is Mine, ⁶ you will be for Me a kingdom of priests and a set apart nation.*" Shemot 19:4-6.

[72] *Ancient Egypt*, Lorna Oakes and Lucia Gahlin, Barnes & Nobles Books, 2003, Page 283.

[73] The word "Bible" has traditionally been the word used to describe the collection of documents considered by Christianity to be inspired by Elohim - I prefer the use of the word Scriptures. The word Bible derives from Byblos, which has more pagan connotations than I prefer, especially when referring to the written Word of Elohim. This subject is discussed in greater detail in the Walk in the Light Series book entitled *The Scriptures*.

[74] The Scriptures provided Appointed Times that are described by YHWH as "My Appointed Times" (Vayiqra 23:2. In other words, they belong to Him. The Appointed Times described in Vayiqra 23, as well as other portions of the Torah, are often erroneously referred to as the Jewish Holidays. This is a grave mistake, because YHWH specifically says that these are "My Appointed Times." They belong to no ethnic or religious group. This topic is discussed in greater detail in the Walk in the Light series book entitled *Appointed Times*.

[75] The concept of "The Trinity" is one which derives from pagan father, mother, son worship. Examples of trinitarian worship can be traced back to Babylon. For more detail on this important subject see the Walk in the Light series book entitled *Restoration*.

[76] This is why Torah observance is critical – it teaches us

distinctions between acceptable conduct and unacceptable conduct. It tells us how to live righteous lives. We often hear about a person acknowledging that they are a sinner, but the only way to know if you are a sinner is the Torah.

[77] The significance of forty (40) days and forty (40) nights cannot be overlooked. It was present when Noah and his family were protected in the Ark and it is used repeatedly in the life of Mosheh, another man that was delivered through an Ark. The twelve who spied out the Land did so for forty (40) days and forty (40) nights, and we should expect to see this type of time period, or rather cycle, repeated when dealing with the Covenant and the Land. The number forty (40) is repeatedly connected with the Messiah.

[78] It was in 922 BCE that the Kingdom of Yisrael was divided into two Kingdoms.* The Northern Kingdom, Known as the House of Yisrael, would consist of ten (10) of the Tribes. The Southern Kingdom, known as the House of Yahudah, consisted of two tribes plus the Levites. It is interesting that we see the same numerical division as the reports given by the twelve (12) spies concerning the Land before they enter into the Land. That, of course, was a pattern in the Covenant cycle. While the two who gave a good report were still made to wander in the Wilderness for forty (40) years with the others, they would inherit the Land while the others died. In similar fashion, when the tribes were divided in 922 BCE, the House of Yisrael, representing the ten (10) spies were removed from the Land and essentially "disappeared" – like death. The House of Yahudah was given different punishments, one of them being symbolically represented by the prophet Ezekiel as he laid on his right side for forty (40) days, signifying a forty year punishment for the House of Yahudah – a year for a day. (Ezekiel 4:6). YHWH always punishes Yisrael exactly as He said He would according to the Covenant. The House of Yisrael was punished in the same fashion – only for 390 years. (Ezekiel 4:5). It was prophesied that the House of Yisrael would essentially lose their identity, which they did, after the 390 years was multiplied by 7 for a total of 2,730 years according to the Covenant. (Vayiqra 26:14-28). Finally, it was prophesied that they would ultimately be

restored with the House of Yahudah. (See Hoshea 1, among others). This issue is discussed further in this book, as well as the Walk in the Light series book entitled *The Redeemed.*

79 According to Shemot 16:31 "the House of Yisrael called ✗✗ the name of it Manna." This is the first time that we see the term "The House of Yisrael" in the Scriptures. Obviously, it is consistent with the Covenant language that we have seen so far, although there may be a deeper connection with a group of people in the future called The House of Yisrael and the Messiah – the revelation of the true meaning behind this Manna from heaven. The presence of the Aleph Taw (✗✗) stresses this fact.

80 Yahudah (יהודה) is the proper English transliteration for the Hebrew name often pronounced as Judah.

81 As we have seen, the name changes in the Scriptures are directly related to the Covenant. When Abraham and Sarah eached experienced a name change we saw two heys (ﭏ). We saw that as part of the Name of YHWH (ﭏﻱﭏﺯ) separated by a vav (ﻱ), which is actually a connector in Hebrew. The letter vav (ﻱ) symbolizes a nail or a stake - something used to affix things or holds things together. So through Abraham and Sarah we saw a connection that would result in the yud (ﺯ), the Hand of the Covenant – The Hand of YHWH. So we are looking for the Arm or Hand of YHWH to be revealed and we see this man named Hoshea (salvation) who has a yud (ﺯ) added to his name, making it Yahushua. This points to Yahushua being The Arm or Hand of YHWH. When we look at this man Yahushua we see one who came out of Egypt, was a servant first and then a great leader of Yisrael. He spent forty (40) years in the Wilderness, despite the fact that he gave a good report. He came out of this forty (40) year period and was "immersed" in the Jordan. He circumcised the Yisraelites and celebrated the first Passover in the Land. He then went on to conquer and divide the Land. This was a pattern for the Arm of YHWH accomplishing the Covenant promises and this will have profound implications in the future as we look for One to renew the Covenant. This issue is discussed

in more detail in the Walk in the Light series book entitled *The Messiah*.

82 The reason that I point this out is because it is very significant and prophetic. The fact that these two sons were born in a pagan context and later adopted by Yisrael speaks to their future redemption, a time when a future generation of Yisraelites who are born in "Egypt" will be "adopted" by YHWH and grafted back into Yisrael. These apparent pagans will be regathered into the family of YHWH – Yisrael.

83 The modern State of Israel is more properly called a "Jewish" State. It does not constitute the set apart Assembly of Yisrael, and using the name Israel has caused great confusion for many. Some of the people called "Jews" likely have genetic lineage with the Tribe of Judah, thus the label Jew. They tend to practice their own, man-made religion called Judaism, which derives from the Pharisee sect. They are not following Mosheh, as Ancient Yisrael did. They have a secular government, but prohibit citizenship from those who cannot prove they are "Jewish" through their mother. The modern State of Israel does not follow the Torah and the Covenant is not a qualification for citizenship. In fact, they allow every sort of pagan practice to exist in the Land, as well as Atheism. To become part of the Covenant people, the Assembly of Yisrael, you must enter into the Covenant and obey the Torah. The qualifications for citizenship in the modern State of Yisrael are based on genetics or conversion to the religion of Judaism – not the Torah. As a result, the modern State of Israel is not Yisrael, the Covenant people of YHWH.

84 Despite the fact that Mosheh was the direct mediator with YHWH, even he was not immune from punishment. This is a good example of how YHWH expects more from those who have been given much. Mosheh was commanded to speak to the rock and water would come forth. Instead, Mosheh struck the Rock twice. (Bemidbar 20:10). Even though water poured forth, it was not the way YHWH intended and He was not glorified through the act. While this shows how we need to diligently listen and obey (shema), there are other deep teachings hidden in the event.

85   The Covenant was renewed in Moab. YHWH specifically commanded: *"No Ammonite or Moabite or any of his descendants may enter the assembly of YHWH, even down to the tenth generation."* Debarim 23:3. We have an example of this happening with Ruth who was, by no coincidence, a Moabite from the very land where this Covenant was renewed. The story of Ruth provides a beautiful picture of a foreigner being grafted into Yisrael and becoming an important part of the Messianic bloodline. Her famous words are the formula for becoming grafted in to Yisrael: *"For wherever you go, I will go; and wherever you lodge, I will lodge; Your people shall be my people, and your Elohim, my Elohim."* Ruth 1:16. Through this story we see a vivid example of redemption.

86   See Rashi's Commentary on Deuteronomy 29:10, S.S. & R. Publishing Company, 1977, p. 263.

87   The name of the man often called Samuel in English translations of the Scriptures is more accurately pronounced Shemuel (שמול). In modern Hebrew it is often written and pronounced as Sh'muel.

88   The Tabernacle, also known as the Mishkan, was constructed by Mosheh and the skilled craftsmen of Yisrael while they travelled through the Wilderness. It was made to be moveable – as a tent and it was the House of YHWH. The physical appearance and layout of the Tabernacle is a pattern of the Garden of Eden. It is also provides an image of a person's body and is intended to show us how YHWH desires to dwell or "tabernacle" within us. Combined this Tabernacle shows us how YHWH desires to dwell with us and in us. The description of the building of the tabernacle is provided in Shemot 25 – Shemot 28.

89   See Judges (Shoftim) 19-20.

90   We repeatedly see the word "shamar" (שמר) throughout the Scriptures although we do not always recognize the consistency because it can be translated as "watch," "guard," "keep" etc. The word is meant to stress to us that we are to act as watchmen over the commandments so that we are diligent to obey. Adam was supposed to watch over the Garden as he was commanded, and the serpent (nachash) entered and deceived Hawah and himself – the

consequences were devastating. Shaul, as the King of Yisrael, was supposed to keep watch over the Commandments, which he too failed to do. Over and over again we are instructed to <u>keep</u> the commandments and to <u>watch</u> the commandments and to <u>guard</u> the commandments. This is the same word <u>shamar</u> and we are given this instruction so that we stay within the hedge of protection provided by the Torah - so that we don't fall into temptation - so that we are kept from evil. The purpose of a hedge is to make a separation between those things on one side and those things on the other side. The Torah provides us with distinctions and draws a line for us to understand right from wrong, clean from unclean, righteous conduct from abominable conduct. On that foundation the Kingdom is established and it will only be populated with those who will also OBEY.

[91] Tehillim (תהלים) is a proper transliteration for the word Psalms. The Book of Psalms would thus be rendered Sefer Tehillim. King Dawid repeatedly extolled the Torah throughout the Tehillim. In fact, the entire Tehillim 119, the longest of the Tehillim, is about the Torah. I would encourage every reader to read this portion of Scripture, recognizing that the entire text is about the Torah.

[92] Jesse is the English translation of the Hebrew name more accurately pronounced Yeshai.

[93] We know from the text that Abraham went to the "region" or "land" of Moriah better translated as Moriyah (מריה) which means "shown by YHWH." Tradition holds that this was the same sight that the altar was built before the Temple site was selected by David and built by Solomon although the Scriptures do not specifically state that fact.

[94] There are two similar, but also differing accounts of David's purchase of the threshing floor of Araunah. According to 2 Shemuel 24:18-25: *"[18] On that day Gad went to David and said to him, 'Go up and build an altar to YHWH on the threshing floor of Araunah the Jebusite.' [19] So David went up, as YHWH had commanded through Gad. [20] When Araunah looked and saw the king and his men coming toward him, he went out and bowed down before the king with his face to the ground. [21] Araunah said, 'Why has my lord the king come to his servant?' 'To buy your*

threshing floor,' David answered, 'so I can build an altar to YHWH, that the plague on the people may be stopped.' [22] Araunah said to David, 'Let my lord the king take whatever pleases him and offer it up. Here are oxen for the burnt offering, and here are threshing sledges and ox yokes for the wood. [23] O king, Araunah gives all this to the king.' Araunah also said to him, 'May YHWH your Elohim accept you.' [24] But the king replied to Araunah, 'No, I insist on paying you for it. I will not sacrifice to YHWH my Elohim burnt offerings that cost me nothing.' So David bought the threshing floor and the oxen and paid <u>fifty shekels of silver</u> for them. [25] David built an altar to YHWH there and sacrificed burnt offerings and fellowship offerings. Then YHWH answered prayer in behalf of the land, and the plague on Yisrael was stopped." The weight of the silver was around 1 ¼ pounds or .6 kilograms. According to 1 Chronicles 21:25-26: "[25] David paid Araunah <u>six hundred shekels of gold</u> for the site. [26] David built an altar to YHWH there and sacrificed burnt offerings and fellowship offerings. He called on YHWH, and YHWH answered him with fire from heaven on the altar of burnt offering." The amount is a weight equivalent to about 15 pounds or seven kilograms. Notice the difference in prices which appears, on the surface, to be a discrepancy but at second glance is not. The writer in Shemuel simply stating that David purchased the threshing floor and the oxen to sacrifice and paid 50 shekels of silver for them – meaning the oxen. The writer in I Chronicles was concerned about the site and indicated the price for the threshing floor was six hundred shekels of gold. Notice also that fire came down from heaven, as with Eliyahu.

[95] en.wikipedia.org/wiki/Threshing_floor

[96] It is important to note that the House of YHWH was built upon a threshing floor. This is significant because all of the adult males of Yisrael were commanded to appear before YHWH three times a year at the place where He chose to put His Name – In other words - where He lived. That place has been Jerusalem ever since David set up the Tabernacle there. The Appointed Times were centered around the harvests and no one was to come empty handed. In other words, they were supposed to bring the best – their firstfruits – just as Hebel had done long ago. It is there, at

the threshing floor of YHWH, that the hearts of men would be sifted as they did business with their Elohim.

97 There are significant parallels between the Tabernacle in the Wilderness and the House that David planned to build for YHWH. The House of YHWH took a journey with Yisrael and was portable while Yisrael was moving and even during the period of the shoftim (judges). It was only when David became King and established his throne in Jerusalem that we see the transition of the House of YHWH from a movable tent to a permanent building. This is significant and is a Messianic reference to a future time when Messiah will rebuild the House as foretold to David: "*⁷ YHWH declares to you that YHWH Himself will establish a house for you: ¹² When your days are over and you rest with your fathers, I will raise up your offspring to succeed you, who will come from your own body, and I will establish His kingdom. ¹³ He is the one who will build a house for my Name, and I will establish the throne of His kingdom forever.*" 2 Shemuel 7:11-14.

98 Shlomo (שלמה) is the proper English transliteration for the Hebrew name that is traditionally pronounced as Solomon.

99 This is all that YHWH asks of His people and they continually refuse to do what He says. There are rich blessings for those who obey – like David. There are also curses for those who disobey – like Shlomo.

100 www.uhcg.org

101 Yehezqel (יהזקאל) is the proper Hebrew transliteration for the Prophet commonly called Ezekiel.

102 Nelson's Illustrated Bible Dictionary, Copyright (c) 1986, Thomas Nelson Publishers (Names corrected for consistency).

103 Debarim 31:16.

104 Fausset's Bible Dictionary, Electronic Database Copyright (c)1998 by Biblesoft.

105 Yirmeyahu (ירמיהו) is the proper transliteration for the Hebrew name of the prophet commonly called Jeremiah.

106 It is believed that Joseph was born on the Appointed Time of Yom Teruah, which occurs on the first day of the seventh month. This was also the date when he was revealed to his brethren while they were in Egypt, looking for salvation from famine. (Eliyahu David ben Yissachar).

This is a Messianic pattern that we should see repeated by the Messiah ben Joseph. For a further examination of this date as it relates to the Messiah see the Walk in the Light series book entitled *The Messiah*.

[107] The 280 years (7 x 40) concerning the punishment of the House of Yahudah was fulfilled during the reign of Alexander the Great. (Eliyahu David ben Yissachar).

[108] The pattern of Joseph is like a death and resurrection. This was the same pattern and belief demonstrated by Abraham on the Mountain of Moriah. The notion of the Messiah ben Joseph dying and being resurrected is well established in the Scriptures. There is a major push against this belief in Judaism, which is inconsistent with ancient traditions and appears simply to be a backlash against Christianity.

[109] These cycles and the specific calculation is described in greater detail in the Walk in the Light series book entitled *The Messiah*.

[110] We know from the Dead Sea Scrolls, which were written just prior to this time, that the Sect of Yisraelites, known as the Essenes were anticipating Messiah. We also can read in the New Testament writings that people were expecting the Messiah during this time period, and the roles of The Prophet, The Messiah and Elijah were unclear.

[111] While Christianity has a belief in the Messiah, they fail to properly represent the One that they refer to as Jesus Christ. They also fail to properly understand how the Messiah operates in fulfilling the Covenant cycles. This subject is discussed in greater detail in the Walk in the Light series book entitled *Restoration*.

[112] The subject of the Name of Yahushua is discussed in greater detail in the Walk in the Light series books entitled *Names* and *The Messiah*.

[113] The operation of the Covenant through the cycles of time has been touched upon in this book. For an in depth discussion of these cycles see the Walk in the Light series books entitled *Appointed Times* and *The Final Shofar*, which talks about the end.

[114] This is arguably one of the greatest mysteries in the Scriptures, although it was given as a pattern throughout the text. Just as YHWH took a part of Adam and made a

Bride for him, so too YHWH did to make a Bride for Himself. He inserted some of Himself into the Covenant womb and brought forth His Son, His Only Son, to complete the work that began in the Garden. This Son, The Messiah, has been building a House and gathering a family to dwell in that House. The Cycle will be completed when all of YHWH becomes reunited as One – Echad.

[115] Yeshayahu 41:8 and 2 Chronicles 20:7. It is also interesting to note that the word ahav (אהב) is the word for father – ab (אב) surrounding the spirit – hey (ה). This links closely with the fact that Abram had a hey (ה) added to his name making it Abraham. YHWH placed His Spirit within both Abraham and Sarah revealing the love that He intended through the Marriage Covenant.

[116] It is important to stress that no one can earn their way into the House. The path was made open by the mercy, often referred to as the grace, of YHWH. After we step on that path, it is then incumbent upon us to walk, and stay on that path. A good start is the weekly Shabbat and the annual Moadi, The Appointed Times. As we begin to observe these times we synchronize our lives with the Creator and His Covenant. These issues are discussed in more detail in the Walk in the Light series books entitled *The Sabbath* and *Appointed Times*.

A Note on Dates

Historical dating has long been a subject of controversy and debate in the academic community. While certain dates involving particular aspects of a civilization may be agreed upon, others remain in dispute. This sometimes leads to problems creating a complete timeline of history. Very recently some intensive and compelling work has been completed by using astronomical data, particularly eclipse data, which can then be used to lock together histories of various cultures, thereby providing an accurate view of history in totality. The dates used in this book may not always be the same as academia purports, but they are believed to be the most accurate available. Dates provided

by Eliyahu David ben Yissachar, Jerusalem, Israel, through the work displayed on www.torahcalendar.com have been denoted by placing an asterisk (*) next to them.

Appendix A

Tanak Hebrew Names

Torah - Teaching

English Name	Modern Hebrew	Transliteration
Genesis	בראשית	Beresheet
Exodus	שמות	Shemot
Leviticus	ויקרא	Vayiqra
Numbers	במדבר	Bemidbar
Deuteronomy	דברים	Debarim

Nebi'im - Prophets

Joshua	יהושע	Yahushua
Judges	שופטים	Shoftim
Samuel	שמואל	Shemu'el
Kings	מלכים	Melakhim
Isaiah	ישעיהו	Yeshayahu
Jeremiah	ירמיהו	Yirmeyahu
Ezekiel	יחזקאל	Yehezqel
Daniel	דניאל	Daniel
Hosea	השוע	Hoshea
Joel	יואל	Yoel
Amos	עמוס	Amos
Obadiah	עבדיה	Obadyah

Jonah	יונה	Yonah
Micah	מיכה	Mikhah
Nahum	נחום	Nachum
Habakkuk	חבקוק	Habaquq
Zephaniah	צפניה	Zephaniyah
Haggai	חגי	Chaggai
Zechariah	זכריה	Zekaryah
Malachi	מלאכי	Malachi

Kethubim – Writings

Psalms	תהלים	Tehillim
Proverbs	משלי	Mishle
Job	איוב	Iyov
Song of Songs	שיר השירים	Shir ha-Shirim
Ruth	רות	Ruth
Lamentations	איכה	Eikhah
Ecclesiastes	קהלת	Qohelet
Esther	אסתר	Ester
Ezra	עזרא	Ezra
Nehemiah	נחמיה	Nehemyah
Chronicles	דברי הימים	Dibri ha-Yamim

Appendix B

Hebrew Language Study Chart

Gematria	Letter	Ancient	Modern	English	Picture/Meaning
1	Aleph		א	A	ox head
2	Bet		ב	B, Bh	tent floor plan
3	Gimel		ג	G	foot, camel
4	Dalet		ד	D	door
5	Hey		ה	H	man raised arms
6	Waw		ו	W, O, U	tent peg, hook
7	Zayin		ז	Z	weapon
8	Het		ח	Hh	fence, wall
9	Tet		ט	T, Th	basket, container
10	Yud		י	Y	closed hand
20	Kaph		כ	K, Kh	palm, open hand
30	Lamed		ל	L	shepherd staff
40	Mem		מ	M	water
50	Nun		נ	N	sprout, seed
60	Samech		ס	S	prop, support
70	Ayin		ע	A	eye
80	Pey		פ	P, Ph	open mouth
90	Tsade		צ	Ts	hook
100	Quph		ק	Q	back of the head
200	Resh		ר	R	head of a man
300	Shin		שׁ	Sh, S	teeth
400	Taw		ת	T	mark, covenant

Note: Gematria in a very simple sense is the study of the various numerical values of the Hebrew letters and words. Since there is no separate numerical system in the Hebrew language, all Hebrew letters have a numerical value so it is a very legitimate and valuable form of study. There are many different forms of Gematria. The Gematria system used in this chart is "mispar hechrachi," also known as Normative value. The Ancient font used is an attempt to blend the ancient variants into a uniform and recognizable font set that accurately depicts the original meaning of each character.

Appendix C

The Walk in the Light Series

Book 1   Restoration – A discussion of the pagan influences that have mixed with the true faith through the ages which has resulted in the need for restoration. This book also examines true Scriptural restoration.

Book 2   Names – Discusses the True Name of the Creator and the Messiah as well as the significance of names in the Scriptures.

Book 3   The Scriptures – Discusses the ways that the Creator has communicated with Creation. It also examines the origin of the written Scriptures as well as the various types of translation errors in Bibles that have led to false doctrines in some mainline religions.

Book 4   Covenants – Discusses the progressive covenants between the Creator and His Creation as described in the Scriptures which reveals His plan for mankind.

Book 5   The Messiah – Discusses the prophetic promises and fulfillments of the Messiah and the True identity of the Redeemer of Yisrael.

Book 6   The Redeemed – Discusses the relationship between Christianity and Judaism and reveals how the Scriptures identify True Believers. It reveals how the Christian doctrine of Replacement Theology has caused confusion as to how the Creator views the Children of Yisrael.

Book 7   The Law and Grace – Discusses in depth the false doctrine that Grace has done away with the Law and demonstrates the vital importance of obeying the commandments.

Book 8   The Sabbath – Discusses the importance of the Seventh Day Sabbath as well as the origins of the tradition concerning Sunday worship.

The series began as a simple Power point presentation which was intended to develop into a book with twelve different chapters but ended up being twelve different books. Each book is intended to stand alone although the series was originally intended to build from one section to another. Due to the urgency of certain topics, the books have not been published in sequential order.

For anticipated release dates, announcements and additional teachings go to:
www.shemayisrael.net

Appendix D

The Shema

Deuteronomy (Debarim) 6:4-5

Traditional English Translation

Hear, O Israel: The LORD our God, the LORD is one!
You shall love the LORD your God with all your heart, with all your soul, and with all your strength.

Corrected English Translation

Hear, O Yisrael: YHWH our Elohim, YHWH is one (unified)!
You shall love YHWH your Elohim with all your heart, with all your soul, and with all your strength.

Modern Hebrew Text

שמע ישראל יהוה אלהינו יהוה אחד
ואהבת את יהוה אלהיך בכל־ לבבך ובכל־ נפשך ובכל־ מאדך

Ancient Hebrew Text

𐤔𐤌𐤏 𐤉𐤔𐤓𐤀𐤋 𐤉𐤄𐤅𐤄 𐤀𐤋𐤄𐤉𐤍𐤅 𐤉𐤄𐤅𐤄 𐤀𐤇𐤃
𐤅𐤀𐤄𐤁𐤕 𐤀𐤕 𐤉𐤄𐤅𐤄 𐤀𐤋𐤄𐤉𐤇 𐤁𐤊𐤋 𐤋𐤁𐤁𐤇 𐤅𐤁𐤊𐤋 𐤍𐤐𐤔𐤇
𐤅𐤁𐤊𐤋𐤇 𐤌𐤀𐤃𐤇

Hebrew Text Transliterated

Shema, Yisra'el: YHWH Elohenu, YHWH echad!
V-ahavta et YHWH Elohecha b-chol l'bacha u-b-chol naf'sh'cha u-b-chol m'odecha.

The Shema has traditionally been one of the most important prayers in Judaism and has been declared the first (resheet) of all the Commandments. (Mark 12:29-30).

Appendix E

Shema Yisrael

Shema Yisrael was originally established with two primary goals: 1) The production and distribution of sound, Scripturally based educational materials which would assist individuals to see the light of Truth and "Walk in the Light" of that Truth. This first objective was, and is, accomplished through Shema Yisrael Publications; and 2) The free distribution of those materials to the spiritually hungry throughout the world, along with Scriptures, food, clothing and money to the poor, the needy, the sick, the dying and those in prison. This second objective was accomplished through the Shema Yisrael Foundation and through the Foundation people were able to receive a tax deduction for their contributions.

Sadly, through the passage of the Pension Reform Act of 2006, the US Congress severely restricted the operation of donor advised funds which, in essence, crippled the Shema Yisrael Foundation by requiring that funds either be channeled through another Foundation or to a 501(c)(3) organization approved by the Internal Revenue Service. Since the Shema Yisrael Foundation was relatively small and operated very "hands on" by placing the funds and materials directly into the hands of the needy in Third World Countries, it was unable to effectively continue operating as a Foundation with the tax advantages associated therewith.

As a result, Shema Yisrael Publications has essentially functioned in a dual capacity to insure that both objectives continue to be promoted, although contributions are no longer tax deductible. To review some of the work being accomplished you can visit www.shemayisrael.net and go to the "Missions" section.

We gladly accept donations, although they will not be tax deductible. To donate, please make checks payable to "Shema Yisrael Publications" and mail to:

Shema Yisrael
123 Court Street • Herkimer, New York 13350

You may also visit our website or call (315) 939-7940 to make a donation or receive more information.

CPSIA information can be obtained at www.ICGtesting.com
Printed in the USA
LVOW04s1649230315

431520LV00032B/335/P